DATE		
DEC 2 0 1993		

Artful Scribbles

The Significance of
Children's Drawings

ARTFUL SCRIBBLES

The Significance of Children's Drawings

BY

HOWARD GARDNER

BASIC BOOKS, INC., PUBLISHERS

New York

Library of Congress Cataloging in Publication Data

Gardner, Howard.
    Artful scribbles.

    Includes bibliographical references and index.
    1. Drawing, Psychology of.   2.   Children as artists.
3. Cognition in children.   I.   Title.
BF723.D7G36   155.4′13   79–2777
ISBN: 0–465–00451–2

Printed in the United States of America
DESIGNED BY VINCENT TORRE
10   9   8   7   6   5   4   3   2   1

For Rudolf Arnheim

CONTENTS

ACKNOWLEDGMENTS

THE preparation of a book featuring words and pictures in equal measure has posed an assortment of challenges. I have been extraordinarily fortunate to have generous help from numerous friends, colleagues, and artful scribblers. I wish to thank the following individuals:

Tom Carothers, Judy Gardner, David Pariser, Ellen Winner, and Dennie Wolf for their careful and critical readings of earlier drafts of this book;

Alexander Alland, Larry Fenson, Al Hurwitz, David Pariser, Frank Peros, Brent Wilson, Marjorie Wilson, and Joan Travers of the Brooks School for providing information, advice, and materials;

Midge Decter, Vincent Torre, and Phoebe Hoss for competent and sensitive editorial support, and Donna Wilke for preparing the index.

Kerith, Jay, and Andrew Gardner for patient and loving tolerance of their father's curiosity;

Dean Askin, for his careful photographic work;

Judith Fram, once again, for her flawless preparation of the manuscript and her willingness to help with whatever was most pressing;

The Demos, Helm, Jingozian, McIntosh, Kaempfer, Polonsky, and Weber families for allowing me to view (and then disguise) the milieus in which youthful artistry takes place;

Eve Mendelsohn for hundreds of hours cheerfully spent helping me with every aspect of this book, ranging from the securing of difficult-to-obtain figures to the identification of errors in reasoning or presentation;

Finally, I owe an incalculable debt to Professor Rudolf Arnheim, the foremost psychologist of art in our time, for his consistent encouragement of my still fledgling work in this area, for his wonderful teaching and teachings, for his brilliant critique of the first draft of this book, and, above all, for his gift of friendship. I am honored that he has permitted me to dedicate this book to him.

I want to thank the following individuals and publishers for permitting me to reproduce copyrighted materials:

To Professor Alexander Alland for permission to reproduce examples of children's artwork from different cultures.

To Professor Rudolf Arnheim, the University of California Press, for permission to reproduce an "X-ray drawing of a gorilla eating dinner" from R. Arnheim, *Art and Visual Perception*, 1974; and for permission to quote from R. Arnheim, *The Genesis of a Painting: Picasso's Guernica*, 1962.

To Mrs. Nane Cailler, Galerie La Gravure, for permission to reproduce the figure of faces from Rodolphe Töpffer's *Essai de Physiognomie*, 1845.

To Professor M. Fortes, Kings College, Cambridge, England, for permission to reproduce drawings from M. Fortes, "Children's drawings among the Tallensi," *Africa*, 1940.

To Professors N. H. Freeman and S. Hargreaves, University of Bristol, for permission to reproduce figures from N. H. Freeman and S. Hargreaves, "Directed movements and the body proportion effect in pre-school children's human figure drawing," in *The Quarterly Journal of Experimental Psychology*, 1977.

To Drs. R. Allen Gardner and Beatrice Gardner, University of Nevada, for permission to reproduce drawings by Moja from R. A. Gardner and B. T. Gardner, "Comparative psychology and language acquisition," in *Psychology the State of the Art*, edited by K. Salzinger and F. Denmark, Annals of the New York Academy of Science, May 1977.

To Professor Gertrude Hildreth for permission to reproduce drawings of trains from G. Hildreth, *The Child Mind in Evolution: A Study of Developmental Sequences in Drawings*, Kings Crown Press, 1941.

To Dr. Elizabeth M. Koppitz for permission to reproduce drawings by retarded children from E. M. Koppitz, *Psychological Evaluation of Children's Human Figure Drawings*, Grune & Stratton Publishers, 1968.

To Dr. Diana Korzenik, Massachusetts College of Art, for permission to reproduce "drawings of jumping" from D. Korzenik, "Children's drawings: Changes in representation between ages five and seven," unpublished doctoral dissertation.

To Mrs. Joan Travers and the Brooks School, Concord, Massachusetts, for permission to reproduce children's artwork.

To M. Jean Vertut, for supplying photographs of and granting permission to reproduce examples of Ice Age art.

To Professor John Willats, North East London Polytechnic, for permission to reproduce drawings from J. Willats, "How children learn to draw realistic pictures," in *The Quarterly Journal of Experimental Psychology*, 1977.

To Drs. Brent Wilson and Marjorie Wilson, Pennsylvania State University, for permission to reproduce drawings by Anthony.

To Academic Press for permission to reproduce drawings from N. H. Freeman and S. Hargreaves, "Directed movements and body proportion effect in pre-school children's human figure drawing," and from J. Willats, "How children learn to draw realistic pictures" (copyright © by Experimental Psychology Society), in *The Quarterly Journal of Experimental Psychology*, 1977; and for permission to reproduce drawings by Nadia from L. Selfe, *Nadia: A Case of Extraordinary Drawing Ability in an Autistic Child*, 1977.

To Fratelli Alinari for supplying photographs of Leonardo da Vinci's *The Last Supper* and Andrea del Castagno's *The Last Supper*.

To Arts in America Publications for permission to reproduce Jackson Pollock's *No. 5*.

To the British Museum for supplying the photograph of and granting permission to reproduce Albrecht Dürer's *The Rhinoceros*, reproduced by courtesy of the Trustees of the British Museum.

To Brunner-Mazel, Inc., for permission to reproduce drawings by retarded children from J. Di Leo, *Children's Drawings as Diagnostic Aids*, 1973.

To Diablo Press for permission to reproduce drawings from H. Read, "Art as a unifying principle in education," and from H. Schaefer-Simmern, "The mental foundation of art education in childhood," in *Child Art: The Beginnings of Self-Affirmation*, edited by Hilda Lewis, 1966.

To Elsevier Sequoia S.A. for permission to reproduce figures from Phillips, Hobbs, and Pratt, "Intellectual realism in children's drawings of cubes," in *Cognition*, 1978.

To Grune & Stratton, Inc., for permission to reproduce drawings from E. M. Koppitz, *Psychological Evaluation of Children's Human Figure Drawings*, 1968. Reproduction by permission of Grune & Stratton, Inc., and E. M. Koppitz.

To Harvard University Press for permission to reproduce drawings of tadpoles from J. Goodnow, *Children Drawing*, 1977.

To International African Institute for permission to reproduce Tallensi drawings from M. Fortes, "Children's drawings among the Tallensi," in *Africa*, 1940, *13*.

To Kunstmuseum, Bern, for supplying photographs of, and granting permission to reproduce, early works of Paul Klee. Permission from the Paul Klee Foundation, Museum of Fine Arts, Berne, and copyright © by COSMOPRESS, Geneva, and S.P.A.D.E.M., Paris.

To Little, Brown and Company, for permission to reproduce a drawing from *Make a World* by E. Emberley, by permission of Little, Brown and Company, Copyright © 1972 by Edward R. Emberley.

To Mayfield Publishing Company for materials from *Analyzing Children's Art* by Rhoda Kellogg, by permission of Mayfield Publishing Company (formerly National Press Books). Copyright © 1969, 1970, by Rhoda Kellogg.

To Charles E. Merrill Publishing Company for permission to reproduce the figure of Clark's experiment from B. Lark-Horovitz, Lewis, and Luca, *Understanding Children's Art for Better Teaching*, 1973.

To Mouton Publishers for permission to quote materials from R. Weir, *Language in the Crib*, 1962.

To Museo de Castelvecchio for permission to reproduce Giovanni Francesco Caroto's *Portrait of a child of the early 16th century, holding a schematic "man" drawing*.

To the Museum of Modern Art for supplying photographs of and granting permission to reproduce works by Theo van Doesburg and Pablo Picasso.

To the National Gallery, for supplying the photograph of Paolo Uccello's *The Rout of San Romano*, reproduced by courtesy of the Trustees, The National Gallery, London.

To Pantheon Books, a division of Random House, Inc., for permission to reproduce the "Mice" poem from E. Richardson, *In the Early World*, 1964.

To Routledge & Kegan Paul Ltd., London, for permission to reproduce drawings from H. Eng, *The Psychology of Children's Drawings*, 1931, and from H. Eng, *The Psychology of Child and Youth Drawings*, 1957.

To Simon & Schuster, Inc., for permission to reproduce H. Farley's "I love animals" poem from R. Lewis, *Miracles*. Copyright © 1966 by Richard Lewis.

To the Smithsonian Institute for supplying the photographs of and granting permission to reproduce Helen Frankenthaler's *Small's Paradise*, Adolph Gottlieb's *Three Discs*, and Willem de Kooning's *Woman VIII*. Courtesy of National Collection of Fine Arts, Smithsonian Institute.

To Société de la Propriété Artistique et des Dessins et Modèles for permission to reproduce early works of Paul Klee. Copyright © by S.P.A.D.E.M., Paris; COSMOPRESS, Geneva; and for permission to reproduce early works of Pablo Picasso, copyright © S.P.A.D.E.M., 1979.

To the University of California Press for permission to reproduce the x-ray drawing from R. Arnheim, *Art and Visual Perception*, 1974; for permission to quote materials from R. Arnheim, *The*

Genesis of a Painting: Picasso's Guernica, 1962; and for permission to reproduce a drawing from H. Schaefer-Simmern, *The Unfolding of Artistic Activity,* 1948.

To the University of Chicago Press for permission to quote materials from E. H. Gombrich and Q. Bell, "Canons and values in visual arts: A correspondence," in *Critical Inquiry,* 2(3), 1976.

To Ernst Wasmuth for permission to reproduce examples of primitive art from L. Adam, *Nordwestamerikanische Indianerkunst,* 1923.

Cambridge, Massachusetts
August 1979

Artful Scribbles

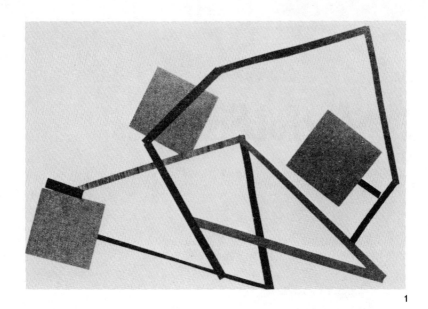

1

2 Theo van Doesburg. *Simultaneous Counter-Composition.* 1929–30. Oil on canvas, 19¾" x 19⅝". The Sidney & Harriet Janis Collection, The Museum of Modern Art, New York.

CHAPTER 1

Introduction:
Looking through
Children's Drawings

ACENTURY or two ago few individuals could have conceived of, let alone taken seriously, a book on children's drawings. The mere suggestion that these youthful productions should be pondered, or considered as works of art, would have seemed ludicrous. At that time childhood itself was not considered an important period of life, and so the activities in which young children engaged were hardly considered a topic suitable for scholarly inquiry. Further, any thought of children's drawings as beautiful or intriguing could not have held currency. A society that valued the realistic drawings of an Ingres, a Millet, or a Constable would find little reason to cherish the seemingly careless scribbles of its children.

From today's vantage point our ancestors appear blind to the charm of youthful drawings or, at the very least, short-sighted in assessing their significance. Consider the way in which the set of works reproduced here resonates with significant currents in the history of art. The first, by Danny, was made by juxtaposing narrow strips of contact paper (1);* in its sharp angles, variously proportioned enclosures, and triumvirate of squares, it is reminiscent of the minimal constructions of Theo van Doesburg (2) and Kazimir Malevich. Kathy's brilliant watercolor was made in less than fifteen minutes (3); its painterly streaks, vivid primary colors, and fiery explosiveness call to mind the work of Jackson Pollock (4) and other abstract expressionists.

* Throughout this book numbers in parentheses are keyed to relevant illustrations.

3

3

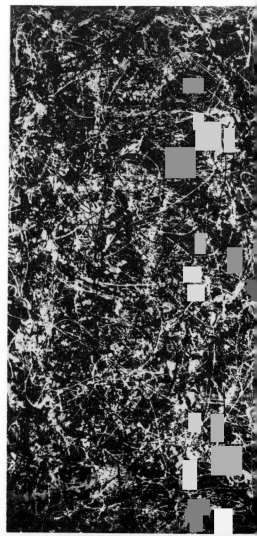

4

In sharp contrast is the simple figure portrayed by Thomas
(5); in its gaiety, liveliness, and playful romping it is linked in
spirit to "childlike" works from the hands of such twentieth-century
artists as Miró, Picasso, and Klee (6). And equally different is the
dramatic equestrian scene sketched by Nadia (7): in precision of
line, foreshortening, and vivid motion, it partakes of the style of
such Renaissance masters as Paolo Uccello (8). So diverse is this
set of works that they reverberate with a range of schools and
periods, styles and masters; all the more amazing, then, that they
were each fashioned by a child who had yet to celebrate his seventh
birthday.

Even as children's drawings now evoke considerable interest,
the phenomena surrounding their production have also proved
compelling. The child of two grabs a marker and scribbles enthusiastically on every available surface. A three-year-old produces a
vast array of geometric forms, including the enigmatic mandala—a
cross ensconced in a circle or a square. The four- and five-year-old
ceaselessly creates and re-creates representations of objects, often
rendering familiar entities in precisely the same way as youthful
draughtsmen from remote regions and diverse backgrounds have
rendered them. The drawings of young schoolchildren are often
their most striking creations: vibrant, expressive, exhibiting a

5   6

7

strong command of form and considerable beauty. In fact, children's drawings can be said without exaggeration to undergo a complete life cycle of their own. It is as if the young child, hardly out of the crib himself,* has begun to create his own offspring—a wholly separate world, a world stocked with marks, forms, objects, scenes, and fledgling artistic works. No one shows the child how to do this—and, equally amazing, each normal child, progressing at his own rate, seems to go through just this sequence. By now we would consider it a sign of ignorance, if not of gross neglect, to disregard these products of our children's hands or to overlook those fashioned by youngsters anywhere.

Nonetheless, the life cycle of children's drawings raises a number of troubling if fascinating questions. One set of questions addresses the issue of which factors make possible, and which shape, the course of childhood drawings. We are led to ponder whether striking works like those in figures 1, 3, 5, and 7 characterize every child or issue forth only from a few preternaturally gifted youngsters. We search for the origins of such works: Are they skillful copies? Do they depend on the instructions of teachers, or do

---

* To avoid the awkward concatenation of feminine and masculine forms, the sex of our prototypical child will alternate from chapter to chapter.

they instead reflect natural processes of unfolding? Are they happy accidents or the result of meticulous planning? We become curious about their antecedents: Did they follow upon a lengthy and arduous process of intellectual and social development, or did they emerge "ready-made"—courtesy of a "preset" hand and mind? And we ponder as well the fate of youthful artists: Will such children go on to produce ever more interesting works, ones that not merely charm but also inspire? Or will their interest in drawing wane as these youngsters discover more appropriate (and more adaptive) vehicles with which to express their feelings, beliefs, and thoughts? In short, a collation of such drawings coaxes a developmentally conscious age to ponder their sources and their fates.

Just as we have become intrigued about the factors spawning children's drawings, many of us have come to ponder their ultimate merit and significance. Controversy has arisen about the question whether they should be considered genuine works of art, worthy participants in the traditions associated with Uccello, Mondrian, or Klee; or whether these drawings are better viewed as youthful exercises which, however pleasing to the contemporary Western mind, reflect processes and capacities remote from those that characterize acknowledged masters of painting.

Eminent authorities can be cited on either side of the debate over the aesthetic status of children's works. As far back as 1848 an influential Swiss pedagogue and artist, Rodolphe Töpffer, intrigued his contemporaries with the suggestion that "there is less of a difference between the young scribbling Michelangelo and Michelangelo as an immortal artist, than between the immortal Michelangelo and

8

Michelangelo as an apprentice";* and just a few years later the poet
Charles Baudelaire dubbed the child a pure archetype of "the painter
of modern life." In our own century many artists have studied
children's works and paid them homage. Jean Dubuffet collected
children's art, read widely on the subject, and even conducted a
special investigation of graffiti on Parisian streets. Pablo Picasso
pored over drawings by children and eventually published a set of
sketches based on youngsters' renditions of the bullfight. In an
intriguing aside the great master on one occasion commented, "Once
I drew like Raphael, but it has taken me a whole lifetime to learn to
draw like children."

Yet strong reservations have been raised about the practice of
attributing significance to children's drawings. In a probing assessment of the relationship between child and adult art, the critic
André Malraux commented, "Though a child is often artistic, he is
not an artist. For his gift controls him; not he his gift. His procedure is different in kind from that of the artist's, since the artist
treasures up his acquired knowledge—and this would never enter
the child's head. . . . Children's works are often fascinating because
in the best of them, as in art, the pressure of the world is lifted. . . .
The charm of the child's productions comes of their being foreign
to his will; once his will intervenes, it ruins them. We may expect
anything of the child, except awareness and mastery; the gap between his pictures and conscious works of art is like that between
his metaphors and Baudelaire. . . . The artist has "an eye," but not
when he is fifteen." Similar sentiments have been voiced by a contemporary art educator, Nancy Smith: "The child and the artist
have different approaches to the relation of form or composition to
subject matter . . . the child and the adult experience these funda-
mentals differently." The educator Maria Montessori ridiculed the
notion of an artistic child: "The eye of [the] child is uneducated,
the hand inert, the mind insensible alike to the beautiful and ugly."
And one of the foremost artists of our epoch, Paul Klee, who studied his own childhood drawings, watched his son Felix draw, and
devoted as much time as any painter to a study of the works of
young children, finally admonished:

> Don't translate my works to those of children. . . . They are worlds
> apart. . . . Never forget the child knows nothing of art . . . the
> artist on the contrary is concerned with the conscious formal com-
> positions of his pictures, whose representational meaning comes
> about with intention, through associations of the unconscious.

---

* The sources of quotations and research findings will be found in the
notes, pp. 271–274.

Given wide-ranging discussion by noted authorities on the nature and status of children's art, we might well expect that a definitive consensus had been reached, or that, at the very least, considerable progress had been made toward clarifying the issues. After all, countless educators, parents, and other interested parties have collected the artwork of children, and dozens of books about children's art have been written over the past few decades. Similarly, given the sustained attention in the art world to the works of naïfs, primitives, and other twentieth-century artists whose works have been considered childlike, one might legitimately anticipate that the relation of these works to those of young children would long since have been fixed. In truth, however, the issues raised here have remained in a state of relative limbo: considerable interest but relatively little progress. For an understanding of some of the reasons for this state of affairs, it is helpful to review briefly the history of interest in children's artwork.

As soon as one searches for a history of children's art and examines the attitudes toward it in earlier epochs, one discovers how recently the scribblings of children have entered into public consciousness. No doubt children have always drawn; and no doubt proud parents have looked admiringly at their youngsters' marks on the sand, daubings on windowpanes, or scribbles upon rocks. Yet one looks in vain through prehistory, classical accounts, and even writings at the time of the Renaissance for conclusive evidence that children drew, let alone that such drawing mattered. (An early sixteenth-century portrait by Giovanni Francesco Caroto (9), which features a child holding a schematic drawing of a man, and a sketch

9

10

on a child's slate from Minoan times (10) are the only exceptions to this statement that I have been able to locate.) Clearly, prior to modern times few people cherished and preserved works by children.

Moreover, such inattention to graphic activity is entirely consistent with the general attitude toward children which permeated Western civilization until the last few centuries. To be sure, children were enjoyed and loved, but until they reached an age of reason (sometime after the seventh year), they were not deemed to be serious individuals. And once this pivotal moment of rationality had arrived, children were treated essentially as miniature adults. Indeed, until the time of Jean-Jacques Rousseau in the mid-eighteenth century, there was little suspicion that children might pass through stages of development, even less that their language, thoughts, behavior, and drawings might reveal (or reflect) qualitatively distinctive conceptions of the world.

By the latter half of the nineteenth century the Rousseauian attraction to the innocence of children, together with the growing scientific interest in the development of the mind, had led educators and scientists to attend anew to the drawings of youngsters. At the same time paper and markers became more widely available (and affordable), making for more opportunities to draw. Reflecting the new preoccupation with the growth and education of children, a number of pedagogues undertook examinations of children's drawings; they soon discerned strikingly similar development across thousands of miles and dozens of cultures. As the result of these examinations a number of major points about children's drawings became firmly established.

According to the emerging consensus, a child begins making marks during the second year of life, at first enjoying the motor sensations of banging marker on paper, but soon coming to prize instead the contrasts between the dark scribbled lines and the white surface. The contriving of certain geometric forms—circles, crosses, rectangles, triangles—coupled with an increasing proclivity to combine these marks into more intricate patterns, is a fundamental development of the third and fourth years of life. The child is establishing a vocabulary of lines and forms—the basic building blocks of a graphic language—which, like the sounds of language, eventually combine into meaningful, referential units. And, indeed, a pivotal moment occurs some time during the third, fourth, or fifth year of life: the child for the first time produces a recognizable depiction of *some thing* in the world—in most cases, the ubiquitous "tadpole man" who stands for Everyman.

The preschooler evolves fixed patterns, or schemas, for the familiar objects of his world—a line abutting a circle for a flower, a rectangle harboring enclosed crosses for a house with windows, a circle with radiating lines for the sun. And once he has mastered such graphic strategies and has gained some understanding of the spatial possibilities offered by the paper, he produces organized scenes—sometimes happy combinations of familiar objects and persons, at other times more abstract configurations in which diverse geometric forms are arrayed.

In either case, according to most authorities, a summit of artistry is achieved at the end of the preschool period. As suggested by our opening examples, drawings by youngsters of this age are characteristically colorful, balanced, rhythmic, and expressive, conveying something of the range and the vitality associated with artistic mastery. One has the strong feeling that such drawings constitute an important and perhaps a primary vehicle of expression for the young child. And the often striking products reinforce a general notion of the child at this age as a young artist—an individual participating in a meaningful way in processes of creation, elaboration, and self-expression.

This apogee, this flowering, does not last, however. Instead, during the early school years the child's interest in free graphic expression is widely believed to wane: it is sometimes replaced by a correlative preoccupation with language, games, or social relations, or, at other times, by a single-minded determination to achieve photographic realism in drawing—to show everything just the way it appears to the lens of a camera. Whatever the case, however, the exuberant high point of earlier years is submerged, at least for a time; it resurfaces only in a select group of youngsters—perhaps those with special talent, perhaps those with no alternative means for self-expression, perhaps those with a supporting environment, unusual motivation, or even marked obstinacy.

This much, then, has been common coin—a description of

children's drawings which most experts can endorse. Why, then, is our knowledge still so fragmented? Why do we but partially understand this topic? In my view, one standard approach to children's drawings, while basically accurate, has remained far too disinterested: by reviewing in neutral terms the stages through which the drawings pass, it has simply characterized children's drawings, much as one would describe a recently deciphered ancient code or the stages in the unfolding of an embryo. And so we are left with a sterile, static view of the child drawer: nowhere do we glimpse the young child clad in a tattered smock surrounded by the smell of paint and the feel of brushes, engrossed in drawing, actively trying to make sense of his world, and of his own thoughts and feelings, through the act of putting marker to paper. An account of drawing as part of the overall developmental process remains to be effected.

To be sure, there has been another approach to children's drawings—one decidedly "interested," perhaps overly so. While the authorities I have quoted have for the most part been content with dispassionate description, other investigators have attempted to figure out the "meanings" or even "the meaning" of children's art. These writers have often gravitated toward a one-sided and therefore misleading view of children's work—a view oblivious to the variety of processes that such work may in fact entail.

Consider the various causes to which children's drawing has in the past been sacrificed. Some writers treated it as a simple reflection of a child's affective state: contemplating a youngster's drawing of a gorilla, whose stomach with its partially digested food is visible from the outside (11), they would dwell on his fear of that animal, his desire for oral satisfaction, the gloomy mood that dictated the choice of the color black. Subject matter served as a "royal road" to the child's unconscious concerns. Other analysts would replace this excessive emphasis on the child's emotional life

11

with an equally heavy-handed embracing of a cognitive point of view: they would view such an effort as an attempt to draw "what the child knows rather than what he sees." In this spirit they would stress the child's compulsion to register the contents of the stomach, to show that he indeed knew where the food had gone; or they would stress his still primitive mastery of spatial relations, as exemplified by his failure to realize that certain organs are situated behind others and thus cannot be fully exposed in a veridical representation. Selecting yet another angle of this cognitive orientation, other writers exploited children's drawings as a measure of intelligence: the child who included several features of the gorilla would be deemed more intelligent than the child who included just a few, irrespective of how expressive or stylized the latter's rendering of the animal happened to be. And still other experts simply waxed enthusiastic about children's drawings. One commented: "Children's drawings are indications of more general phenomena of life. They may be regarded as expressions of our search for order in a complex world, as examples of communication, as indices of the type of society we live in, as reminders of our own lost innocence and verve." Another expert saw devastating effects of a lack of opportunity to draw: "The child without access to a stimulating arts program is being systematically cut off from most of the ways in which he can perceive the world. His brain is being systematically damaged." While such well-intentioned remarks may have helped call attention to drawings, they were ultimately counterproductive: for if drawings relate equally to every aspect of a child's existence, they would be as difficult to explain as would life itself.

In so classifying and criticizing these early students of child art, I do not intend to deny, minimize, or distort their achievements. As I've indicated, most of what we know about the nature, the course, and the significance of children's drawings has come from workers in one or another of these traditions: and much of what I present here builds directly upon their pioneering contributions. Still, to my mind, the major task of understanding the meanings and the import of children's drawing will not be accomplished until we consider facets that have thus far received scant attention: the reasons that children's art follows its characteristic course (as well as the reasons behind any deviations); the precise relations between the child's drawing and other aspects of his mental, social, and emotional development; and the aesthetic status of the work that he produces. These questions will loom large in the pages that follow.

Let me say an initial word about each of these issues. To begin with the drawings themselves: I find it insufficient simply to say that children first scribble, then make geometric forms, and then draw tadpoles. Science properly begins with such descriptions, but it should not end with them. Even though final, exhaustive explanations will continue to elude us, we must still seek them. Thus I will attempt here a fine-grained analysis, in an effort to tease out the factors that guide children's drawings from one to another stage. Indeed, at each stage I will ponder the challenges confronted by the child: for instance, how in early childhood single lines come to form enclosures; what factors enable young schoolchildren to organize objects into scenes; which processes the preadolescent invokes in attempting to fashion forms that faithfully resemble their referents. And at the same time I will offer an explanation for certain deviations: why selected youngsters may evolve a characteristic style during the preschool years; why some continue to draw even during the middle school years; and how an exceptional youngster like Nadia, the autistic drawer of horses mentioned earlier (7), can achieve heights of representational grandeur.

In regard to the relation between drawing and development, it seems to me patent that drawing cannot—and should not—be considered apart from the rest of the child's evolving capacities. Yet a kind of isolation of the "drawing organ" has characterized most descriptions, quite possibly because people with the strongest interest in children's drawings have rarely possessed deep knowledge of human development. As a developmental psychologist I have been repeatedly struck by the intimate yet generally ignored links between the child's drawing and the rest of his burgeoning powers: the child who first wields a marker is learning in many areas of his young life about tool use; the toddler who hits upon simple "thing-like" enclosures has been establishing basic categories and object classes in every realm of life; the six-year-old "artist" is engaging in rampant symbolic play in other areas, producing figures of speech, stories, dances, and songs which in charm and originality often rival his more tangible drawings; the dogged realism manifested in the schoolchild's drawings mirrors with amazing fidelity the embracing of literal language in school and the pervasive rejection of any deviations from norms and conventions across the fabric of social life. Even the enigmatic features of adolescent art—an emerging interest in pure design, a concentration on the human figure, a preoccupation with rendering spatial volume, a repudiation of works that do not meet one's own increasingly exacting standards—are all tangible manifestations, in the realm of drawing, of factors that pervade the consciousness of individuals on the threshold of adulthood. Such considerations underline the pressing need for a developmental analysis; and yet, with few exceptions, the affinities between drawing and development have been totally bypassed or left implicit.

Finally, I turn to perhaps the most delicate and challenging question of all: the artistic status of the works of children. That such works may move us and have the potential to stir others is not at issue: indeed, these works would not now be so widely examined had they not originally allured many of us. Yet we cannot escape the issue of whether they hold the same meanings for a youngster as they do for an adult; whether a youthful drawer is significantly involved with the product or is wholly enveloped by the processes of creation; and whether, whatever his attitude toward his work, his skills utilize processes akin to those marshaled by gifted adult artists.

In confronting this question of artistic status, I shall be stepping directly into a dangerous crossfire involving sharp-witted philosophers, learned aestheticians, reflective artists, and indeed every lay person who has ever contemplated the nature of aesthetic experience, of aesthetic purpose, or of aesthetic achievement. Few areas prove more daunting to define or to investigate. Yet we cannot hope to make any progress in ascertaining the aesthetic status of children's artwork unless we are willing to define what is involved in artistic activity. Moreover, it is my contention that little progress has been made on this issue *precisely* because most authorities, whatever their ultimate views, have failed to consider which criteria "count" for artistry and have thus begged the very issues they sought to clarify.

The approach to art embraced here can perhaps be best conveyed through an example drawn from another realm, that of figurative language. Consider a four-year-old youngster who says of the traces left by a skywriting airplane, "Look at that scar in the sky." We do not wish to credit a preschool child with command of metaphor if he simply uses the word "scar" inappropriately or if he does not know its precise meaning. On the other hand, if we can establish that he does indeed know what a scar is, that he is not confusing the airplane (or its trace) with some other entity, and that he gains some pleasure from the production of this figure of speech, we would be inclined to conclude that he is engaging in artistic activity. By the same token, we do not automatically want to call a child—or a chimpanzee or a computer—an artist just because he happens to create a set of lines that we find pleasing. But if the child reveals to us on other occasions that he knows how to vary the use of line, that he attends to such aspects as color, expressiveness, and shading, that he intends to produce a certain effect, and that he (and others) are gaining pleasure from the results of his activity, then we might properly view that child as a young artist.

Our perspective on artistry, then, is decidedly cognitive. We are looking for evidence of knowledge in at least two senses. On the one hand, the artist must know *how*: he needs to be able to use the medium productively, to vary its basic elements, to combine them in diverse ways, to achieve certain effects. But in addition, the artist must also know *that*: he needs to know that options are available to him, that each entails various benefits and costs, and that his ultimate products will have effects both upon an audience and upon himself.

In the end, I do not expect to succeed where the wisest have failed. I shall not solve the issue of what is—and what is not—art: I shall not prove that children's works are—or are not—art. The posing of this question will, however, be justified if it enables one to make progress in assessing the significance of the child's graphic activity. Certainly children's artwork is not identical to that fashioned by adults, but I shall also try to show that by no means is it a totally separate entity: in its sources, its processes, its ultimate significance, it possesses distinct and specifiable parallels to the artistry of gifted adults.

I think it possible to draw a line, though one by no means devoid of contortions, between the paces of those youthful scribblers glimpsed earlier and the activities of the most gifted artists—be they the dedicated traditionalist Gérôme or the constantly experimenting Picasso. But specifying the relations—and the distances—between these two "end points" will take many pages. It becomes essential to consider how a child learns to look at what he has drawn, how he learns to look at what others have achieved, and how he gradually gains control over the medium which, at the beginning, is foreign and implacable to him. The normal trajectory of development, as achieved by most children in Western culture and quite possibly throughout the world, will form the basic scaffolding for my story, the framework against which one can contemplate its central riddles.

In traversing the several stages of artistic development, I shall encounter quite naturally some other intriguing questions. I shall consider, for instance, the relationship between the art produced by children and that wrought by the hands of various "special populations": the drawings made by nonhuman primates, the sketches produced by brain-damaged individuals, and those intriguing works created by individuals raised in different cultures, including prehistoric cave artists, contemporary artists in preliterate cultures, and those occasional naïfs still lurking today in certain remote pockets of our own culture. I shall consider, in addition, the relationship between drawing and other activities undertaken by the young child: of special interest is the increasing separation of drawing from writing and other cultural notations, the emergence of mapping and other nonartistic kinds of graphic activity, and the relationship between drawing and efforts involving other art forms, ranging from music to storytelling.

For the most part I shall focus on behavior typical of normal children; after all, we are seeking a portrait of artistic development as it has been realized in the species. Most examples presented here are therefore taken from children without special talents in the artistic sphere. But any inquiry in art, and especially one concerned with the sources of artistic accomplishment, must necessarily confront the issue of talent—the status of those individuals who, owing to nature, nurture, or some indissoluble blend, possess special gifts. Several talented child artists have offered themselves for intensive analysis; they have generously allowed me to speak with them, to photograph their work, and to observe them as they engage in artistic activities. Because they are still young, and because I cannot anticipate what will happen to them eventually or what they will ultimately think of their youthful cooperation with an inquiring psychologist, I have not identified them by name: but I want herewith to record my profound thanks to them and to their families for helping me to convey the nature of a complex and deeply personal activity.

There is yet another challenge that I must meet here, one with an even greater meaning for me personally. In preparing this book I have for several years been collecting and studying the drawings of my three children. They, too, have generously allowed me to reprint their drawings and, in an effort to afford them at least a modicum of privacy, I have transformed the names of Kerith, Jay, and Andrew into a hypothetical pair—Kay and Jerry. Not surprisingly, they have become interested in their father's curious activities, and herein resides the ultimate challenge.

Recently one of my children began visiting my study and poring over the drawings that he and his siblings had been producing. Having learned of my intention to write a book on children's drawings, he one evening asked, "Dad, why do children draw differently as they get older?"

As an inveterate developmental psychologist, I returned the question forthwith: "That's just what I want to write about. Why do *you* think that they change?"

My son paused for several moments and then answered, in his most thoughtful way, "As you get older, I think you look differently. You look more carefully at things. Also you think a lot, you plan before you actually make the drawing."

If this book succeeds in reaching beyond the common sense of a sensible young boy without at the same time becoming unnecessarily obscure or needlessly provocative, it will have achieved the goals that I have set forth.

CHAPTER 2

First Scribbles

WHEN he was eighteen months and three days old, my son Jerry grabbed hold of a marker lying on the table in front of him. He swung the marker against a piece of paper, repeated this action again, and then stopped. Noting that no mark had been made, he then turned the marker around, so that now the felt tip, rather than the blunt end, could strike the paper. When still no mark was forthcoming (because the felt had dried up), Jerry dropped the marker and went to fetch another one. He curled his hand around the new marker, loosely enough to retain flexibility, yet secure enough to ensure some control over the direction of his movements.

This time his swipes were crowned with success (12). Using his elbow as a pivot, he unleashed a rapid, semicircular motion which produced an arc on the page; and as he repeated this circular gesture several times, a number of overlapping arcs came to cover the center of the sheet. Looking deliberately at the paper and continuing to gesture as feverishly as only an excited young toddler can, he then proceeded to bang the marker against the paper a number of times, letting out a squeal with each bang, and in the process producing a series of little dots. Breaking out into a broad grin, Jerry then dropped the marker, lifted the piece of paper, and handed it to me, announcing in a satisfied manner, "Daddy."

Jerry had produced a scribble, not his first and possibly not even his most appealing, but unquestionably a scribble, a series of markings on a page which recorded two minutes of activity of the musculature of his hand, wrist, and forearm. Few would want to apply to this product a more honorific term than scribble, and, indeed, the term scribble is often used by individuals—including educators who should know better—as an expression of disparagement. But this scribble represented an achievement for Jerry—as indeed such scribbles do for every young child.

To be sure, the gap between what Jerry had drawn, in the

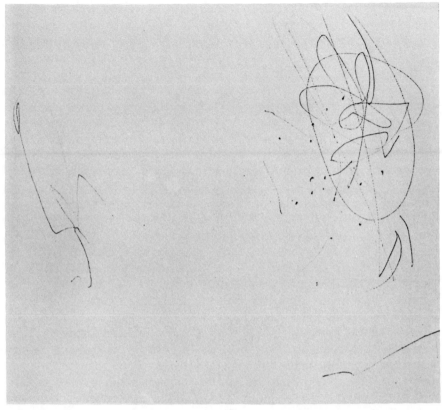

12

middle of the second year of his life, and the kinds of finished pictures produced by an adult, or even a child artist of six or seven, is enormous. There was none of the control over geometric forms routinely found in the "prerepresentational" drawings of the two- or three-year-old; none of the recognizable schemas* of humans, animals, and houses (with chimneys!) found in the sketchbook of many a five-year-old; none of the artfully balanced and colorfully embroidered scenes fashioned by the young schoolchild; none of the photographically realistic renderings of ships, airplanes, horses, or houses within the ken of the normal ten-year-old.

Still more vast is the distance between Jerry's scribble and the everyday activities of the practicing artist. Almost any skilled painter of our day can produce, with modest effort, a satisfactory likeness of the persons, objects, and events in the world around

---

* Following common terminology in psychology, the word "schema" is used to refer to the basic graphic forms for depicting objects. In contrast, the word "scheme" is used to denote any repeatable behavoral act. Children use a variety of perceptual and motor schemes to produce a schema of a human being.

him. Key aspects of expression, mood, and character are also within the grasp of the competent technician (though only the genuine artist can capture a nuance with precision). More remarkably, the various skills in the artist's repertoire can interact productively with one another. She can convert the many forms and objects that she sees—in the world before her or in her mind's eye—into accurate likenesses on the canvas. Or, proceeding from what is already on the canvas, she can transform even the most casual doodle (or scribble) into an arresting design or a convincing representation. Nor is she simply an apparatus, or program, for converting perceptions into contours and contours into likenesses. The talented artist will also encourage a ready congress between her feelings and her palette. She can convey emotions and expressions of significance; and she can evoke in the viewer of her work some of the feelings and experiences that have possessed importance for her.

Such interplay amongst perceptions, behavior, and feelings is clearly beyond the ken of the young child, even one much further along in artistic development than my scribbling toddler. And yet if the distance that Jerry must still traverse is vast, so, too, is the portion of the journey that he has already realized. Indeed, after less than two years in the world, he may have progressed to the threshold of artistic achievement.

Consider, in contrast, the infant's meager behavioral repertoire at birth. Though possessing a set of well-developed reflexes, the newborn infant has scant control over the movements of her fingers and limbs. They flail about almost at will, reflecting perhaps the degree of her arousal but devoid of any purpose. At most, an incipient relation to the perceived world can be demonstrated: the newborn child will focus reliably on points of contrasting light, on edges and angles, and (in the opinion of some researchers) on the "eye portion" of a face. But there is no evidence to suggest that the newborn can see a world of objects and persons or, for that matter, a complete geometric form.

When it comes to the feelings of the newborn child (or, for that matter, the feelings of any "subject"), psychologists can only speculate. While it seems reasonable to assume some discrimination on the part of the infant between comfort and discomfort, between pleasure and pain, finer discriminations seem unlikely. And the thought that the child might somehow be able to express her feelings in a symbolic medium—such as a line upon a paper—seems as remote at this time as the possibility that the rhythms of neonatal reflexes might harbor the basic structure of a symphonic poem.

Race the film of development forward six or eight months and one encounters an organism that has adapted with amazing rapidity and skill to the world in which it has found itself. The child already sees persons and faces as organized totalities, as meaningful gestalts rather than a conglomeration of presumably unconnected features. She recognizes familiar persons, smiles readily at them, and unambiguously signals her discomfort at unfamiliar (or threatening) sights. Household objects—teddy bears, rattles, the bottle—also rapidly evoke signs of recognition as well as appropriate sequences of action. She smiles at the rattle, then shakes it vigorously as soon as it has been placed in her hand.

The motor system has also matured to a considerable degree. The child can now swipe reliably at an object, seize it tightly, and try out a surprising grab bag of actions with it. Seeing a marker, she will grasp for it, probably capturing it successfully on the first swipe, then place it in her mouth, bite on it, and, probably finding it tasteless, drop it on the floor. Or she may discover that she likes the sound it makes when she hits it against a surface, and will continue to bang it for long periods of time. And if she is attracted by the sound that another person makes with the marker, she is likely to repeat the actions in which *she* herself has been involved, on the mistaken (but charming) belief that her own actions have given rise to this interesting noise.

Nonetheless, still shy of her first birthday, the infant is notable for what she fails to understand. For her, the marker is simply an interesting object on which to practice her most familiar activities —mouthing, eating, sucking, throwing, banging—an object that is fun to hold, fun to cast away. She holds it whichever way she grabs it and makes no effort to orient it correctly (or even consistently). Nor does she show any interest in the marker once it has disappeared from her view; for her, objects exist only in the here and now, and once out of sight they are equally out of mind. Her recognition of the world of objects has progressed, but she still seems to lack knowledge about the world of pictures. To be sure, she will attend to a picture, as well as a three-dimensional display, and she will focus on "informative aspects" of the pictorial array, such as thick lines. But it is not yet clear that she can relate a freehand representation to the corresponding "real life" object.

Finally, our child of half a year has yet to separate herself from the world about her. She still lacks any sense of herself as a discrete being, with her own thoughts, beliefs, and needs. Her own actions remain indistinguished from those of others; her own mirrored reflection is seen simply as another person; and while she has evolved bonds of attachment to certain close individuals, her involvement with them remains totally practical. Such persons function as sources of food and bodily comfort, or possibly also as participants in the first furtive exchanges of peek-a-boo.

Let another year go by and the changes in the child's world are as cataclysmic as they were the first year. In fact, one might go so far as to claim that the child has taken a series of decisive steps —steps that make her quite unambigously a young person in her own right. In particular, she has come to understand the two principal worlds about her—the world of objects and the world of persons. She now appreciates that objects exist in space and time and will continue to do so even when they are no longer in her view. This knowledge—seemingly simple but actually decisive—allows the child to live in a world that is predictable rather than chimerical, reliable rather than random. She now can expect to find things (for the most part) where she left them; she can expect things to do what they have done before; she can expect the same causes to yield the same effects, the same acts to entail the same consequences. Her world is now comfortably Newtonian, and all's well in that world.

Even as the child now inhabits a world of predictable objects, she has come to live in a world with a regular cast of persons. First and foremost there are those reliably situated about her—parents, siblings, and valued caretakers. To each of these individuals she has gradually formed a relation of attachment, a feeling of security and well-being in their midst. The painful price of this comfort is distress as they depart or when they are absent. But if development has proceeded normally, the child is also able on her own to undertake small trips away from these individuals—to establish initial autonomy. Gracing this realization is an even more important development. Now aware of the existence of other persons, with their own names, bodies, needs, appearances, and views, the child is well on the road to differentiating herself from these others. Phrased more positively, she is on the threshold of recognizing herself as a person in her own right, of knowing that she has a name, a body, and a discrete existence. No longer will she stare perplexedly in the mirror at the stranger there. Rather she will try out experiments, examine her own body, compare it with her reflection, and ultimately offer unmistakable and cheerful signs of her own existence as a separate entity—a human person in a social world.

Acquisition of knowledge about a world of objects and a world of persons is a monumental achievement. The child now has firm expectations about what she will encounter in her daily activities and increasing confidence in her ability to master the world about her. Such knowledge also multiplies the ways in which she can relate to the world. Equipped with knowledge about the properties of objects and the ways of persons, she need no longer simply react to them mechanically; she can make use of them, exploit them, even outmaneuver them to achieve her own ends.

At long last, tool use becomes possible. Objects are no longer restricted to single functions: instead they become viewed—and valued—in terms of their potential for eliciting a range of desired consequences. If the child wants a piece of food, she need no longer just grab for it. She can make use of any of a number of implements —such extensions of her limbs as a stick, a stalk, or a spoon—to pull that desired morsel toward her. By the same token, she may use another individual as a tool, either calling on that person by name to retrieve the food or simply giving a tug on the skirts, which, quite reliably, will result in the same desired outcome. Persons and objects are no longer mere entities; they have become a reliable and frequently exploited means for securing an infinitude of ends.

We can see these various discoveries at work in Jerry's explorations. When he now sees a marker, he no longer simply tries out each of his most practiced (and often inappropriate) schemes. Rather he entertains an expectation—that it will make a mark. If this expectation is initially thwarted, he initiates a program of action: He first flips it around to make sure that he has placed the right end upon the surface. Later he will know enough to discover by inspection which end is correct. Should this check fail, he has yet another option, for he has come to expect that marks will come not just from this one marker but from any of the now familiar class of markers, ranging from a pencil to a paintbrush. And if he is thwarted even there, he can shift to another order of tool: a sign or call to his father will fetch for him a marker that works.

Jerry's pleasures in using the marker are still primitive. One could hardly say he has any grand representational schemas up his sleeve. But the delights are far from nil. Earlier he gained satisfaction merely from the cool feel of the marker in his hand and the rough muscular movements of his forearm. Now he wants to behold the impression made by the marker, he is frustrated when no mark is made, and he gains satisfaction from beholding the paper filled with the fruits of his labors. The marker is beginning to function as a tool, a means for securing the desired end of lines across a piece of paper. And before long Jerry will discover that he does not need a writing implement in order to adorn surfaces with such lines. In the months ahead Jerry will make marks that please him by smearing porridge in a bowl, dew on a windowpane, water in a bathtub, a melting candy bar, and part of a bowel movement which he cleverly extricates from the interstices of a poorly fastened diaper.

This satisfaction is not just for him alone, however. Jerry is now cognizant of the existence of other persons, persons who display their feelings toward him, their likes and dislikes, their hopes and fears. And so it is natural for him, upon completion of his own labors, to share his product with them. Even as he scans the room eagerly for recognition and approval when he has uttered a word, spilled a glass of water, or shut out the light, so too, he seeks to establish a link with others by virtue of his drawing. He gives the picture to his father, but the gift is secondary. What is important here is the drawing's link to communication—its role in social exchange. Furthermore, at times Jerry will incorporate his drawing into a ritualized social exchange, making a noise each time someone else makes a mark, placing lines directly atop those made by someone else, or imitating as faithfully as he can the movements made by another individual who has put marker to paper.

To be sure, in these early markings Jerry has yet to discover the full potentials of his behavior. He has not a glimmering that his marks can stand for objects or events in the world; he cannot fashion discrete forms such as circles or crosses; his activity is limited to just what it is called—sheer scribbling. Yet, something of moment has already occurred. For in the transition from the infant who is not cognizant of the products of his pen to the child who cares deeply about whether a mark has been made, a crucial realization has come about: the awareness that, by the actions of his own hand, he can create something—something that lasts, something that has importance for him, and (judging by their responses) something that has significance for those about him. The potential to create a product that matters—a mark that can stand on its own—is one of the first indications to the child of his own efficacy, his nascent capacity to use a tool and to create a product with it. At this time when the child is gradually breaking away from his caretakers and attempting to establish autonomy, this evidence (as clear as a black line against a white backdrop) that he can himself produce something assumes critical developmental importance. Even as the child's ministrations to a treasured teddy bear illustrate that he can now assume some of the roles ordinarily occupied by the powerful adults in his midst, that he too can love and care and scold, so too the capacity to produce lines on a page shows that he can wield the tools of his culture to create a trace that matters. Just how, and how much, it matters will be his task to discover as he makes the transition in the months ahead from mere marks to marks that can designate those objects and persons he has come to know.

FIRST INTERLUDE

The Developmental
Course of Scribbling

JUST shy of twenty-three months of age, Jerry sat down at the kitchen table one sunny spring morning and, equipped with the requisite materials, produced in rapid succession a series of twenty-four drawings. Though several markers were available, he stuck resolutely to a blue one, making only occasional stabs with a nearby pink marker. His intense concentration suggested that he knew exactly what he wanted to do; he seemed equally in control whether filling in one page fully or simply placing a single mark and saying, "One more picture" (my translation: "another sheet of paper"). From one perspective the series of drawings was not remarkable, for there were many other days when Jerry had produced much the same sort of series. Yet such sessions of scribbling seem worth pondering, for it is from such apparently casual but actually event-filled sessions that the messy and wayward scribbles of early drawings slowly give way to the control of geometric form, the achievement of representational depiction, and the precision of faithful likenesses.

In this heated frenzy of scribbling Jerry was displaying "live" that process termed *microgenesis*—the minute-by-minute, step-by-step sequence whereby human activity evolves. At any point in development the individual possesses a certain set of skills, a given cluster of perceptual and motor schemes, and a more or less explicit sense of direction. It may well be that this orientation, this movement toward a goal, is only dimly perceived, but the forward progress of the growth process in normal individuals is no less real and no less potent for eluding consciousness. In Jerry's case, he already possessed a series of schemes or "moves" in the graphic sphere: he could run through circular motions, dotted patterns,

25

twisted writing like lines. Each of these schemes, just like a developing muscle, called for continuous exercise so that its full potential could be explored and realized, and the overall thrust in this practice was decidedly forward. Rather than remaining at a point of equilibrium or stasis, Jerry's activity progressed every day, so that from one week to the next a distinct evolution could be detected. As we examine in detail the passage of events from one drawing to the next, we can gain a feeling for, and perhaps even glimpse directly, the developmental process itself.

Let us therefore follow Jerry as he proceeds from one drawing to the next. He began by making a series of wild blue circles built upon a single continuous stroke and expressed in a whirlwind of activity (13). The next drawing (14) came close to featuring a single circle. It in fact looks like a deliberately fashioned circle, but because of his inability to repeat this feat for several months, it is better described as a happy accident, one of those occasional tantalizing anticipations of a future achievement. After completing the circle, he placed inside it a number of letterlike forms, by means of some rapid jabs. The overriding circular form, subsequently filled in with some more precise jabs, also dominated the next two drawings (15, 16); in the latter one, the placement within the borders seemed distinctly purposeful.

The next five drawings saw a shift from a concentration on circular enclosures to a reciprocal stress on the making of small marks, produced by bending intently over the paper and emitting a single sound with each blow—"oh," "ah," "oh." The first drawing (17) was presented without comment; the next (18) was called "a picture." The motifs of circles and little marks were combined in the next two drawings (19, 20), as he seemed eager to keep alive the circular as well as the mini-marking schemas.

Jerry spent a good deal more time on the ninth drawing in the series (21) and indeed managed to fill up most of the page. The circular motif once again came to the fore, but, particularly at the bottom of the page, some of the little marks again made an appearance. There was also a sustained attempt to take lines in various directions, an effort accentuated by the twisted contortions of Jerry's wrist.

Series of drawings produced over a short period of time exhibit a characteristic rhythm. They seem to come in sets, with each cluster of three, four, or five drawings an exploration of one particular motor scheme, gesture, or motif. Having once "worked through" a scheme, for however long that takes, the child seems to move on to a somewhat different problem or challenge and again rehearses that scheme for a time. Earlier schemes are seldom dropped completely, however; initially kept in reserve, they are either resur-

3

14

15

6

17

18

9

20

21

rected explicitly in later sequences or, more commonly, become partially incorporated into subsequent explorations with related forms.

Another shift in tempo can be seen in the next several drawings. While Jerry had exerted considerable effort in filling out the page in his ninth drawing, the next four papers (22–25; done in pink) were executed very rapidly. Just one or two lines, almost like the signature of a busy executive, constituted these drawings. One senses a pause, possibly designed to gain new energy. Significantly more involvement characterized the next drawing (26). Here Jerry invoked once more both the circular and the writing forms; and then, suddenly, he hit upon a new type of activity—a burst of a dozen dots which filled the upper right-hand corner of the sheet. Jerry clearly enjoyed this plosive activity and, for reasons which I am afraid remain obscure to me, called this peppered section "a birdie."

The newly discovered and instantly favored dotted patterns also dominated several drawings that followed. They were geographically localized in the first (27), extended more leisurely across the page in the next three (28, 29, 30), and indeed supplanted the writing marks as a rival for the dominant circular motif. Concentric circles propelled at considerable speed returned to the fore, however, in the next set (31, 32); but little dots still could be discerned, this time occupying the center of the circle as the little marks had done earlier.

Determination finally began to flag in the last four drawings in the series (33–36). Jerry had the energy to make only a few incomplete circles, a handful of lonely dots. Whether he would have continued the series, and perhaps even discovered new sources of

22   23   24

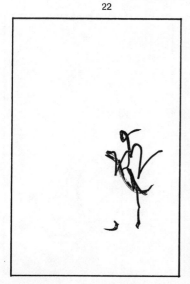
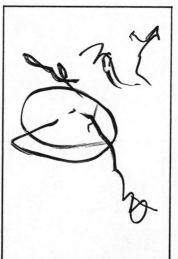

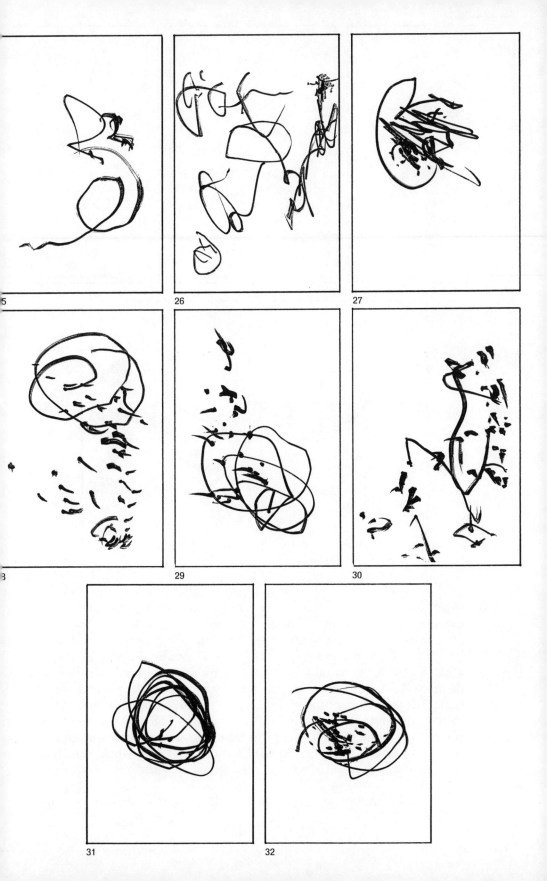

25

26

27

28

29

30

31

32

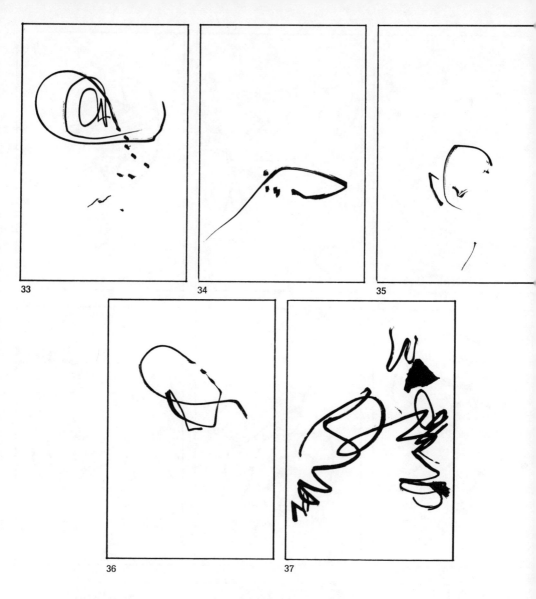

33 34 35

36 37

inspiration or energy, will never be known, because his older sister came along and began to imitate her brother instead (37). So much for controlled and undisturbed experiments within one's own home!

Two dozen drawings in less than ten minutes—a rate of output almost any artist would envy. Nor can this graphic effluence be dismissed as random activity. Jerry was too heavily involved in what he was doing, too delighted by some of the products, too intent on naming, repeating, and varying his several schemes (and schemas), to allow the conclusion that this activity was mindless or purposeless. But how then should we think of this work, and how best to chart its place within the gallery of drawings by young children?

Finding rough analogies to a child's drawing proves tantalizingly easy. Clearly, what the two-year-old draws has resonances in his linguistic activity—the child's babbling, his early linguistic forays, his nighttime monologues—all these partake of the flavor of drawing, proceeding at their own rate, and following the beat of their own mysterious purposes. Much the same parallels can be noted for the child's singing—his humming at eight months, his chaotic combining of tonal fragments at two years, the invention of new melodies toward the beginning of school—all these progressions share some of the spirit and directed energy of the child's graphic activity. Building with blocks, putting puzzles together, dancing and cavorting about the room, learning the number series, engaging in "pretend play" with teddy bears, tea sets, and daddy's typewriter—these activities, too, are linked in sundry ways to Jerry bent over the kitchen table at play—*and* at work.

A challenge lies in going beyond such loose affinities. Is it indeed possible to characterize in a more precise manner the numerous activites undertaken by the child bent on mastering the various symbol systems of his culture? At times the behavior of the child seems infused with planning and direction—each drawing seems to build upon the previous one, the child seems deliberately to attempt certain effects, to pose and then solve certain problems. At other times the activities appear to be without rhyme or reason —the drawing could have started or stopped at any point, proceeded in any direction, and lasted for two seconds or twenty minutes. At still other times the drawing activity seems to an observer to be strongly patterned yet beyond the child's control: one is reminded more of a squirrel burying nuts than a schoolchild computing sums.

But perhaps it is a mistake to embrace one of these descriptions at the expense of others. Processes of development may include skeins of each of these descriptions. Indeed, drawing seems to provide an especially illuminating model of how the individual invades and makes progress in the various domains of expression provided by his society. Each child may in fact exploit a number of skills, proclivities, and sources. Part of his output is indeed determined by forces beyond his control—the urge to grab the pencil and to rub it against the page seems a dividend of primate heritage. But part of his activity is quite purposeful: he has tried out a certain pattern of behavior and he wants to repeat it (indeed, he insists on repeating it) because he finds the sheer activity and contact pleasurable, or because he wants to vary its form, or because he wants to achieve a certain result and has not yet done so effectively. And sometimes the drawing simply fills time; neither the child's attention nor his planning capacities have been mobilized— he is drawing "because it's there."

But what of the particular series we have seen? Surely there is more here than sheer instinctive behavior or random activity. Indeed, what seems to have unfolded in the ten-minute segment that I happen to have witnessed was that Jerry was busily trying to perfect and to realize the various combinations and interrelations among a number of schemes that emerged naturally from the movement of his arm and wrist. We see the ovals of his circular wrist motion, the dots of his jabbing hand motion, and the intricate writinglike forms made by a marker grabbed tightly in the fist and twisted back and forth. Sometimes he worked on one of these components alone, sometimes they were merged, juxtaposed, or contrasted. Surely Jerry was not in any strong sense aware of what he was doing. He had no way of talking about (or otherwise reflecting upon) these various schemes at his disposal because his consciousness of his own actions was still emerging. Yet at a tacit level there is clearly some monitoring of the various possibilities, some satisfaction in seeing them gradually mastered, some sense of direction as the youngster makes increasingly elaborate forms and eventually achieves genuine representations.

Perhaps the closest analogy to this drawing activity occurs in the language play of the child. Consider, for example, a three-year-old attempting to count an array of eight items:

> One, two, three, four, eight, ten, eleben. No, try dat again. One, two, three, four, five, ten, eleben. No, try dat again. One! two! three-e-four-five, ten eleben . . . One! two, three, four, five, six, seven, eleben, whew!

Even more dramatic parallels occur in the child's prattle as he rests in bed. The common flavor comes across in the following example, part of a verbatim transcript of the nighttime monologues of a boy of two and a half named Anthony:

1. That for he	15. Look at Daddy her
2. Mamamama with Daddy	16. Look at Daddy . . .
3. Milk for Daddy	
4. OK	51. Daddy put on a hat
5. Daddy dance (two times)	52. Daddy put on a coat
6. Hi, Daddy	53. Only Daddy can
7. Only Anthony	54. I put this in here
8. Daddy dance (two times)	55. See the doggie here
9. Daddy give it	56. See the doggie
10. Daddy not for Anthony	57. I see the doggie (two
11. No	times, falsetto)
12. Daddy	58. Kitty likes doggie
13. Daddy got	59. Lights up here
14. Look at Daddy (in falsetto)	60. Daddy dance (3 times)

As in Jerry's drawings, there is not a single clear message expressed here, nor does a systematic theme run through the entire set of utterances. Yet at the same time the sequence seems anything but random. There are certain recurring sounds (of *m* or *d*), phrases (Daddy dance, Daddy put on a . . . , See the doggie), and characters (I, Daddy, Anthony, the doggie, Mama) which surface regularly, sometimes in the same phraseology, sometimes embedded in different turns of phrase. And, as in the drawing, rehearsals tend to occur in sets of three or four phrases, which move to "reserve" for a while, only to resurface in a new verbal environment and, perhaps, a somewhat altered form. Rather than trying to communicate meaningful messages to other persons, Anthony is more or less systematically running through a corpus of words and sounds that he is in the process of mastering, combining them in various ways suggested by the rules of the language, and, possibly without any awareness of the fact, often producing a combination that proves pleasurable, even poetic, to our ears. What seems to characterize both the daytime drawing activity and the nighttime monologues is that they take place with a notable concentration of energy but in a half-conscious state. Impersonal developmental forces, the stuff of growth itself, rather than the child's own emerging skills of planning seem regnant. If either the child's drawings or his personal conversation were to be interrupted, the whole chain of activity might well cease: the youngster is immersed in a world of his own making, one of tremendous creative significance, but one that can be readily dissolved.

Both examples of playful symbolic activity are characterized by an extreme versatility, as the child moves effortlessly from one set of schemes to another, and indeed seems to be exhibiting his full set of schematic wares. However, the drawing system can also specialize. In the months following Jerry's initial rehearsal of basic forms, I witnessed a number of sessions where he concentrated with exclusive, indeed exhaustive, attention to just one or another scheme. Three weeks after the initial session, for example, he produced nothing but overlapping circles, sometimes using just one marker, at other times harnessing in rapid succession every marker within reach. Two days after his second birthday he orchestrated a session in which spiral-like forms (the extended concentric circle) dominated his drawing activity (38). And a month after his birthday Jerry worked for almost two weeks exclusively on the jagged lines that may be early attempts to copy adult cursive script (39, 40). But as if to dissolve all generalizations and to remind us that he was capable of coordinating his efforts, Jerry also produced, on his birthday, one super picture (41)—a many-colored, full-page effort which contained within it instances of every one of the schemes he

38

40

39

41

had hitherto practiced. It was as if he had uttered a sentence using every part of speech and type of word he had ever encountered before, not to express an unequivocal meaning or attain a specific end, but rather to prove that he indeed had at the tip of his tongue the entire periodic table of linguistic elements.

I have suggested that these series of drawings reflect general processes of development. But they may also have had a more specific end. Three months after the first series of twenty-four papers, Jerry became totally preoccupied with the desire to have faces drawn. I invoke the infelicitous construction "have drawn" because much of his activity consisted in convincing the adults and older siblings around him to produce faces. When he succeeded in this, he would dictate the particular features desired and sometimes he would roughly indicate—by waving his pen or placing a mark near the spot—where a specific feature should be placed.

Jerry's own efforts to draw a face remained unsuccessful for a few months, but he signaled the nature of his attempts at "face-hood" through an oscillation of two strategies. Sometimes he would try to extract a single circle from his customary volley of concentric circles, by starting the series and then trying to stop—a ploy that often resulted in an aborted circle or a circle with an angry line trailing off at its periphery (42). At other times, proceeding from his writing strategy, Jerry would very slowly try to make a wiggly line that would eventually come back in upon itself to produce a bounded form (43). Neither of these efforts was initially successful but both pushed him along toward his desired goal of a circle that could house features (44). Ironically, he had already produced the much-vaunted circles as early as three months before—but then they had been accidents. The challenge he now faced was to mobilize these schemes not simply by accident but by design, so that he could produce a visage when he desired one. The first successful faces finally did occur when he was about twenty-six months old—individual circles, named as "faces," which were immediately filled with one or more smaller circles, termed "eyes" (45–48).

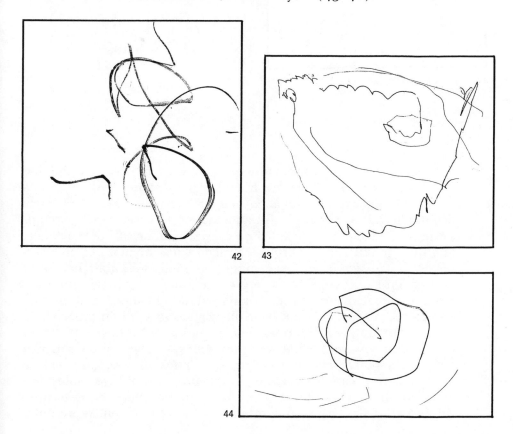

42   43

44

Those awaiting complete explanation of the origins and the microgenesis of drawings are bound to be disappointed. Attempts to provide an explanation *à la* classical physics are in my view doomed to fail. One can devise an equation to describe the circumstances in which given weights on a lever will, or will not, balance, and then go out and perform the crucial experiments. But one cannot write an equation for turning the nonrepresentational child drawer into one capable of representational depiction and then execute the relevant study. Behavioral development and mental development simply do not lend themselves to such an antecedent-consequent frame of reference (do x, and y will follow). What we *can* anticipate—and what we may forever have to be satisfied with—is *an increasingly accurate description of what happens*, a slow-motion cinematic portrait of the progress of one child, two children, many children, as they follow the arduous but pleasure-tinged path from sheer random motor activity to patent representational form. We are free, of course, to offer a model of what happens—to search for that language, that analogy, that figure of speech, that example from another realm which most successfully captures what we see the child do and illuminates its nature. Such a model will surely be complicated. If nothing else, the reprinting of drawings from one two-year-old child reveals that no simple set of factors is likely to provide a satisfactory, let alone an exhaustive, accounting of how drawing skills develop.

Do not mistake this point: I do believe that experimental methods can enhance our understanding of such phenomena. We should be able to gain information concerning the effects on the skill of drawing when there is a choice of various markers or papers of different sizes; we should be able to assess the effects on the form of drawing attributable to other individuals, the influence of graphic models, the role of language, the nature of the marking instrument, and no doubt countless other variables. In such ways we may discover how to speed up, or to slow down, the process whose mainsprings we have been trying to delineate. And we will uncover valuable pieces of the puzzle of drawing that has been scrutinized here.

But to my mind all of these efforts will be simply playing with the levers of development which, in the case of early drawing, have been rather tightly set by the individual's birthright. They provide detailed commentary and relevant elucidation of particulars but do not alter the basic text. The explanation of how children draw in these early stages can only—and then only if we are very fortunate —come to resemble the form of explanation embraced by embryologists of how the zygote gives rise to the blastula, or how the fetus gives rise to the newborn. We can expect increasingly fine descriptions and increasingly greater awareness of the environmental factors that contribute to its course, but we will not be able to find a final—or even a first—cause for what is intrinsic to the processes of development. And we will encounter the same impasse whenever we attempt to explain the processes of creation, be they the equally striking ontogenetic sequences one finds in the four-year-old representational drawer, which we will contemplate in the Second Interlude, or the explorations undertaken by Picasso in the production of *Guernica,* to which we will turn in the last chapter.

CHAPTER 3

The Romance of Forms

IT IS DIFFICULT to envision two twentieth-century scholars more different from one another than the Swiss psychiatrist Carl Gustav Jung and the California-based nursery-school teacher Rhoda Kellogg. Jung, an early colleague and for several years heir-apparent to Freud, deeply involved in studying the psyche of man, in its collective as well as its individual manifestations, ministering to the curious and the troubled, corresponding with the great personages of his time, involved over the years in increasingly arcane studies of mythology, rites, and even the minutiae of medieval alchemy. Kellogg, on the other hand, the no-nonsense American-bred schoolteacher, basically self-taught, for years dismissed as a crank surrounded by her huge collection of children's drawings, gaining recognition late in life as a result of her methodical classification of hundreds of thousands of drawings from thirty lands, finally opening a library and school in which these products can be pored over by students, educators, and even rival analysts of children's art. So far as I know, Kellogg and Jung met but once; the content of their conversation has not been published. But it is safe to guess that they talked animatedly about the mandala.

Mandala (Sanskrit for "magical circle") is a term sometimes used to designate all symbolic representations that include a circular motif, and sometimes used specifically to designate those circular forms that incorporate within them a rectilinear form. Mandalas can be found in the productions of various cultures, dating back at least to paleolithic times (49). These forms are also found very commonly in the drawings of children, particularly those who are two or three years of age (50). And it is this frequent occurrence which, independently but with equal compellingness, impressed itself upon the analyst of human dreams, Carl Jung, and the student of children's drawings, Rhoda Kellogg.

Jung was struck by the frequent appearance of the mandala in

50

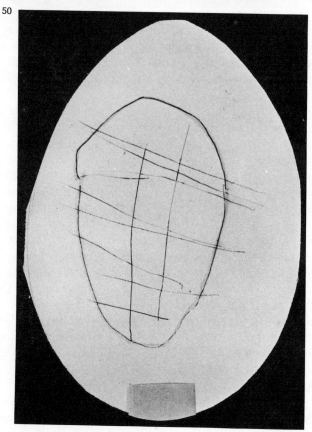

the dreams of his patients. For instance, in one set of four hundred dreams from a single patient, a mandala-like symbol involving four separate pockets or corners appeared no less than seventy-one times. The circular portion appeared in such guises as a serpent around the dreamer, a clock, a round target for shooting practice, a round table, a basin, and a ball. The rectilinear part made its appearance as a town square with a fountain in the center, a square prison cell, an empty square which was itself rotating, a taxi driving around a square, four children in a circle, and the like. Often the center was highlighted, as when an egg was placed in the middle of a ring, or when a precious stone or a pole dominated the "dream field."

Following upon this series of dreams, the patient suddenly underwent an epiphany—"an impression of the most sublime harmony." He dreamt of two circular forms with a center common to both. The more vertical circle, a blue disc with a white rim, was divided into thirty-two parts with a hand rotating upon it. The more horizontal circle, of four colors, featured four little men standing upon it. Together, the two circles made up a world clock consisting of three basic rhythms or pulses: a small pulse, with the hand of the blue vertical disc moving on one thirty-second at a time; a middle pulse, consisting of one complete rotation of the hand, while the horizontal circle moves on by one thirty-second; and a great pulse of one complete rotation of the golden ring which is equal to thirty-two middle pulses.

As interpreted by Jung, "the vision sums up all the allusions in the previous dreams. It seems to be an attempt to make a meaningful whole from the formerly fragmentary symbols [previously] characterized as circle, globe, square, rotation, clock, star, cross, quarternity, time and so on." Soon after this epiphanous experience, the patient underwent a religious conversion: the disparate parts of his experience were synthesized into a harmonious composite pattern. Indeed, exhibiting its mystical powers, the mandala enabled the patient to solve the problem of the Trinity—to reconcile the female element, the earth, and the body. "It was the first intimation of a possible solution of the devastating conflict between matter and spirit, between the desires of the flesh and the love of God . . . the mandala would express the deity through the three fold rhythm, and the soul through the static quaternity, that is, the circle divided into four colors. And thus its innermost meaning would simply be the union of the soul with God." In this fashion the patient's vision provided a symbolic answer to questions that had been wrestled with over the centuries.

Jung saw man and woman in perpetual quest for meaning in life, a meaning that frequently required the reconciliation of opposite forces, and particularly the paradoxes spawned by religion. This struggle, which generally occurred at an unconscious level, led spontaneously to the elaboration of symbols, usually visual, which captured (and sometimes clarified for the individual himself) the nature of his dilemma. Unique to the mandala was its widespread, seemingly inevitable, appearance across time, nations, cultures, and individuals. This universality marked the mandala as a symbol that had evolved as part of the unconscious shared by all human beings—"the wholeness of the celestial circle and the squareness of the earth, uniting the four principles or elements or psychical qualities, express completeness and union. Thus the mandala has the dignity of a reconciling symbol . . . mandalas are expressions of a certain attitude which we cannot avoid calling 'religion.'" In Jung's final analysis the psyche possesses a substratum which transcends all differences in individual cultures and individual consciousness; forms like the mandala constitute a psychic expression of the identity of brain structure common to all members of the species. And the completeness or totality expressed in the "four-foldedness of the one" represent the Deity as well as the self—the most central issues confronted by human beings. A visualization of these entities clarifies their nature, and this is why a mandala is found—and savored—everywhere.

Where Jung looks to the structure of the human brain and the nature of human consciousness and unconsciousness as the ultimate source of mandala-like configurations, Kellogg finds the origins of the mandala in the drawing history of the young child. And because she has examined this history with microscopic care, she can locate the mandala's origins with specificity. Where other authorities have simply noted that youngsters scribble, Kellogg has classified the scribbles of children the world over into twenty basic types (51). And where others note that youngsters mark at different locations on the page, Kellogg has in fact identified seventeen different "placement patterns" (52).

Let us run through the "progress of drawing" as described by Kellogg. By the age of two or two and a half, children begin to realize (or "draw out") various forms that have been latent in their scribbles and placement patterns. Circular scribbles smooth out to

51

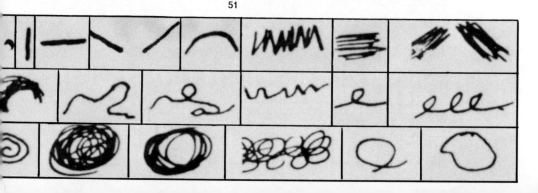

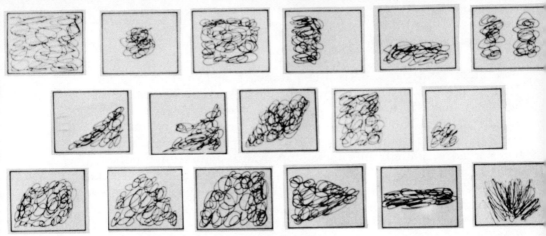

52

become recognizable, discrete circles; or, heightening in angularity, they become rectangular or triangular. Indeed, with each apparent repetition, the form becomes slightly clearer, more differentiated from other forms, more autonomous. The first circles can hardly be differentiated from a series of wavy lines; subsequent forms are distinguished by their extreme oval or elliptical qualities. By the same token, early squares may resemble circles, or the more angular scribbles of the first year; but with succeeding practice the lines become increasingly parallel or perpendicular to one another, angles are sharpened, and the form comes to resemble a rectilinear Platonic ideal.

It is usually only a matter of months before the child begins to rehearse on the same page a number of these forms. Much as the older child practices letters of the alphabet or words in a primer, the three-year-old runs through his vocabulary of forms, making first a square, then a triangle, then a patch filled with color, then a series of dots, and so on, for many hours at a stretch. Virtual juxtaposition of forms occurs after a while and then, either gradually or suddenly, the child comes to superimpose the forms on one another. Kellogg refers to these superimposed patterns—the circle filled with lines, the triangle set in a circle, the square embedded in a triangle—as combines (53); and when three such forms crop up in the same approximate region, she calls them aggregates.

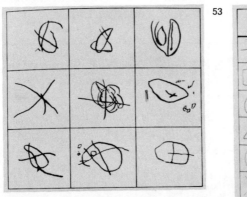

53

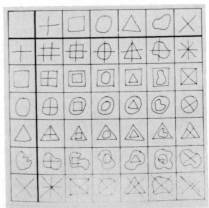

Given such basic diagrams as ovals, rectangles, triangles, and crosses, there are up to sixty-six possible ways in which these can be juxtaposed or superimposed upon one another. But not all hybrids appear with equal frequency, and, in fact, some hardly appear at all. Mandalas are the examples, par excellence, of a combine. Not only are mandalas visible in many combines but, more important, mandalas seem to represent a central tendency of "combining behavior": the simplest and most balanced diagrams, when combined with one another, produce mandala-like forms.

The circular aspect of the mandala is probably the paramount factor contributing to its dominance. Its conformity with the movement of the child's arm, its perfect symmetry, its patent resemblance to so many objects (or "things") in the world, the relative ease of repeating the form (as opposed, say, to the square)—all these factors interact and seem to confer upon the circle its special status. In line with such pioneering students of children's art as Gustaf Britsch, Henry Schaefer-Simmern, and Rudolf Arnheim, Kellogg stresses the graphic potential of the circle: from its variations will grow suns, with their linear radiations, and ultimately the first representations of the human figure.

Both Carl Jung and Rhoda Kellogg find the mandala inevitable—Jung because it is unequivocally encoded in our nervous system and uniquely suited to resolve our existential dilemmas, Kellogg because it is the natural outgrowth of the drawing sequence through which every normal (and many abnormal) children will pass, a sequence marked by a search for order and harmony. I incline toward Kellogg's view, finding it leaner, less grandiose, and less complex. But in my view, neither of these students of human activity, nor any other major muser on the mandala, has adequately taken into account the extent to which a form like the mandala reflects the most pervasive developmental processes at work in the young child.

In coming to know the world, the child is continually called upon to distinguish among objects seen, sounds heard, materials felt, persons encountered. At first the child will be struck by the starkest of contrasts—the loudest and the quietest sounds, the lightest and the darkest hues, the tallest and the shortest persons. Contrasts among moods will be equally dramatic—delight and anxiety are distinguished from one another far earlier, and far more easily, than mild pleasure and slight pain. Just as these polar contrasts prove primary in the realm of perception, so too the young child will in his actions first produce elements decisively different from one another. In the vocal domain, for example, the child initially utters those sound clusters that combine the most closed state of the vocal tract (*m, p*) with those sounds that involve a full opening of the tract (*ahs* and *aws*). Later, sometimes much later, the intermediate sounds (*eh* and *ih, k* and *g*) make their appearance. By the same token, in his play with objects, the child initially brooks no intermediate behaviors. Either the doll or bear is brought close to him, or it is cast out of the crib: keeping objects at arm's length, literally as well as figuratively—maintaining one's "psychic distance"—is a much later phenomenon. And, in time, the juxtaposition of opposites permeates the semantic sphere: just consider the clash of opposites that forms the core of fairy tales.

This principle of maximal contrast, as it has been termed, also governs the realms of visual perception and visual production. Just as the infant first distinguishes a mark or figure against a blank background, just as the toddler can differentiate those members of a class which are most distinct from one another (ducks from sparrows) and only eventually gains the ability to discriminate among more closely related instances (sparrows from wrens), so, too, in his drawings the child first features the sharpest kinds of contrasts. We have noted that certain portions of early scribbling are circular or wavy: in these actions the child's elbow remains fixed and his forearm rotates widely back and forth. Such "roundish" forms stand in decisive contrast to a number of other early scribbles. To produce incisive dots, the child's entire arm (fingers to elbow) is raised up high and lowered sharply in one movement; to make straight lines, the ends of the fingers must remain at the same distance from the body while the angle of the elbow is constantly readjusted; to create angular forms, the orientation of the wrist must be abruptly readjusted halfway through the motion. The pleasure—and the exercise—gained from these distinctly different movements may well explain the prevalence of these forms in early scribbles and placements. No doubt the distinctive visual appearance of each of these marks adds to its appeal.

In addition to yielding different graphic effects, these contrasting "graphic moves" also entail distinctive "qualities." Producing dots is a sharp, hard-pounding activity (like punching a bag); producing wavy lines is a calmer, more regular unfolding (like decorating a cake); producing angles involves a shift of energy and pressure midway through the gesture (like signaling penalties in a football game). Such differences in "quality of production" constitute another important part of the child's early activities, noticeable in the child's productions as well as in his perceptions. Thus, when I took a marker and began to pound on the page, Jerry, at twenty months, imitated my actions with great concentration and enthusiasm. What was likely to be imitated, however, was not the resulting graphic configuration but rather the dynamic properties of the banging itself; and Jerry banged with his fist or with a spoon, as well as (or even in preference to) the marker. Similarly, when I waved my marker back and forth, or alternated a series of angular motions, the "vectoral" properties of my activity were likely to be seized upon. In Jerry's virtually compulsive reproduction of his father's activities, it was characteristically the action—the directed energy—and not the product which occupied center stage.

Eventually, however, such involvement with sharply contrasting behavior, such preoccupation with the dynamic properties of a display, gave way to concentration on the actual properties of what had been drawn. At eighteen months Jerry had just begun to notice whether the marker had indeed left a trace. A year or so later he was concerned not only with whether he made a mark but also with the nature of that mark. And, more specifically still, the mark began to acquire finitude—a beginning and an end, a unitariness of some sort.

Here again, we can discern interesting links to other arenas of the child's life. At a year or so, a baby simply produces an individual sound or set of sounds; by two and a half the child is producing recognizable, meaningful entities, specifically words and phrases. At a year or so a baby stumbles (or crawls about) in a relatively aimless fashion; a year and a half later his activities are determinedly goal-directed. At a year or so a baby simply pushes blocks around or bangs them together; a year and a half later he places them on top of one another, in towerlike fashion (before, of course, gleefully knocking them down). And so, too, it no longer suffices to produce some wavy lines, a set of dots, or a few random angles. Instead the child at two and a half produces finite forms—a closed circle, a finished triangle, a balanced rectangle—in short, an enclosure of some sort, with its own undeniable quiddity.

We must note, however, a fundamental difference between this achievement of enclosures in the graphic realm and the production of tales, tunes, or towers. Put succinctly, at a time when these latter creations can already signify elements in the world, the young drawer is still preoccupied with the production of forms for their own sake. At a time when words undeniably refer to objects and events, and symbolic play sequences denote dressing, going to bed, or playing house, the forms that are drawn remain just forms, still unconnected to the world of objects and experience beyond. Indeed, drawing remains for many months an experience little influenced by the perception of the everyday, meaning-laden world. To be sure, the child looks, and with an increasingly critical eye, at the shape and size of the forms being drawn; and yet at the same time it is equally true that he makes little effort to see and shows little concern about the relationship between the forms made on paper and the forms in the "real world." A line for a child at two and a half years is still a path that is followed for its own sake; he is only beginning to see it as a boundary of an enclosed space; and so, even though the child has long since acquired the ability to "read pictures" in books, he has not yet effected that important mental leap which recognizes the enclosures of his own pen as isomorphic to the bounded forms of the real world.

The linkage of the world of graphic activity to the universe of experience does not occur until the age of three: still, it scarcely happens with total suddenness. In fact, intimations of this ability emerge during the second and third years of life. As early as seventeen months, Jerry, after making a mark, said the word "birdie." While clearly he was imitating what I had said after making a mark, this remark at least testified to his emerging awareness that one can name something one has drawn. In the following months numerous additional remarks were addressed to drawings. For instance, at twenty-three months, crossing out a face in a book, he said, "bye-bye face"; at twenty-five months he asked me to make a drawing and then declared, "Now I draw a monkey"; at twenty-seven months, already at the threshold of graphic representation, he made a series of lines and circles and then informed me that "this is Peter Pan. Clap your hands and Tinkerbell will be OK."

Such allusions, made quite regularly, disclose a clear ability and inclination on the part of the "prerepresentational" child to speak about his drawings and about the act of drawing itself. Because such remarks promise representations which are not, however, delivered, the child is said to be "romancing." What unites this disparate chatter is that the child is indicating what he would *like* to accomplish (in the case of Jerry and the monkey or bird), or is effecting an extremely general link between the realm of drawing and the realm of language (in the case of Peter Pan or the face). What is lacking is the actual achievement, within the confines of the drawing itself, of a recognizable likeness between the forms produced and entities in the world. In other words, in the eyes of observers, there is little, if any, objective basis for the romanced name. The names seem a random comment, a non-visually inspired afterthought, part of a game or interchange between the child and his society, rather than a label grounded at least tangentially in the particular form that the child has fashioned.

Just what the romanced name means to the child remains a mystery. Does the child really discern a resemblance that happens to be missed by everyone else? Does he seek to "wish" the form into being by so anointing it; might he even be performing some kind of magical or totemistic act? Does the child see labeling as a game in which the culture participates, or is it done simply to please adults who may well have been bombarding him with the inevitable "What is it? What are you drawing? Tell me what it is." May the child be involved in some kind of record keeping, with each mark simply a primitive kind of notation standing for the object (just as a word is, at least initially, an arbitrary way of designating something in the real world)? Or is romancing the child's way of making a transition from mere scribbling to genuine representational depiction?

I do not think that romancing lends itself to a simple explanation, particularly in view of the fact that it does not occur with equal frequency, nor on analogous occasions, in all youngsters. A clue to romancing, however, can be found in the behavior of young children whom my colleagues and I have studied, children of equal intelligence and charm who nonetheless exhibit strikingly different approaches to their daily experience.

On the one hand we have encountered a cadre of young children whom we have come to call *patterners*. These youngsters analyze the world very much in terms of the configurations they can discern, the patterns and regularities they encounter, and, in particular, the physical attributes of objects—their colors, size, shape, and the like. Such patterners enthusiastically array blocks on top of one another, endlessly experiment with forms on the table or in their drawings, constantly match objects with one another, build pairs and trios and the like; but they spend little time re-enacting familiar scenes in play and they engage in relatively little social conversation (though they certainly understand what is said).

Sharply contrasted with these youngsters is the population whom we have touted as *dramatists*. These children are keenly interested in the structure of events that unfold in their vicinity— the actions, adventures, clashes, and conflicts that befall the world of individuals, as well as the fantastic tales describing even more gripping events, which they ask to hear over and over again. While patterners cling to the activities of drawing, modeling with clay, and arrangement of numerical arrays, the dramatists prefer to engage in pretend play, in storytelling, in continuing conversation and social interchange with adults and peers. For them, one of life's chief pleasures inheres in maintaining contact with others and celebrating the pageantry of interpersonal relations. Our patterners, on the other hand, seem almost to spurn the world of social relations, preferring instead to immerse (and perhaps lose) themselves in the world of (usually visual) patterns.

Both patterners and dramatists enjoy putting the marker to the paper, but they seem to have quite different pleasures in hand. As can be seen in figure 54, a drawing by a typical patterner, such children enjoy exploring visual possibilities, taking a line in varying

54　Drawing by a three-and-one-half-year-old patterner. The child made the drawing without comment but with rapt attention to each detail. As he connected the dots, he counted them.

directions, and this activity usually suffices for them; they feel relatively little need to label their products. Sensitive to the gap between their drawings and the visual configurations of real objects, they are unlikely to label their drawings spontaneously but may well "romance" just to silence or appease their elders. In contrast, as a drawing by a typical dramatist indicates (55), such children find the social interchange surrounding drawing as engrossing as the actual scribbling activity itself. They offer names—perhaps funny or silly ones, sometimes related to events that have recently transpired, at other times inspired by familiar stories or even wholly imagined ones—and this "romancing" becomes a central element in the draw-ing activity of the dramatists. Indeed, because they are relatively insensitive to visual configurations, the disparity between "real" and "depicted" objects seems of little moment to them. Of course there are children who do not exemplify either of these tendencies, and there are as well children who seem to oscillate between patterning and dramatizing guises. Every child indulges in some romancing, but the reasons that prompt these namings and the apparent pleas-ures attendant upon them seem to differ greatly depending on the particular child who offers an invented name.

Not all romancing, to be sure, is equally unrelated to the product at hand. In fact, in the months before the first "genuine representations" one can find clear evidence that the child is begin-ning to link depictions—including his own—to the world beyond his drawing. Perhaps the first clue comes toward the end of the second year of life, when the child will discern a resemblance to a real-life entity in some accidentally encountered configuration in his surroundings. Thus a two-year-old we have studied walked through the woods one day and pointed out resemblances to vari-ous objects and letters in the angles of branches; for example, she sighted a letter T, a letter K, a gun, and an umbrella. Another step in the journey from arbitrary to motivated naming occurs when the child looks at a form or diagram he has made and then proposes a

55 Drawing by a three-and-one-half-year-old dramatist. As he proceeded, graphic and nar-rative effects were freely combined: "Once upon a time, there was a little fish" (draws oblong on right), "and he had a mommy fish" (draws larger oblong shape on left). "Once the little fish went swimming away" (draws loop above the little fish). "The mommy chased after him" (draws loop above the larger fish). " 'Bad, bad, you,' she said. 'I'm going to have to put a gate on'." (draws the stripes on top of the little fish. " 'I will have one too' (adds stripes on the larger shape), 'and I want eyes to see you' " (adds eyes on both the fish).

series of names. Jerry, for example, at twenty-eight months looked at a circle he had drawn and then announced, "Oh, that's a balloon, a circle, a poopoo." In such cases a visual resemblance may in fact obtain between the depiction and the referent, but since the naming is clearly arrived at after the fact and seems a search for any possible fit rather than a planned likeness, it still partakes of romancing.

The child is clearly beyond sheer romancing, however, when he can place features appropriately into a form furnished by an enterprising parent or experimenter. We have found that, when requested to do so, many prerepresentational two- and three-year-olds can accurately locate features in outlined human or animal bodies. My daughter Kay, for example, was scarcely two years old when, given a large circle, she was able upon request to place hair at the top of the circle, dots for eyes near the top, another dot in the center for a tummy, and various protuberances at the bottom as legs. I would not speak here of genuine representation, for the impulse to represent came from outside the child. At the same time, once offered the relevant suggestion, the child was able to add features that clearly reflected some topological fidelity to the human body. Such marks go beyond sheer romancing.

The issue of whether one wants to award to the two- or three-year-old the unambiguous epithet of "graphic symbol-maker" has recently attained special significance. After all, what is one to make of the activities of selected members of the species of *Pan*

56

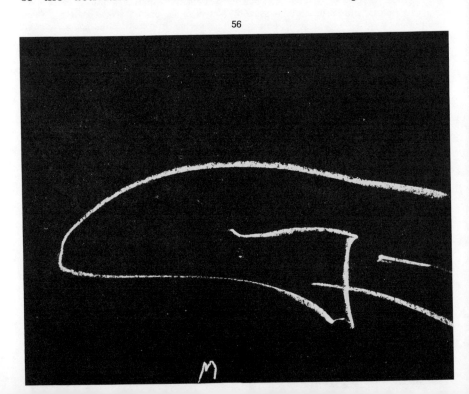

troglodytes—the chimpanzee? Fresh upon reports of Lana, Sarah, and Washoe, the three most illustrious chimpanzees who are mastering various linguistic systems, comes the claim from R. A. Gardner and Beatrice Gardner that a young chimp they have been studying is now producing representational drawings. To do justice to the claims of the Gardners, one should look first at the drawings they have published and see whether the likenesses claimed by three-year-old Moja can in fact be seen there. Then it is fair to reveal that one drawing was described by the chimpanzee as a bird (56), while another was called a berry (57). Moja (58) also was able to indicate upon questioning the name of the artist responsible for the drawings and the subject of her drawings.

With every passing year chimpanzees seem to become more able. There is every reason to believe that this rise in ability will persist, not because the IQs of chimpanzees are rising but rather because experimenters are becoming more clever, and methods for training performances are undergoing continuing refinement. A few years ago the primatologist Desmond Morris could write with confidence that chimpanzees were incapable of representational drawing. To be sure, they passed through scribbling stages, just like human infants, and they even fashioned an occasional mandala; but because they did not monitor their visual images, they would not reliably repeat what they had done before, and thus they could not effect the crucial leap to genuine representationality. After all, if chimpanzees could not name things, how could they draw them?

57

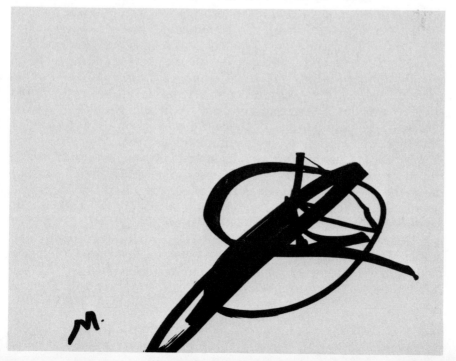

58

The Gardners have now demonstrated linguistic abilities in chimpanzees far greater than most researchers had believed possible. And they are claiming that their chimpanzees are equally able to produce genuine representations. We may well want to retain some skepticism about the testimony of young Moja, even as we remain agnostic about the romancing answers of two- and three-year-olds. Yet in view of the colossal strides made by teams of psychologists and chimpanzees over the past few years, it would be a bold scientist indeed who would dare to bar chimpanzees forever from the world of representational art! Even as our two-year-old subjects are but a few months away from the world of "tadpole humans," the chimpanzees of the world may be on the threshold of drawings whose identity is so unambiguous that the labels they supply will but confirm what is clear to every open-eyed viewer. In the meantime we can ponder the meanings of the mandalas they draw and consider, in particular, whether the factors that prompt human children to draw mandalas might also be at work in the products of our closest phylogenetic relatives.

Just what has our inquiry suggested about the nature and status of the ubiquitous mandala? How does this figure fit in the chain linking simple scribbling to genuine representation? To my mind, three factors appear relevant.

First of all, the mandala juxtaposes and contrasts two of the most popular and stable of geometric shapes—the circle and the cross. As such, it reflects the pervasive tendency among young children to focus upon, and revel in, highly contrasting elements.

Second, and relatedly, the mandala is a memorable and highly pleasing visual form. Just as children come to like certain tonal patterns because (like the universal chant of a minor third) they are readily produced and can carry appealing messages, so, too, the mandala is a well-balanced form, easy to recognize, repeat, and remember and readily exploited for a variety of graphic purposes.

But to my mind the central reason for the pervasiveness of the mandala lies in its location en route to genuine representation. At the time of the mandala's appearance—somewhere near the end of the third year of life—the child is beginning to understand the representational nature of drawing. True, he does not himself depict, but he can participate in the depicting process when given the opportunity to do so.

It is then that the mandala assumes its special role, standing midway between purely formal exploration and genuine representational depiction. The mandala is at once an acceptable, indeed admirable, geometric form, yet its appearance and complexity presages subsequent depictions. The circular portion anticipates any bounded object; the two lines of the cross can prefigure legs, arms, facial features, hair, or even clothing. When prompted to romance, children may in fact offer any of these labels, yet they feel no compulsion to do so—the mandala can also stand merely for itself. In my own view the mandala appears universally and has awesome significance because its occurrence is overdetermined: by virtue of the child's visual processes, schematic reservoir, sense of simplicity, balance, and opposition, he is predisposed to produce the mandala; and just because this form contains the germ of eventual representation, it serves as an actively felt hint of pivotal events ahead.

CHAPTER 4

Tadpoles as Things

OTHER human beings play an important part in the life of the infant from her very first days. The newborn baby is "wired" to attend particularly to eyes, such as those of her mother, and does so from birth. The two-month-old can transcend such compulsive attention to the region of the eyes and take in the face as a whole. By six months the child can recognize with a smile individuals most familiar to her even as, within a month or two, she displays anxiety in the presence of a stranger. And by the end of the first year the child can readily recognize and identify depictions of other persons: the "other" is known already via pictorial media as well as from personal acquaintance.

Knowledge of other individuals continues to expand and deepen during the second year of life. The child is strongly attached to certain valued individuals, and much of her behavior is motivated by a desire to remain in their company. The child also comes to know many other persons, to associate specific properties with each (Aunt Sally is a "tickler," the postman always comes toward the end of the morning), and to behave (more or less) appropriately in their presence. She learns that other individuals—and even dolls—can act as agents to accomplish things. Nor does this knowledge of others remain dissociated from more personal growth. In fact, only through coming to know others well, only through appreciating the range of human behavior, as we have seen earlier, does the child eventually come to understand that she, too, is a separate being, a person in her own right, a self.

Such self-knowledge does not, of course, coalesce at a specific time, nor for that matter is it ever fully completed. Yet one notes during the second and third years of life certain milestones in the child's understanding of self. The child comes to recognize her own name and to respond to it; she can offer the appropriate name upon seeing a picture of herself; and she also comes to know that the reflection in the mirror is not some other person but rather that special being who is "me." Acquisition of this important bit of knowledge has been monitored by Michael Lewis. Following up similar work on "self-knowledge" in chimpanzees, Lewis surreptitiously placed red rouge on the faces of infants and then gave them the opportunity to examine their own reflections in the mirror. Infants who simply stared at their reflection or who touched the mirror were not credited with knowledge of self; infants who, upon sighting the rouge, placed their hands against their own faces presumably understood that the reflection in the mirror was theirs. One-year-olds rarely displayed self-knowledge; two-year-olds nearly always did.

The child's knowledge of other persons and increasing awareness of self have developed sufficiently in the first twenty-four months of life to raise a thorny question: why, given such knowledge about the world of persons, does the child not depict them in her graphic activity? Why does the scribbling child continue to produce sheer graphic patterns for one, two, even three years before producing a mark that resembles those depictions of human beings she sees all about her? Why, in other words, don't toddlers draw persons?

A telling clue comes, I think, from a consideration of the ways in which the growing child comes to know the world. In the first year or two of life, as we have had the chance to observe, the child gains a tremendous amount of knowledge about the world. She comes to understand both the regularities governing the behavior of people and objects in the surrounding world and certain exceptions to these regularities, along with the nature of her own enmeshment with the persons, dolls, toys, furniture, clothing, and assorted paraphernalia of her culture.

This knowledge, however, has one severe limitation. It is direct, practical, unmediated—knowledge completely tied to an immediate active physical contact with the world. When an infant sees a ball, she will reach for it, throw it, bite it, squeeze it. On seeing a person, she will crawl over to him, embrace him, smile at him, perhaps cling to him. But the child has no *independent* way of denoting, signifying, or relating to these entities—either she performs an action upon them, reacts to something that they perform, or (so far as we can tell) fails to partake of their worlds.

The pivotal change in this relation to the world begins in the second year of life. At that time the child becomes able to make contact and relate not only directly through her actions but also through the mediation of diverse entities invented by the culture, by means of words, pictures, gestures, or numbers—in other words, by virtue of the panoply of symbols that come eventually to dominate and regulate the human experience. The child need no longer be in the presence of a ball in order to direct appropriate actions toward this object or to think about it: she can undergo equivalent experiences on hearing the word *ball*, beholding a picture of a ball, or observing a papier-maché representation of a ball. By the same token, the behavior and responses that once occurred exclusively in the presence of mother herself, can now be evoked by her name or her picture, as well as by other sights, sounds, smells, and objects associated in the child's mind with that now conceivable entity known as "Mommy."

Needless to say, such a transition from a world of tangible objects to a world of symbols does not occur from one day to the next. Nor is there direct yoking between the ability to appreciate the symbol and the ability to produce it. A child may understand a word for weeks, months, or even years before she can produce it herself. She may understand a gesture (for "come here" or "bye-bye") well before she can herself produce the gesture appropriately. By the same token, she will be able to "read" pictorial depictions of balls, birds, other persons, and mice for perhaps two or three years before she herself can produce such symbols; and it will be several years before her own depictions are as clear as those fashioned by the culture.

It would be simple to attribute to motor difficulties the particularly lengthy gap between the perception of pictorial symbols and their production by the child: perhaps it is very difficult to wield a pencil or marker in such a way that a recognizable human being emanates from it. And indeed, it seems physically less demanding to say "Mother" or to gesture "bye-bye" than to create a pictorial equivalent of a person. Yet there are problems with this explanation. If we look back at the combines and aggregates produced by the two-year-old, we can see all the "raw ingredients": all the partial linear and circular schemes that will ultimately be "drawn upon" when the child produces her first human likeness. Similarly, as Kellogg notes, sunlike figures (59) are very common during the mandala phase but are rarely labeled as such. One might respond to the issue raised here by pointing out that, for the child, the production of pure forms is a satisfying experience, and the child feels no need to represent "real-life" objects. But once again, this explanation seems unsatisfactory because, whatever the child's agenda, it is clear that the forces about her—just as in the case of language—are "holding their breath" until the birth of representationality. Thus we must again ask: Why do these ingredients not combine immediately to produce that graphic entity that clearly occupies such importance in the young child's mental world?

59

In order to gain some insight into this issue, it may help to consider each symbolic medium as a separate realm, one having its own characteristics, potentials, problems, obstacles, and evolutionary course. This perspective is perhaps most evident in the realm of language, where one can follow the child's steady course from babbling to individual sounds to the first "all-purpose" words (like "Mama" and "hi"), and from there to simple two-word phrases, three-word sentences, and the eventual introduction of questions, negations, and the like. No doubt the child's language unfolds in this way at least in part because of the language that she hears and the world in which she lives. But just as clearly, there are multiple problems involved in the very course of mastering the medium of language: producing specific sounds, attending to word order, gaining sufficient vocabulary, coming to understand tense, plural, and aspect. Indeed, in a way reminiscent of the lag between producing aggregates and depicting humans, the child has the capacity to link words together—to utter two-word phrases—months before she actually succeeds in such concatenation. Clearly, the various "properties of the medium" which each child must confront are instrumental in determining the highly regular course of language acquisition in cultures around the world.

Such a constrained course seems to govern the acquisition of competence in other symbolic media. Consider, for another example, the case of music. To be sure, one observes vast individual differences in children's musical capacities, with some children singing tunes quite accurately by the age of two, others taking several years before they can produce, or even reliably recognize, a set of familiar tunes. Yet even here, the nature of music imposes its own developmental course. Whatever her natural gifts and cultural setting, every child must come to understand the structure of the scales, the nature of rhythmic organization, the possibilities of pitch variation and harmony, the role assumed by different instruments, the constraints operating on the use of her own voice, and the ways in which her vocal resources of effort, breathing, tension, and the like can be orchestrated. And that is why one encounters significant parallels in musical development across a wide range of children and cultures.

The case, I submit, is analogous with plastic media. Whether it be modelling in clay, building with blocks, or wielding a brush, a pencil, or a magic marker, the child must first spend many months coming to know the medium. She must learn what each of her actions can readily accomplish, what they can accomplish with effort, and what they cannot accomplish at this moment in development. In the case of blocks, she must know how they can be combined with one another, which configurations will remain standing and which will fall down, how they will fall down, what noises they will make, what shapes they can assume. She must explore spatial relations unceasingly, so that she can eventually build an arch, a staircase, a house, a rocket ship. In the case of clay, she must come to learn how malleable the clay is, what shapes she can make out of it, which shapes will fall apart and which will last, what she can do with each of her fingers separately, with her fingers used in consort with her fist or with various other tools, such as hammers, pokers, markers, and the like. Each of these bits of information will contribute to the actions and symbolic enactments which she eventually comes to carry out with the clay: the snakes, houses, horses, and balls of later years will be the natural products of intensive exploration of the Play-Doh medium.

To be sure, these tasks need not be burdens for the child. In fact, playing with sounds, squashing clay, and humming tunes are among the pleasurable moments in the life of the toddler. The child would be unlikely to proceed further with the media unless she found them rewarding. But just because each of them does prove engaging and each involves the child for many hours, we must ponder why representationality emerges across different media at such varying times.

We have already encountered the various challenges posed by

the graphic medium. First of all, the child must come to know what she can accomplish with the marker: what lines can be made, how thick they may be, what pressure she can apply, how wide an arc can be realized. By the same token, she must explore the terrain of the paper: what pressure it will withstand, how many marks can be made on it, how she can embroider, utilize, and relate to the center, the edge, and the four corners of a drawing sheet.

Here, then, is the agenda—by no means an oppressive one— confronted by the child as she traverses the course from scribbles to lines, diagrams, aggregates, combines. The youngster is coming to know what she can do with her body, a marker, and a piece of paper. And while there is much that she can do, there is much that she cannot—so this exploration takes considerable time. Indeed these factors constitute the principal reason years pass before the child is ready to depict the world—before she is ready to assert, and to realize, a graphic equivalent between marks on the page and the entities of the environment.

Two major factors ultimately stimulate the realization of graphic equivalents. First of all, there is romancing: at the very least this verbal adventuring indicates to the child that she (like others) has the potential for making marks that depict entities. The second factor, of equal importance, is the emerging capacity to produce configurations that function (and begin to look) like things. As long as a line is merely a path, merely an exercise in which one moves one's hand across the page to see what kind of traces it happens to leave, there is little possibility of graphic equivalence (except, conceivably, to a road or river). But once the child becomes able reliably to produce bounded shapes—circles, squares, triangles—and once these shapes can stand on their own, untrammeled upon by other lines, the child discovers that she can make things—enclosures, bounded entities which, like the objects of the world, have a limited shape, operate as a "figure" against a background, create an impression of solidity, substance, "thing-ness."

The differences between enclosures on the paper and objects in the world remain vast. Objects actually occupy three dimensions, have tangibility, depth, and solidity, and lend themselves to a plethora of actions and interactions. Depictions on the page are two-dimensional, typically offer no clues regarding depth or solidity, cannot be handled, and seem intermeshed principally with their surrounding canvas. And so the translation (and transition) from graphic enclosure to depicted object is by no means immediate. Indeed one can predict which graphic forms are most likely to be seen, and treated, as depictions in terms of how convincing their "thingness" is—how equivalent to the real object the graphic configuration seems to be. The forms produced in modelling with clay are much more objectlike, hence it is easier to associate their shapes with other objects in the world. That is why the child makes clay "balls" months before she sketches graphic "balls." Even within the graphic medium, those drawings that most closely resemble real-world objects are the first candidates for successful depictions. Thus circles that are completely filled in are more likely to be seen as balls than circle outlines, which could equally well denote a ball but which do not, on the face of them, seem as solid, tangible, and ready to bounce. Some children even seem to consider the piece of paper itself as the depicted object—surely a barrier to genuine two-dimensional representation.

Despite all these obstacles en route to the first human representation, the magic moment eventually comes (60). Sometime in the opening four years of life the child produces the first figure that merits the label "man," "person," "mommy," "me," or some other humanoid description. Occasionally the debut is a false alarm, and several more months will pass before the child even attempts (or announces) another person. Much more frequently, however, this debut signals a long run. In the ensuing days, weeks, and months

60

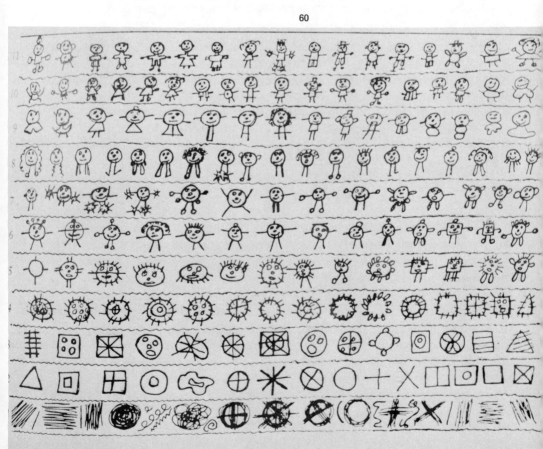

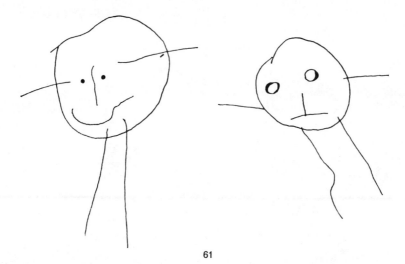

61

the child will produce hundreds of such figures, designating every
manner of person, a veritable feast of humanity, albeit in suspi-
ciously nonhuman forms. The various necessary factors—a quiver
of graphic schemas, the ability to discern similarities between
physical entities and line configurations, the capacity to fashion
and execute a plan—have finally come together in a decisive manner, and representational drawing is the inevitable consequence.

Because they are reminiscent of the first stage of the frog, with
its elliptical end and lengthy tail, these early depictions have often
been called tadpoles or tadpole figures (*hommes têtards* by the
French; *Kopfflüssler* by the Germans). Not all authorities see it
quite this way: for instance, Rudolf Arnheim, who believes that the
circular portion designates both head and body, rejects any implication that the child has left out the trunk of the person. But perhaps because the term "tadpole" captures not only the physical
appearance of the drawing but also something of the fledgling,
unfinished, yet germinal nature of young children's drawings, it has
prevailed.

Tadpole figures come in various sizes and shapes. Sometimes,
in their simplest forms, they are but a circle with a line or two
extending from the bottom. Sometimes the circle has facial features
in it—particularly eyes, but occasionally an entire assembly of features. Some of the tadpoles have arms sticking out the side of the
circle (61), while others have buttons or a belly button injected into
the center. A collage of such tadpoles from around the world can
be seen in figure 62.

But whatever their precise form, there is something singularly
odd about tadpoles. While they tend to have two protuberances at
the bottom, which are usually seen as legs, and may (less frequently) have two extensions on the side, which are perhaps arms,
they consist of but a single central circle. This circle could stand

Argentina   The Philippines   Japan   China   Syria

Iran   Hong Kong   Denmark

62

for a head; it could stand for a body; or, as Rudolf Arnheim insists, it could stand for both, serving as an equivalent of the whole person minus appendages. The fact that facial features are often included suggests that the circle stands for the head; but this move would imply that the child is unaware that the human being actually has a torso several times larger than the head. Even though the child may value the face and head more than the torso, it still seems most unlikely that the child has simply ignored the rest of the body. But has she?

One way to find out whether the child is aware of this other part of the body is to probe her knowledge of the human body. Studies by Claire Golomb and others document that the typical three- or four-year-old is well aware of stomachs, necks, chins, arms, belly buttons, and the like. The child can point these out on herself, locate them in drawings that have been begun by others, and, when pressed, even add them to her single-circle tadpole. Ignorance of the torso is no defense.

Another way to unravel the funny form of the tadpole is to intervene experimentally in the drawing process. Noting that tadpoles often have arms protruding from them, Norman Freeman, a British psychologist, wondered whether children saw these arms as extending from a head, a body, or some undifferentiated amalgam. He therefore produced a number of tadpolelike figures, which differed from one another in the ratio between the head and the trunk (63). Sometimes the head was very small and the trunk very large; at other times the trunk was very small, and the head very large. He then asked children simply to complete the drawings by adding arms.

63

In Freeman's view, if children wanted arms to emanate from the head, they would invariably add the arms to the top circle. If, on the other hand, they associated the arms with the trunk, then the arms could be reliably appended to the lower circle. But neither of these straightforward patterns turned out to be the case. Young children instead exhibited a "body-proportion" effect: they added the arms to whichever circle was larger, thus indicating that the arms were associated in their minds with the more massive moiety of the human figure. And so, despite Freeman's ingenious study, the meaning of the circle in the prototypical tadpole remains an enigma.

The first tadpole figures do not follow any grand design. Indeed, typically the very first drawings are happy accidents, circles with lines protruding, which seem sufficiently humanlike (or tadpolelike) to merit the epithet *man*. Once the child discovers that she can achieve this effect reliably, however, she has entered a representational stage, which, as we have noted, is often pursued with a vengeance. Intent on mastering this form, the child produces person upon person, and before long she has been admitted forever into the realm of representational drawing.

The discrepancy between the differentiated person that the child sees (and knows) and the simplified figure that she draws does not disturb the child. The issue of what the circle "stands for" seems a matter that vexes adults, not children. It seems reasonable to conclude that the tadpole stands for the person, much as the words *mother* or *ball* stand for the entities they denote. There is no need for a point-by-point isomorphism between the drawing and its referent: no need for a mirroring between the symbol and the thing symbolized. A general correspondence suffices between what is drawn and the object in the world. The thing on the page stands for the thing in the world—the circle is the body mass, the protuberances are the limbs.

But in children's early drawing, things never stay the same for long. Drawings of human beings rapidly expand along twin lines.

First of all, the child becomes able to produce individuals more differentiated from one another. The single circle of the tadpole becomes two circles of varying size, the lower, larger one coming to stand for the trunk, the upper, smaller one designating the head. The tadpole becomes a hook on which to hang appendages: arms sprout fingers (at first one, two, or many, eventually five); legs spawn toes; faces are soon adorned with ears, eyes, mouth, teeth, eyebrows, ear lobes, hair, and even freckles (64). Soon the graphic human being contains all the features the child can list. By the same token, the parts of the body eventually become less discrete from one another, better differentiated into a single form. The head comes to flow into the torso, the fingers come to grow out of the arm, limbs are double lines, thus conveying an appearance of volume. Each of these features comes to take on a shape that is less notationlike, more graphically equivalent to its human counterpart. The person comes to look like a person.

Even as persons become humanized, the child's repertoire of depictable entities increases. Where there were only persons, there are now individuals of different sizes and statures: babies, parents, witches, fairies. Animals of various species emerge: dogs, cats, horses, birds. At first these seem virtually indistinguishable from

64

65

persons. The dog may simply be a tadpole with four bottom legs, or a tadpole reclining on its side; the bird may be a smaller person, a person with a line on its head, a person with two protruding bodies. Houses also emanate from the same central schemas—rendered more rectilinearly—with a few internal marks substituting for limb extensions (65). Numerous other objects, ranging from dolls to suns, trees, and flowers, evolve naturally, if slowly and fitfully, from the initial form of the person.

One important and interesting feature limits these early drawings. With rare exceptions they do not—and they are not intended to—depict specific entities in the world. The child does not draw Lassie, Pluto, or her own dog Fido—she draws "a dog." She does not draw her house or the house next door—she draws "a house." Trains, planes, suns, and stars—these stand for the entire class or represent an ideal type, instead of depicting particulars that can be identified and then paired up with their realization in the "real world."

One reason the child draws the general rather than the specific may be her still limited abilities: she lacks the skill needed to make those fine distinctions that allow the identification of one dog as against another, one person in contrast to another. But a more powerful factor also seems at work here. At the time the child is making such representations, her conceptual organization of the world is itself constituted at a rather general level. Rather than having a well-articulated, hierarchical structure of classes, one organized (Linnaean-fashion) from the broadest superordinate member (living things) to the most specific entity (Fido), her categorical structure is relatively flat and one-dimensional. Moreover, the child tends at this age to categorize elements at the level most useful to her in light of her habitual commerce with them. And so, with rare exceptions, she is content to think of all dogs simply as dogs and to resist further distinctions within the class; she will rarely think of them as animals, since this level of abstraction has very little utility in her life; and she will never view them as "living objects" or "physical entities," since she has not yet developed categories at this level of generality. She in fact thinks in terms of general prototypes within a category and therefore she draws in that way.

Yet another related factor propels the child to produce consistently a schematic dog, man, or house. Children of this age tend to organize specific categories of their world in terms of good "central instances" or prototypes. Rather than treating all dogs as equally acceptable exemplars of the category, they naturally come to focus on one instance (quite likely a terrier or a spaniel), to view it as the "best" or representative dog, and to see others as greater or lesser deviations from this prototype. Much the same occurs across a range of categories—robins (not ducks) are prototypical birds, apples (not Granny Smiths) are prototypical foods, sedans (not convertibles) are prototypical cars. It thus becomes natural for the child to have a single prototypical procedure for rendering all members of a category, and to do so regularly. Indeed, errors are read initially as a "wrong dog," rather than a running dog, an injured dog, a dachshund, or a collie.

The reasons prompting these two tendencies—to think of objects at a certain level of categorical generality and to ferret out prototypical instances of these categories—are a subject currently in debate. It has been traditional to assume that children gravitate to these basic categories and prototypes because that is what they most frequently encounter in their culture; and, to a lesser extent, because this level of generality most closely parallels their current interests and level of knowledge. It has also been suggested that the child's nervous system may actually be wired to discover (or posit) prototypes. According to the latter argument, neither the surrounding culture nor principles of economy in making sense of the world, compel children to view certain dogs as "good" dogs. Rather, they do so because of the way they (and we) have been built. If this view is valid, we may begin our symbolic life by naming (and drawing) instances of what we have been built to notice.

Even if such a strong assertion cannot be fully supported, early naming practices do reinforce this general conception of the mind of the child. Almost irrespective of what the child hears around her, she is given in her early months to talk of general exemplars: birds, flowers, man, dog—and to overextend these terms to the point of applying them to any entity that shares a reasonable number of features with these all-purpose terms. Thus anything that looms in the air becomes a bird; anything that grows on the ground and has some vague green attached to it becomes a flower; anything that moves around and speaks is a man, while anything with four legs that does not talk is a dog.

By the same token, prototypes are prevalent in the experience of the young child. The inclination to invent, and gravitate about, central instances can be noted across a range of symbolic domains. For instance, in early symbolic play certain prototypical scenes are enacted over and over: serving dinner, having a tea party, administering to a patient, and putting a child to bed are the kinds of scenarios in which two-year-old children regularly participate as they explore the world of persons and roles. Such tendencies to cling to prototypes can also be discerned in lengthier linguistic creations. Thus the child of three or four constantly revisits a few basic story frames, such as those in which a victim (often a little child or little animal) is at first chased and eventually devoured by a villainous animal, spirit, or elemental force. And even in the realm of music children soon come to prefer a certain simple tune structure which recurs again and again in their own play activities, nocturnal monologues, and zestful dances.

We can infer how these general tendencies in the use of symbols color the child's first representational drawings. The child wants, and is perhaps driven to invent, graphic equivalents for those categories that occupy her thought processes; and so it becomes natural for her to develop a formula, or prototypical schema, which can represent or stand for the full range of instances of this category. Perhaps here we can locate the reason nearly every four-year-old comes to have a way of drawing *a* house, *a* dog, *a* man, *a* bird, and *a* flower—she seeks to draw the sorts of things she knows about. And at the same time we glimpse here the reason it takes many more years before the child develops schemas sufficiently specific to differentiate in a useful manner among instances from these classes.

While our characterization of the tadpole-drawing child may have accentuated her limitations, each discovery of a basic schema actually constitutes a significant achievement. The child not only has to fashion, through the relatively paltry tools of a marker and paper, a graphic equivalent of objects in the world, but also has to design each solution so as to differentiate the marks from others that she makes. The child cannot merely offer any mark or set of

marks as a dog, a bird, a flower, a person. Rather, building upon the
same basic mandala-like forms, she must produce graphic equivalents that bear similarities to the object in the world and that at
the same time differ from other schemas.

This challenge drives the child to invent solutions within the
medium of drawing: how to render the petals of the flower so they
differ from the rays of the sun; how to distinguish the branches of
the tree from the arms of a person; how to differentiate the doors
and windows of the house from those of an airplane; how to make
the tail of a dog different from the tail of the bird, the elephant, or
the kite. Of course the child does not always succeed at first; she
soon discovers entities that she wants to draw but cannot; and she
often gets help from people about her, including people who may
(well meaningly but perhaps wrongheadedly) model a convention
or a trick (such as the V-form bird or the smiling sun). At times,
moreover, her schemas are highly rigid: many children must draw
an object the same way each time and are stymied when asked to
draw parts in a different order or to supply a missing feature. Just
as frequently, however, children make successful adjustments on
their own; and when they do devise their own solutions, the depictions often display a special charm.

Consider, as one instance, how young children typically depict
objects with a number of informative sides. The child can of course
simply draw one side—the one that faces her; or, in an effort to be
perceptually veridical, she may draw the two or three sides that
would actually be visible at any one time. More typically, however,
the child decides to expose all important facets. And so, in drawing
a car, she may depict the top and all four sides, simply letting each
one extend out from a central core (66). Or in portraying a city
block (67), she so arrays the buildings and people that each is completely visible (and completely recognizable).

Another problem emanates from attempts to render the interior of an object—for example, the inside of a house. Here the
child will sometimes produce a transparency or "x-ray" drawing

66

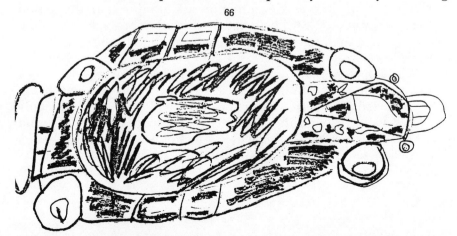

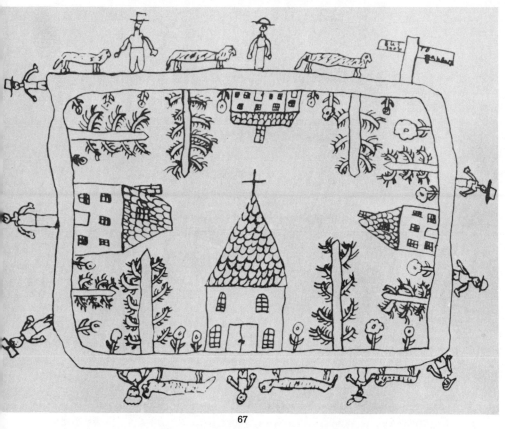

67

—a sketch from which one receives information about both the interior of the house (bathrooms, bedrooms, cellar) and its crucial external features (the roof, chimney, and front door). When necessary, this solution is also adopted to show the internal organs of a person, though ignorance of anatomy, coupled with a certain squeamishness, makes this mode of depiction somewhat less likely.

A classic experimental demonstration of "transparent drawings" occurred in 1896 when the educator Arthur B. Clark asked his subjects to draw an apple with a pin stuck through it. He found that, until the age of seven or eight, children strongly resisted veridical depictions in which the pin disappeared as it penetrated the flesh of the apple. Instead they would fashion a flat two-dimensional disk, with a line that went right through it, a disk with a line partially through it, an incompleted disk, or one of the other solutions depicted in figure 68. Accurate depictions, where the foreshortened pin entered one side and emerged from the other, rarely occurred until the middle years of primary school.

Proving that at least some experimental demonstrations in psychology are powerful and long-lived, Hilda Lewis replicated Clark's major findings seventy years later. And indeed this kind of solution within a medium is not restricted to young children in

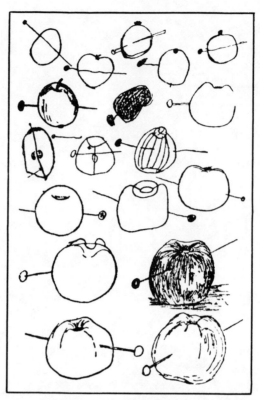

68

Western society. One intriguing, though possibly unsettling, phenomenon is the resemblance between these "childish" solutions and
the graphic practices often encountered in preliterate or primitive
cultures. In such societies one occasionally finds drawings in which
all four faces of an object are depicted; drawings that lack foreshortening; ones rich in transparencies; one as schematized as
those found among preschoolers of our own culture (69, 70, 71).
Nowadays few would want to suggest that the adults or older children in such cultures are mired at an early stage of development,
one conceptually equivalent to that of youngsters in our culture.
(Researchers have demonstrated that when relatively "culture-free"
tests are employed, the apparent intellectual gap between literate
and preliterate societies becomes markedly reduced.) Yet some explanation for this apparent coincidence of solutions is still wanted.

I find it helpful to distinguish between individual and cultural
evolution. It seems that, both in the case of young children in our
society and individuals growing up in other cultures, these sorts of
graphic solutions arise readily; they seem natural consequences of
efforts to depict in a comprehensive and satisfying manner what
individuals see about them. Where cultures differ is in the kinds of
solutions that have evolved over the course of many centuries. In
many preliterate cultures the solutions arrived at in early childhood are considered adequate (as indeed they are for many pur-

69

70

71

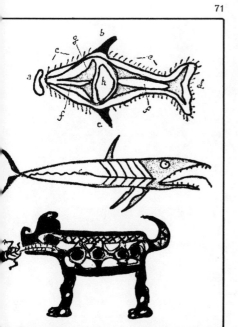

poses); drawings may well evolve in other ways, often becoming quite stylized and full of nuances, but typically not featuring spatial perspective or photographic realism. And where the culture has not itself evolved toward these latter approaches, the probability that an individual artist will hit upon them is very low. In our culture, on the other hand, solutions to certain challenges in graphic depiction have become generally accepted. Thus almost anyone who passes through the schooling of the culture and is exposed to its attitudes and standards will eventually abandon the "improvised" solutions in favor of procedures that yield graphically veridical depictions. Perhaps it is wrong (and ethnocentric) to treat one solution as intrinsically better than others; but I would certainly rate as developmentally more advanced an individual (or culture) that has available to it a range of depicting options, as against an individual (or culture) that has only one.

Yet even this assertion must be considered in context. When my daughter Kay was six, she, like many other children, insisted on drawing arms in such a way that they extended horizontally from the middle of the torso. One day I asked her where arms leave the body and she immediately assured me that they emanated from the shoulder. I then asked if she could draw them in that way and she

72

73

readily complied. I assumed that we had negotiated a developmental milestone: now that her knowledge was aligned with her graphic repertoire, there surely could be no reason for her to insist on locating arms at the center of the torso. But I was wrong. Kay immediately drew another person, with the arms once again coming out of the center of the body. "I know that's not the way you want to do it, Dad," she said sympathetically, "but that's the way I like to do it, at least for now."

In deciding how to render her "person," Kay was exercising a choice, one that made sense to her in terms of criteria of simplicity, symmetry, or some other set of personal standards. In some instances, however, the child seems to have little choice: she compulsively repeats the tadpole (or its successor) in the same rigid and somewhat anomalous way. Such deviant depictions are often symptomatic, sometimes of an emotional disorder, at other times of general retardation (72, 73, 74, 75). Such "diagnoses" must of course be made cautiously: "odd" schemas can derive from a number of causes and are by no means necessarily pathognomic. Yet because the development of drawing at this age occurs so similarly throughout the world, significant discrepancies are readily noted and compel some explanation.

Barring some such disorder of growth, the child of four, five, or six will have evolved a variety of schemas for familiar objects; totally comfortable in the mission of representing reality, she can to some extent adapt her schemas for particular occasions and can begin to organize them into simple scenes. As we have seen, she has also evolved a variety of solutions for problems that arise in the

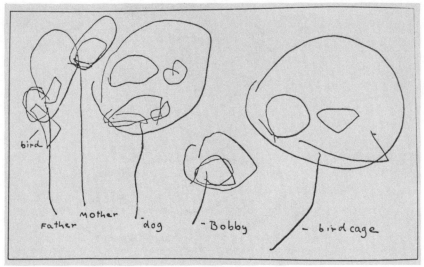

course of drawing: she may allow us to see all four sides simul-
taneously or to view inside and outside from the same vantage
point. But for all that, her drawings remain piecemeal—specific
elements scattered across the page, rather than organized views of a
panorama that she has seen or a vision in her mind's eye. We
observe collections or heaps of entities devoid of spatial organization, not structured works of art; conglomerations of prototypes,
rather than differentiated renditions of particular individuals or
specific experiences. Yet, paradoxically, the child is not far off from
creating a set of productions that can lay genuine claim to expressiveness, pleasantness, and artistry. In fact, in the months ahead an
unparalleled flowering of the child's graphic gifts will ensue.

75

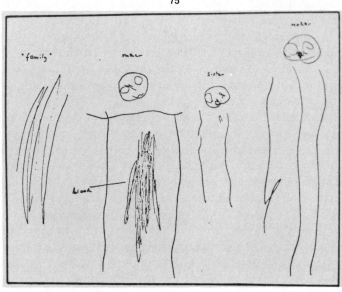

SECOND INTERLUDE

Steps to a Doll House

ON September 3, 1974 Shula Lesser, a young girl of four and a half, produced a most remarkable drawing (76). Dominating the center of a sheet of computer print-out paper was a large square house, itself divided equally into four squarish rooms. The two rooms on the left were bare, but standing next to a broad "railroad-track" staircase, the two on the right were filled with a set of highly stylized objects. A downstairs living room contained a table, composed of three intersecting lines; two chairs rocking upon curved bottoms; a square piece of furniture, probably a television set, with two diagonally oriented men dancing atop it, each sporting a top hat. The bedroom above the living room housed two beds, with a pillow standing upright upon each, as well as two paintings hung on the wall, one autographed by the artist herself.

76

Bordering this house, at the bottom right-hand corner of the "canvas," was a small and richly detailed structure labeled by Shula as a doll house. In many ways this edifice was a charming miniature of the large square house; it too contained four rooms, chairs, tables, beds, pictures, and, interestingly, two men tripping lightly atop a piece of furniture. Most of the stylized features of the large house were preserved: the top hats, the propped-up pillows, the curved-bottomed chairs, the same railroad-track staircase. But in the doll house each of the four rooms contained a roughly equivalent number of objects; an attempt had been made to show the side of the house, presented in a front-face view; a chimney protruded from the top; and there was also a roof. Finally, outside the house stood a few additional features, including two dragonlike figures sailing in the air and a small rectangular apparatus situated between the doll house and the real house.

Any analysis of development should feature an endstate: a description of competent performance in the domain under study, as well as some notion of how an individual might be expected to achieve that competence. Surely the drawing by Shula is in many ways an extraordinary achievement for one not yet five years of age: the amount of detail, the planning involved, the light-hearted mirroring in the doll house of the fixtures of the large house, the endearing stylization of persons, chairs, tables, and beds. At the same time, however, it in many ways typifies drawings by children of this age: it is rich in schematic versions of common objects— figures composed largely of simple geometric forms juxtaposed to one another, static versions of objects and individuals, scenes in which every element is separately laid out rather than artfully organized into a single, spatially convincing composition. Certain practices—for instance, the "x-ray" means of showing interior and exterior, the *en face* depiction of the staircase—also reflect widespread solutions by preschoolers to graphic challenges. But whether one emphasizes the originality and precociousness of the drawing or its resemblance to other pictures by children of this age, the essential developmental question remains: how did Shula advance in a few short years from the scribbles, circles, and crosses of prerepresentational times to such an incredibly rich, detailed, and sophisticated rendition of a pair of houses? To put it in developmental terms: how did she arrive at the endstate of preschool competence?

Because Shula's parents, a young professional couple with a deep interest in the arts and an abiding curiosity about human development, carefully followed the developing of drawing in each of their children, we can provide at least the visual evidence on which an answer to this question could be based. And because the circumstances under which Shula and her siblings drew were constant from one month to the next, we can make a happily close analysis of her progress. In the Lesser household the children, seated at small low tables, drew regularly, often for hours at a time. They had on hand a generous supply of magic markers and, equally important, a virtually infinite supply of computer print-out paper, on the back of which they sketched out their drawings. The major means of "training" were simply *equipping* and *encouraging*: the children were given the supplies they needed and stimulated to draw. Afterwards, mother or father simply jotted down the date and, if available, any comments made by the youngster in the course of the drawing.

And so we can follow through the predecessors of Shula's drawing of the house and identify the points at which the various constituents of the "endstate drawing"—the circular forms, square objects, filled-in patches of color—made their initial appearances, how they came to be used together, and what factors led, seemingly ineluctably, to the charming duo of houses we have just encountered. In so doing, we can gain a feeling for the processes of artistic growth. And because we know what has gone before, and what will follow, we acquire a sense of significance that is impossible to secure from the study of single context-free drawings.

Turning the calendar back two and a half years, we see a very early drawing by Shula, a mere scribble, made in January 1972 when she was just two (77). This unremarkable but typical drawing was produced by the familiar marking motion, in which the child, using her elbow as a pivot, simply swings the pencil back and

77

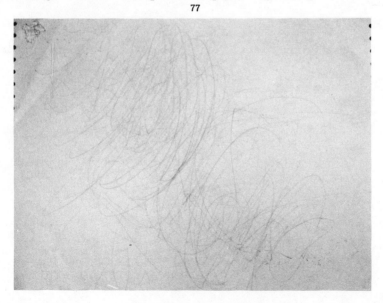

forth across the page. We can assume that Shula was enjoying the vigorous movement and was attending to the scribbles she was making but still had relatively little control over marking and little sense of purpose guiding her drawing.

Two drawings gathered from the summer of that year already signal a major advance, to a point when more lines and forms are already emerging. In the first drawing (78) she shows her emerging ability to control muscular movements: she can more readily stop the movement of the marker; she can experiment with lines of various thicknesses, sizes, shapes, and colors; and she can already effect various curved versions of linear forms. In the second drawing (79) the rough circular stabs of the marker have given way to a much more carefully controlled circular motion, one which cul-

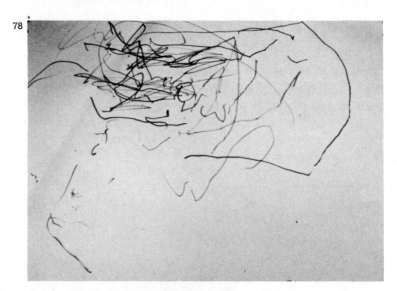

78

79

80

minates in a series of concentric circles. Still, the child does not complete any of the circles: instead she seems compelled to repeat her elliptical motion over and over again, though occasionally pausing to produce tiny, separate patches of color.

By the following spring, circular and linear motifs are both well in hand. In a drawing from that period (80) a number of discrete circles can be seen. Moreover, circles and lines are contained within other circles, as Shula demonstrates an ability to create combines, aggregates, and other amalgams of geometric forms. Quite clearly, Shula can now produce separate bounded entities: the objects of the world have their enclosed equivalences in a graphic medium. A drawing made the following month (81) fea-

81

tures further combinations of these basic forms: it also includes the
first representation to emerge in Shula's entire corpus—a genuine
tadpole person, complete with facial features. In scarcely more
than a year, Shula has progressed from the most elementary scribble to the distinct and unambiguous depiction of a human being.
We see the fruitful integration of circular, linear, and concentrated,
patched forms into a single legible representation.

But other forms of experimentation are also proceeding, and
each of these will eventually find its place in Shula's drawing repertoire. One drawing (82) contains numerous concentrated zones of
marking, where the young artist revisits the same area, producing
several patches, some enclosed with a linear contour, some free-
floating. Experimentation with crossed lines, visible on the right
side of this drawing, becomes a dominant motif in the next one
(83), a depiction that resembles two railroad tracks meeting at right
angles. Such toying with linear forms later becomes the basis of
rectangular enclosures, including not only the favored cars and
trucks but also doors, windows, houses, chimneys, staircases, and
pieces of furniture.

In the following months we observe additional manipulations
of these basic constituents. One drawing (84) spawns a family of

82   83

84

facelike figures, some with suggestions of eye and nose features, others with more concentrated facial patches. Enclosures are now boasting a number of interior elements. The following drawing (85) features a series of mandalas embedded in a large, igloolike

85

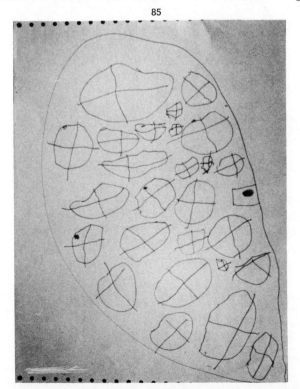

enclosure: here circles and linear forms intersect, like tiny windows, within a surprisingly well-articulated, overarching single frame. These forms also become rehearsed in various ways as the child explores all possible manifestations and ramifications of each basic form. For instance, one drawing displays a preoccupation with writinglike linear patterns, interspersed with windows and doors, and several complexly contoured forms in which lines travel in many directions (86); another "rehearsal" features a veritable explosion of the separate elements, now coming together into a festival of lines, patches, and circular motifs (87).

Up to this point Shula, at three and a half, has been following a path traversed by nearly every normal human youngster, the same course from scribble to tadpole which we have observed time

86

87

and again in the preceding pages. But as an exceptional child, Shula also began at an exceptionally tender age to introduce elements of stylization of her own. These can already be seen in a series of drawings made at the tail end of 1973, just before her fourth birthday. A remarkable lively facelike enclosure, with various mandalas, radials, patches, and featurelike forms, constitutes the subject matter of one drawing of this period (88). A sunlike enclosure stuffed with bright flowers, windows, and fishlike forms enlivens another (89). In the third picture in this series, an initial houselike enclosure, possibly the forerunner of this interlude's initial drawing, is replete with floors, windows, and floral forms (90). And then, in one of those almost totally unexpected achievements which nonetheless occur from time to time in the drawings of creative young children, a rich and richly colored series of patches, with a

88

89

single embedded facelike mosaic, brings the drawing season of 1973 to a close (91).

The emerging spatial organization of these latter drawings is worth noting. No longer does Shula simply continue drawing until the paper is well filled or attention has flagged; instead, she gives evidence of awareness that the paper can serve as a background field against which to array elements in an organized fashion. Deliberate placement, regular distancing between elements, restraint, and an honoring of unfilled or "negative" space mark these drawings. Looking at them, Rudolf Arnheim commented on their "unusual Miró-like balance." To be sure, this nascent feel for composition, this sense of controlled planning, does not dominate every work,

90

91

yet its appearance is sufficiently frequent at this point, and increasingly dominant in later months, to establish it as a legitimate aspect of Shula's repertoire—a telltale sign of talent.

Even as a variety of schemas are evolving and a sense of organization can be discerned, the human figure itself is not remaining quiescent. Shula is not only experimenting with different colors but is also interjecting, in bright reds, oranges, and greens, such motley features as hair, pupils, eyebrows, toes, fingers, and ears (92). These facial attributes initially appear in human beings, but soon they emerge in the vicinity of houselike enclosures—sometimes simply placed in a kind of list configuration (93), at other

92

93

times, in buttoned rows within a houselike configuration (94). In
the last of these drawings, made in February 1974, just two years
after the first scribble, we can already see all the basic constituents
of the houses that will be drawn just six months later. And we note,
too, a charming initial attempt to depict a figure in a noncanonical
aspect—a person lying down.

A few more predecessors of our endstate drawing should be
examined. In one drawing of June 1974 (95) we see for the first
time a full-drawn house, with roof, windows, and door—the model
for the doll house; and we also catch an initial glimpse of stylized
human figures—the man with top hat, buttons, separate torso, and
cane, who will be making a return appearance inside the two
houses. A drawing of August 1974 (96) contains a long series of

94

95

96

haphazardly arranged rooms, as well as such specific features as telephones, chairs, tables, kitchenware, and dancing persons, each of which appears in more organized fashion in the target drawing. Certainly by the time we have seen this drawing and made an initial acquaintance of the various constituents therein, our target drawing, remarkable though it still is, no longer comes as a revelation.

In one sense our story is over; but in another it has hardly begun. After all, Shula was only four and a half when she executed the target drawing, and her drawings continue in the ensuing months to evolve in many productive ways. Indeed, a drawing from the same era confirms that producing houses, with their characteristic x-ray interiors, is a relatively easy matter for our young artist —she can combine the assorted components in numerous ways (97).

97

What has made possible, in a matter of barely two and a half years, this remarkable journey from scribbles to scenes? Can we isolate or highlight a single factor—be it motor maturation, differentiation of visual form, the desire to achieve symbolic competence—and lay this stunning progress at its door? In all probability, no. The entire thrust of our study has intimated the constant and productive interaction of all these forces. We have seen how the child's superior motor coordination makes possible smoother motions—for example, a completed circle or a line that can stop; how in turn this new schema becomes differentiated in the next days through constant practice, observation, and experimentation; how the child strives to produce likenesses of things in the world and will, if necessary, romance a likeness if she cannot achieve it on purely graphic terms. Rather than pointing to the primacy of one developmental factor, a careful examination of the drawing history of a child—of all children—confirms this arena as a scene of perpetual and productive interactions among a host of relevant factors.

Moreover, in her exploration of the graphic medium the child exemplifies characteristic rhythms or cycles—the undulations of creative activity which are a familiar theme in the lives of great artists. Sometimes there is little drawing, at other times feverish activity over several hours, days, or weeks. Sometimes the child rehearses the same figure over and over again, with nary a change, while at other times there is rapid, even sensational, change (and progress) within a day or two. Sometimes the child concentrates fully on the achievement of a particular composed drawing, while at many other times she seems simply to be running through her stock of forms and schemas—rehearsing, varying, exercising, perfecting her skills. Through such drill the youngster masters a set of specific elements and learns how to vary them; then suddenly these forms appear combined in a drawing which, in one sense, is simply a confirmation of what could be done before but which, at the same time, may in its totality represent a reality apart from what the child could do before. And so just as there is remarkable continuity in the child's drawing—even in the case of so rapidly developing a young artist as Shula—there remains the constant possibility of great and unanticipated advances, where from one day to another the child suddenly achieves a wholly new level of competence. Here again the testimony of mature artistic masters comes to mind.

This description of the normal evolution of skills in drawing strongly implies that Shula's houses are a natural occurrence, a kind of evolution of graphic skills almost as ineluctable as the way in which her creeping turned to crawling, her standing to walking, her running to jumping and skipping. But what of other influences to which Shula has been subjected? Might we not with equal justice adopt a more environmentalist pose, looking instead to the forces in the world around her as an additonal, or perhaps even an alternative, line of explanation for the remarkable set of drawings she has produced?

And indeed, this line of reasoning turns out to have considerable persuasiveness. Consider, first, how her brother Gideon, just a year and a half older, produced a pair of houses and their surroundings (98)—more controlled and balanced, to be sure, but at the

98

very least bearing a family resemblance to the drawings she made. The same type of stylization can be seen in another drawing by her brother done at the same period (99); the subject matter may differ, but the curlicues, patches, smiling faces, and other little trappings are again reminiscent of Shula's works.

Other aesthetic influences lurk in the Lesser home. While neither parent is a professional artist, they often discuss artistic matters, both between themselves and with their children. Moreover, Shula's father likes to draw; he occasionally draws for his children, and he also has hung some of his engravings around the house. Who dares claim that his measured geometric forms, colorfully juxtaposed in the computer print-out drawing (100), or the twisted concentric patterns in the engraving (101), have not exerted an impact on the drawing of the two children?

But by far the most striking influence on the children's drawings came from a potent and yet unexpected source—one unavail-

99

100

101

able to children in earlier times but easily accessible in our time, and present in the Lesser household. I refer here to a small compendium of "how to draw" forms by the contemporary American illustrator Ed Emberley. Starting with the simplest geometric forms and adding to each in a piecemeal fashion, Emberley demonstrates how to produce a gaggle of charming animals, vehicles, clothing, domiciles, and various human forms. The example from his book

102

hardly requires comment. This drawing (102), more than anything produced by other members of the family, is father to the pair of houses that has engaged our attention.

Here, then, at the very moment in development when natural processes are supposedly at their height, when the child is allegedly insensitive to factors about her, we encounter a dramatic and persuasive example of the extent to which a model from the culture can contribute to, if not completely dominate, the form and substance of a child's drawing. Those pedagogues who swear by models, as well as those who swear at them, will be reconfirmed in their belief that the artwork displayed around a child can matter, even if the child is using the model as a point of departure rather than slavishly copying its every detail.

I would not wish to suggest (nor do I believe) that such models qualitatively change the developmental course of the child's drawings. Even without the example of Emberley, Shula would still have drawn scribbles, circles, lines, mandalas, tadpoles, and houses in the way she did and in the order she did. Moreover, the general shift from individual forms to organized scenes and from universal tadpoles to more stylized and idiosyncratic persons would have happened had she drawn in Cambridge, Chile, or China, and had she observed around her the models of her father, of Ed Emberley, or of the calendar from the local insurance company. The models about her provided the dialect and accent of her drawing rather than its basic grammar or semantic. But whether she would ever have arrived at the open x-ray version of the house or portrayed the various pieces of furniture in the way and arrangement that she did, or whether she would ever have juxtaposed houses or added accouterments in the way she did without the influence of her environment is far more problematic. Even in children's drawings the final product mirrors the totality of earlier experiences. And if these early experiences include a powerful, persuasive, and pedagogically effective guide to drawing, then the effects will be immediately discernible, even in the works of a child who has yet to reach the age of five. In fact these influences may be even more powerful in the early years than later. After all, such improbable bedfellows as Lenin and the Jesuits agreed: "Give me a child until he is seven and I will give you the man."

CHAPTER 5

Children's Drawings as Works of Art

BETWEEN THE AGES OF five and seven most youngsters in our society achieve notable expressiveness in their drawings. Having mastered the basic steps of drawing and learned to produce acceptable likenesses of common objects about them, they go on to produce works that are lively, organized, and almost unfailingly pleasing to behold (103–108). No longer a simple heaping or stringing out of elements, their drawings come to possess balance and harmony; the various elements unite, yielding a work that is often remarkable for its grace, rhythm, and expressiveness. One feels that the child is speaking directly through his drawings, that each line, shape, and form conveys the inner feelings as well as explicit themes of the young child. Indeed the child himself often seems most at home in expressing himself through his drawings; and the many hours that most children spend putting marker to paper and turning out one drawing after another suggest (if they do not exemplify) the important role played by artistic production in the life of the child.

This eruption of artistry at the threshold of school represents for me the central fact—and the central enigma—of artistic development. One can speak without exaggeration of a flowering of capacities during this period. The expressive forms, lively colors, and stunning compositions bespeak a consciousness that is heightened, if not inspired. Moreover, even if this artistic flair emerges most clearly in the child's visual products, it is by no means restricted to the realm of graphic experience and expression. On the contrary: the child's singing capacities, his ability to tell a story, his constructions with blocks, his inclination to gesture freely and to dance

103

104

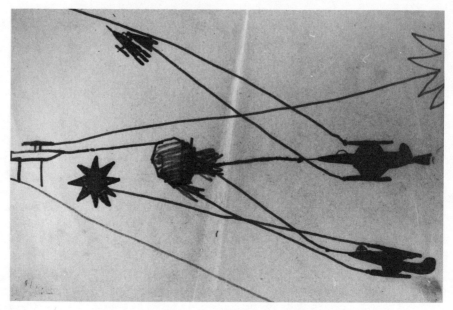

105

106

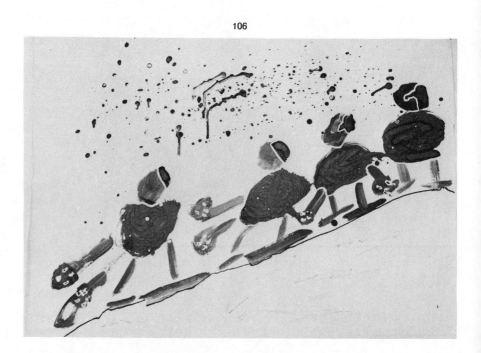

107

108

gracefully—all these areas host a coming of age, a genuine, if initial, "first draft" command of expressive media illustrated by the small set of children's poems and songs reprinted here. Now, instead of merely rehearsing again and again the small group of prototypical schemas of a year or two before, the child has command over a sufficient number of forms, phrases, and figures to produce works that are arresting and powerful. And so, even as the child appears at this time to be a youthful artist, he also may lay claim to be a young musician, dancer, or story teller.

Mice

Creeping mice in the garden
And our cat comes
And bounces on a mice.

(A five-year-old girl)

I Love Animals and Dogs

I love animals and dogs and everything.
But how can I do it when dogs are dead and a hundred?
But here's the reason: if you put a golden egg on them
They'll get better. But not if you put a star or moon.
But the star-moon goes up
And the star-moon I love.

(A five-year-old girl)

Katharine's Phoebe Song

I hear a little Phoebe bird, And he says, "Phoebe - Phoebe",
way off in the woods Where we can't see him.

(A four-year-old girl)

Bill's Green Bird

Oh, beautiful Green Bird! High you fly over the tree tops!
Oh, beautiful Green Bird! High clouds sail over you.

(A five-year-old boy)

But there is even more. It is not just that children of this age often achieve interesting and appealing effects with the various symbolic media of the culture; there is also, perhaps for the first (and sometimes for the last) time, an easy, natural commerce among expressive media. The child sings as he draws, dances as he sings, tells stories while at play in the bathtub or in the backyard. Rather than allowing each art form to progress in its own atelier in relative isolation from the others, children move readily and even eagerly from one form to another, combine the forms, and play them off one against another.

We enter an age of synesthesia: a time when, more than at any other, the child effects easy translations across sensory systems— when colors can readily evoke sounds and sounds can readily evoke colors, when motions of the hand suggest lines of poetry or lines of verse stimulate a dance or a song. Certain expressive properties— elements of rhythm, of balance, of composition and harmony—are so readily shared by these diverse media that a presentation or invention in one form naturally stimulates an analogous patterned activity in another form. As readily as an adult associates from one word to another, so easily do most children cut across domains and categories, often realizing unanticipated (and powerful) metaphors in the process. The battle lines have not yet been formed around each medium: and so it is as natural as it is delightful for each medium to gain sustenance from the media with which it shares certain expressive facets.

Must we therefore conclude that the child of five, six, or seven is a young artist? Are his works, his efforts, and his understandings equivalent, or at least interestingly related, to products wrought by the hands of more mature and seasoned artists? Does the child's drawing partake of and reflect the same capacities, intellectual processes, and expressive powers as those of the masters? And what of the stories or figures of speech so readily produced by the young child at the start of school? Do these bear significant affinities with the figures of speech and the works of literary art which we rightly honor in the adult writer? Many people have chosen to answer these questions in the affirmative, finding in children's art the important seeds, the essential antecedents, of later creative mastery. In their view, the child has now achieved sufficient control over the medium to be aware of what he is doing; at the same time he has not become so entrenched in certain ways of doing things that he has lost the ability to be original, expressive, and artistically fluent. From their viewpoint the years of early childhood represent a golden period in artistic development—one that may rapidly fade and therefore one that teachers and parents are challenged to maintain and nourish.

But there is another, less romantic view which we must also confront. Perhaps these works, whatever their sway over sophisticated audiences, represent something quite different to the child. Perhaps the child is enmeshed in the process of producing components—be they the lines of a drawing or the lines of a song— while having but scant (or fleeting) interest in the eventual product. Perhaps those forms that so please us are but happy accidents—forms the child had no intention of creating and which he would never choose to re-create. Indeed, perhaps the child has no choice about what he feels compelled to produce. Should this be the case, should the child be compulsively following his own agenda, then it would be misleading at best to attribute to him significant command over artistic media. Even as a metaphor by the young child may be a simple overgeneralization, with a word merely carrying a broader meaning for him than it does for most adults, so, too, drawings by the young child may be uncontrolled forms which come forth simply because the youngster is unable to produce anything more faithful to the real world.

We will return to this issue—one central to any discussion of children's art. But first we must establish just what children's art is like. To do so, we should consider some drawings produced by children within our culture. And if we are to bolster our assertion that works by children of this age have a special spirit and life, it is important that we consider children of average gifts rather than those with special talents.

Like nearly all boys (and many girls) who spend their Saturday mornings sprawled in front of the television screen, my son Jerry became obsessed with the array of superheroes who dominate that time period. While intrigued by Superman, Hulk, Spiderman, and Wonder Woman, Jerry soon became particularly enamored of Batman. And so, barely four and a half years old, after a particularly exciting episode, he made his first effort to draw Batman. One can see in a drawing of 19 March 1976 his preliminary attempts to portray this figure (109): a pentagonal body, two protruding legs, a wide cape extending on either side, and the familiar horned head. Jerry's mirrorlike efforts to write the name of Batman, as well as one of his more typically tadpolesque figures, also grace this maiden effort to capture a superhero on paper.

In the following days Jerry was literally obsessed with drawing Batman. Every day after school he would rush home and undertake additional efforts—in color or black and white, in marker or in pencil, on lengthy galley proofs or tiny napkins—to get Batman straight. Shortly after his first attempt, copying from a bubble-gum card, he had already gotten the shape of the cape under better control, attempted its fringelike bottom, separated it from the

hero's body, sought to capture the identifying emblem on Batman's chest, and included the boot-and-pants set that Batman always dons (110). And two days later he produced a whole cast of superheroes, each sporting his characteristic emblem, headgear, and clothing: a veritable line-up of televised heroes, again inspired by models in a comic book (111).

With the passage of another week Jerry had so well assimilated the basic ways of depicting Batman that he no longer required bubble-gum cards or comic books. Instead, seizing a sheaf of papers, he proceeded within an hour to produce no less than a

112

dozen separate sets of superhero figures (see, for example, 112, 113, 114). His command of the forms was now sufficiently well established that he could produce each figure with but a relatively small set of recognizable strokes; like a commercial artist, he had hit upon a formula, a kind of notation, a way of limning the super-heroes so that they were readily recognizable. Excitement and adventure were suggested by the bright colors of their costumes and, in one case, by the dynamic linear patterns with which the cos-

113

114

115

117

116

tumes were rendered. Yet for the most part Jerry remained content simply to align the heroes alongside one another, like suspects in a police line-up or rogues in a gallery (115).

The obsession continued for several months. Jerry rehearsed unrelentingly the specific parts of the Batman (and Batgirl) schemas. By the end of April all the segments—the shape of his head, the cape, the central emblem—were well enough in hand so that they could be produced with but a single motion of the hand, whether it clutched a magic marker or a pencil. Sometimes the schemas, now so well consolidated, were produced in a perfunctory manner (116, 117). But the same basic forms could even be adapted, as in the set of three pirates produced at this time, in an array reminiscent of Picasso's *Three Musicians* (118).

In the fall of 1977 children all over the country, and in many other parts of the world, were enamored of the space extravaganza *Star Wars*. Jerry was no exception. Even before he had argued us into seeing the movie, he began to purchase *Star Wars* cars, *Star Wars* stickers, *Star Wars* books, *Star Wars* records, clothing, athletic equipment, and the like. If *Star Wars* foodstuffs were available, he would no doubt have insisted that we stock up for the winter. Before long he was also deeply involved in drawing the cast of *Star Wars* and had produced dozens of drawings in which every face of the major characters was explored. This time the task of depiction was more daunting, for *Star Wars* included a large array of characters that were not human or even humanoid. But Jerry showed no hesitation in tackling the graphic re-creation of this film. Moreover, he displayed the desire—if not the need—to portray not only the personages themselves but also the melodramatic adventures in which they were constantly enmeshed.

Like a doctor facing a complex surgical operation, Jerry girded himself for the task. Before even seeing the movie, he first undertook to draw—and to master—specific characters. On November

118

119
121
120
122

15, 1977, in the course of drawing an exploding rocket ship, he made an initial attempt to include a spaceship from *Star Wars* (119). The following week, having transcended syncretic work, he created his first full *Star Wars* composition (120). Beneath the title he portrayed the "ship of the good guys", Artoo Detoo, the spaceship, the hero Luke Skywalker, and, as if to balance the forces of good, the villain Darth Vader and the "ship of the bad guys." The iconography of the dramatis personae had already been mastered sufficiently to make each one recognizable. Additional characters were attempted in the ensuing days: for example, See Threepio appeared in the next picture (121). Variations were also instituted: one picture was graced by two versions of Artoo Detoo, alongside a more debonair Luke Skywalker (122).

The basic features of all characters having been mastered, Jerry was ready within a month for the next challenge: the depiction of active scenes involving a number of protagonists. Sometimes these scenes were taken directly from the movie, which Jerry had not yet seen but which he nonetheless knew all about; sometimes they involved liberal invention from the realms of his own imagination, or a wedding of *Star Wars* and other creatures of the media. The following series of ten sketches depict a variety of actions, as narrated by Jerry himself (123*a–j*):

123*a*   "Darth Vader finally kills Ben Kenobi."

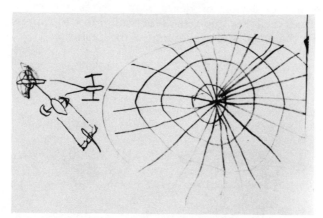

123*b*   "There's a battle with an exploding death star which kills Darth Vader."

123c "Luke tries to burn up death star: this is his first try."

123d "Second explosion of death star." (This picture, in brilliant oranges, yellows, and reds, seems an effort to capture, or exemplify, the mood and excitement of the explosion.)

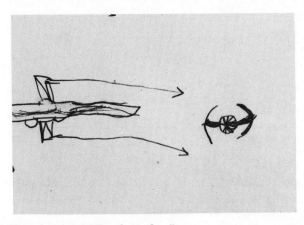

123e "Luke tries to kill Darth Vader."

123*f*   "Darth Vader meets Ben Kenobi again, after Ben teaches Darth Vader."

123*g*   "Darth Vader fighting Kenobi." (Here the actual fight is portrayed, with each character brandishing his weapon.)

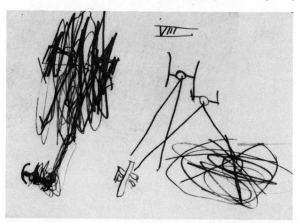

123*h*   "This is a battle in outer space. The bad guy blows up the death star. There's an explosion and Darth Vader gets in the explosion but he's not killed. It's funny, the bad guy shouldn't blow up the death star." (Again Jerry attempts to depict directly the explosion and the battle, with confusing, if well-intentioned, results.)

123*i*   "Luke returns by exploding the death star." (Note the minia-
turization of figures, which facilitates depiction of a whole
scene.)

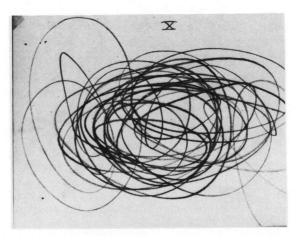

123*j*   "Explosion of the death star." (This time the explosion, which
dominates the whole sheet, is fashioned of circular pencil
strokes.)

    These drawings, all made in sequence on small notepad sheets,
represented a concerted effort by Jerry to "replay" the scenes of
Star Wars for himself. Just three months later another set of materials provided an equally tempting opportunity. Grasping lengthy
cardboard sheets and a fistful of magic markers, Jerry exploited
these instruments to produce even more elaborate renditions of
Star Wars.

    Two of the cardboards were used to sketch all the major fig-
ures in *Star Wars.* On the first one (proceeding from left to right)
Jerry depicted Darth Vader, See Threepio, Artoo Detoo, Chewbacca,

Grand Moff Tarkin, the Millennium Falcon, and the good ship (124). Each figure was portrayed in its own color, with typical expression and expressiveness. The second cardboard sheet (125), emblazoned with two broad *Star Wars* captions, featured storm troopers, Chewbacca, and the trash compactor (in action), as well as two simple scenes: Darth Vader strangling a rebel and Chewbacca hurling a small missile.

Having introduced the characters, Jerry turned his attention to the creation of an organized scene. The first effort, reminiscent of the earlier "line-ups," featured Darth Vader strangling a rebel, ringed by the trash compactor on his right and a storm trooper and Artoo Detoo on the left. Up above floated a good ship as well as the ubiquitous *Star Wars* logo (126). Greater success was achieved in the final scene (127): a fight to explode death star. Here the death

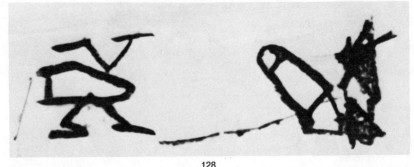

128

star, on the left, is surrounded by a series of black circular explosions, a set of "good-guy ships" and a number of "bad-guy ships," each hosting its own explosion. Though the final product is still static, a clear attempt has been made to capture within a single "frame" the drama and conflict of *Star Wars*.

One more illustration is worth noting. On a tiny piece of scrap paper, Jerry drew some *Star Wars* elements (128). As he described it, "One ship is shooting at a rocket. On the other side is the blood explosion—that's because of the war." In this little episode we can see glimmerings of what will later become the norm in Jerry's and other children's symbolic expression. The verbal story line is beginning to dominate: the line drawings are functioning increasingly as notations to supplement the story, rather than as accurate or fanciful graphic depictions of a scene viewed "in the mind's eye."

Just what is going on in these drawings—the portraits of superheroes, the line-ups of *Star Wars* characters, the depictions of exciting scenes? At times these drawings were prompted primarily by a reportorial function. Jerry seemed simply to want to describe to someone how something looked or how it occurred. Much more frequently, however, one received the unmistakable impression that the act of drawing was in itself an important expression, one essential for the psychological well-being of the child. In describing this act, we may perhaps come to understand why children of this age draw so much, and with such passion, tension, and expressiveness.

We have viewed Jerry at an age when (like so many other youngsters) he was preoccupied with issues of action, power, and violence. No necessity to invoke Oedipal complexes or male aggressive drives here, though one may certainly do so. At a descriptive level these themes are simply ones that rivet his attention, even as the process of baking cookies came to intrigue him some months later. Jerry did not have a vocabulary to discourse on these psychological themes of power and conflict, nor indeed did he seem to exhibit much inclination to converse about these themes. They were not for the dinner table. Yet, as evidenced by his attraction to books, comics, and television shows which presented these themes, they were clearly important to him: his engagement in cops and robbers, spaceman, and other adventure-filled games; his recitation of little stories that highlighted bouts of aggression, violence, even killing; his creation of symbolic play dramas, rich in sharp and penetrating gestures, enacted with his toys, blocks, or "pretend" spaceships.

Jerry's efforts to draw the scenes of *Star Wars* partook of this general passion and enthusiasm. A vast majority of the sketches re-enacted a vigorous scene from the movie or from his imagination, one in which violence, maiming, and conflict were prominently fea-tured. Yet execution of such "ultimate acts" did not prevent them from recurring with the same characters, in even more potent garb, in the very next drawing. Like cartoon protagonists whose fate never extends beyond the next frame, the characters of *Star Wars*— these archetypes of good and evil, power and impotence, friend and foe—appeared again and again in his drawings, enacting and ex-emplifying all of the power, passion, fears, and hopes that can populate the mind of the young child.

Why should youngsters of this age become so obsessed with these "X-rated" themes? Why should they re-enact them innumer-able times, despite the clear signals given by adults that they would much prefer them to be doing something else? In my view, this interest in aggressive acts, this picture of the world as a perennial struggle between evil and beneficent forces, illuminates a central preoccupation of children at this point in their lives.

For several years the children have heard stories about all manner of individuals, even as they have observed countless forms of interaction among adults and peers. Their own actions and be-haviors have also been characterized many times as positive or negative, helpful or injurious, beneficent or malevolent. At first, such characterizations probably make little sense to the young child; after all, he is just beginning to elaborate a world of mean-ing. But by the age of four, five, or six the child has made an initial cut at understanding the behaviors and feelings that are being en-acted, talked about, and worried about in his world. Some of these themes can be quite disturbing, and some of the fears they evoke can be almost disabling.

Accordingly, it becomes very important for the child to try to make sense to himself of these diverse forces and factors. He must come to grips with their meaning, make peace, if at all possible, with the various potent sources and forces in his environment. Such "settling" and "understanding" activity is most likely to take place with those characters and forces that have already made a strong impression on him, are becoming increasingly familiar, and are slowly yielding their meanings—and they are often likely to be characters that loom larger than life, characters whose traits and features prove unmistakably charged. In an earlier day, fairy tales fit this bill; in an even earlier epoch, myths provided the necessary themes, scenes, and characters. Now it is the characters conveyed by the mass media, and particularly ones of such epic status as Batman or Darth Vader, who present themselves as candidates for exhaustive exploration, analysis, and interpretation. Such an exploration can take several forms: the child may speak, sing, dream, or cry about them. But for youngsters four to seven years of age, graphic media present a uniquely rich, flexible, and personal means for exploring the depths of interpersonal relations and personal feelings.

Given the preoccupation of children like Jerry with such fantastic characters, the question arises about the degree to which these characters possess real-life potency. After all, it seems to matter whether the characters of *Star Wars* are seen as purely fictive in nature, remote in time and presence from one's own everyday experience; or whether they have assumed a real-life potency, such that their adventures and fates figure importantly in the experiences, hopes, and fears of the young child.

Questioned directly, most children (like Jerry) will concede that *Star Wars* couldn't really have happened and that the characters they are drawing are "just pretend" or "not real." Their own behavior, however, indicates just as clearly that these characters possess vast potency in the life of the young child; they tend to induce "real fears," such as those associated with robbers, with parental punishments, or with the ghosts that might live in one's house. It is not so much that the child expects Ben Kenobi or the Jawas to enter his house one afternoon and sit down at the dining-room table. (Indeed, should this happen, children would probably be as amazed as their parents.) It is rather that the child does not know for sure which aspects of *Star Wars* are likely to occur in the real world and which are purely fantastic, and so the criteria for whether one should be amused or frightened are much less certain.

An even more potent effect is wrought by the themes and the feelings of which these adventure stories treat. To be sure, a child may not live in constant fear that Darth Vader will one day invade his room. But he knows that there are other villains and bullies (or parents) who can tyrannize him, and he knows the terror of unalloyed fear or anxiety. It is because the adventure stories remind him of these instances that they sometimes frighten him, even as they compulsively captivate his attention and interest. And it is through the drawing activities, I submit, that the child makes his initial efforts to gain some control and understanding and to "work out" his feelings about these potent themes.

We receive, then, in these drawings by one five-year-old child, an initial glimpse of the rich potential of children's drawings. On the thematic side, such drawings can allow the child to explore in his own way themes and traits that weigh heavily on his consciousness. From a formal point of view, the drawings spawn a rapid increase in the child's knowledge of spatial arrangements: in scarcely a year he moves from simple tadpolelike figures to forms sufficiently differentiated to allow easy recognition of a spate of fictional characters; he makes a transition from a simple line-up of characters to the beginning of genuine scenes; and he shows an incipient capacity to portray interactions among characters, conflicts among forces, and the expressiveness of certain heightened motions. In their vigor, use of color, feeling for action, and often strikingly original visual composition, these portrayals of *Star Wars* adventures seem to partake of the elements of artistry.

The question naturally arises whether other youngsters are likely to pass through such rapid graphic growth and explore as well a range of thematic and formal opportunities. It is instructive in this context to be able to examine the products from the hand of someone raised in the same household—Jerry's sister Kay. Precisely because so many of the environmental pressures are presumably similar, the intriguing similarities and differences in these youngsters' early drawings take on added significance.

Even as Jerry's days (and nights) came to be dominated by his experiences with the characters of *Star Wars*, Kay's consciousness (like that of many young girls) became completely enwrapped in the world of horses. Here the impetus was not a product of the mass media (though she collected numerous books about horses as well as innumerable replicas of horses) but rather of her own experiences with horses: at first, during her visits to farms, and soon after, in her own attempts to ride.

Kay first drew horses alone. These horses were simple, graphically as well as thematically: they were elaborated out of a rectangular schema, with initially two, and then four, appendages arrayed at the bottom. The horses were, indeed, little more than elongated tadpole forms.

It soon became apparent, however, that the horse was more than just another schema in Kay's growing graphic armamentarium. She took special care in the elaboration of its form; she began to intertwine her drawings of horses with stories, poems, scenes, and other treatments of these organisms that (like the creatures of *Star Wars* for Jerry) were assuming an increasingly important niche in her daily imaginative life.

Let us examine some early developments of the equine theme. In the summer of 1975, shortly after returning home from a trip to a farm, Kay produced one of her simple schematic horses (129)

A horse is a wild
Animal. a horse Should
Be Free. a horse should
Be Left Like it was built to Be
The horse

129

and captioned it with a poem (which we helped her to transcribe).
In its disarming simplicity of both word and form, the verse captures a feeling she strongly endorsed:

> A horse is a wild animal
> A horse should be free
> A horse should be left like it was built to be.

Two months later, in October 1975, she depicted two of the horses
on which she had ridden the previous summer (130). The body
schema was still elementary, but this time the torso was composed of a single amoebalike contoured line, rather than the juxtaposed geometrical forms of days gone by. And instead of standing
squarely on the ground, the horses were shown heading toward a
little girl—presumably Kay—who, we may assume, was waiting
eagerly for them underneath an apple tree and looking fondly upon
them. Other efforts of this period revealed that Kay was also experimenting with depiction of the riding habit (131) and was placing horses in other simple compositions—for example, in a floral
pattern (132).

Even during this early period it was evident that Kay's vision
was practically the opposite in tone to Jerry's: a quiet pastoral life
where one could love horses, a clamoring for a setting devoid of
loud and harsh activity, a time for contemplation and for the exercise of the deep feelings of love and tender care. Yet one can also
see at work many of the motifs and forms that characterized Jerry's
involvement with *Star Wars*: deeply felt emotions; an emerging

Freedom is A horse.
Star is A horse.

130

Freedom

131

132

sense of compositional form in which the various elements of the canvas join to yield an overall expressive effect; use of color in which the canonical hues of objects were sometimes sacrificed in order to produce heightened emotional expression or to yield a canvas replete with pleasing blends.

Despite these converging signs of preoccupation with horses, we were not prepared for a remarkable work produced by Kay at the end of her sixth year. While visiting her grandparents at the seashore, remote indeed from any horses, she was reminded one day of some pleasant riding experiences she had had the previous summer. Going off by herself, she returned to recite to us a poem she had composed. As it happened, Kay was not yet writing and, like many preliterate children, she had an extremely accurate verbal memory, one bordering on total recall. Her poem has been reproduced below: it reflects her deep feeling for horses and her longing for the kind of life that can be associated with them, even as it indicates that incipient sense of poetic form, the simple moral truths, the modest and charming attempts at rhyme and rhythm characteristic of this age.

The Thing I Wish the Most

I would love to live on a farm
Not the kind with animals and charm
But just with a garden
And one or two horses
Which I could ride down to the store.

And around the neck
Of that horse of mine
A ribbon with baskets on either side
To carry the things that I got at the store
To carry some cloth and a ribbon
Maybe much more.

And a friend and a big place to play
With more space than a garden
And more space to play
And no school would be there
And all days were free
And birthdays would be out and much much more fun
It would be somewhere all year
Never a drop of rain for a year
What a beautiful place to be
Just around the sea.

But Kay did not rest with the composition of this poem. She asked us to write it down so that she could show it to others. And then she decided to illustrate it (133). Rather than composing a single scene, however, she elected to prepare a montage, an ensemble of sketches in which various aspects of her feelings and ideas would be conveyed. No precise order governed the effort: some lines were illustrated after ones that actually preceded them in the poem; a few of the scenes lacked an integral link to the poem; still others were direct depictions of lines from the poem. Perhaps the most striking scene is the fourth one: here the vision of the poem is embodied in a single drawing which features a well-planned and well-executed compositional scheme. Taken together,

133

the poem and its illustration signify how a child can express to others—in a form much more effective than normal discourse—her thoughts about a treasured experience in life.

This effort behind her, Kay did not rest on her laurels. Indeed, at about the same time, she produced another document—this time an illustrated account of an adventure that had befallen her the previous summer. The little book Kay fashioned related the time she and her friends were horseback riding and an errant horse stepped into a hive of bees. The rest is clearly conveyed by the seven drawings, the single abstract design, and the nine pages of narration (134a–f): the horses panicked, the youngsters were thrown, Kay and a friend were discovered by her mother, the owner of the stable was relieved that no one had been hurt, and Kay remembered well her refreshing reward that day—a Coke. Especially striking in this short account is Kay's capacity to divide her efforts between the composition of the narrative—itself quite cogent—the depiction of the principal characters, and the inclusion in the drawings of important interactions. Thus we see the girl and the horse exchanging greetings on the first page (134a); the array of young girls, with different colored hair, and the ponies and pony tails in the second scene (134b); the placing of the horse's rear leg close to the beehive in the third drawing (134c); the unmistakable

134a

134b

134c

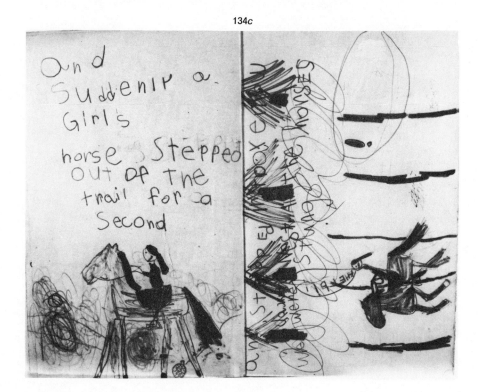

air of chaos, along with the cry for help, in the fourth companion drawing (134c); the fleeing horse bypassing (and dwarfing) the fallen girl in the fifth illustration (134d); the two youngsters tossed onto the ground in the sixth drawing (134e); and the totally unexpected yet fittingly calm colored design, with its equine shapes, which decorates the final pages of the narration (134f).

In this story Kay deliberately simplified the various forms so that she could communicate a considerable amount of information in both words and pictures. In other drawings during the following months she experimented with both the form of the horse and the kinds of scenes in which it could be embedded. A drawing of the same time records an initial effort (with mane flying) to present the body in motion (135). A tracing made but a month later reveals the kinds of exercises to which she gravitated in an effort to sharpen her representational skills (136); it also suggests the feeling of efficacy that can be gained when such efforts prove successful. In a drawing made in January 1976 the horse itself remains simple but it has now been embedded in quite a complex story

134d

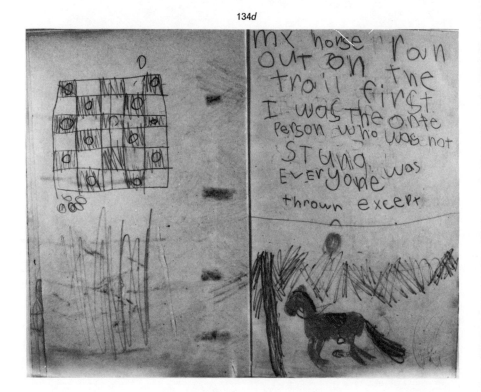

for the owner fo the Stable named Jean. Soon after that my Mother found me and a boy.

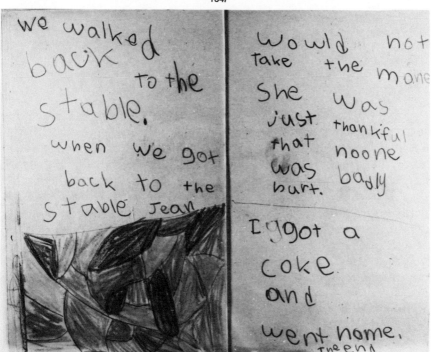

we walked back to the Stable. when we got back to the Stable Jean

would not take the mone She was just thankful that noone was badly hurt.

I got a coke and went home. The end

135

136

(137): we see here an Indian boy who has been left alone for several days in the middle of the woods, on a kind of survival trip. Surrounded by tall trees, two teepees, a pet dog, and his treasured horse, the youth seems well outfitted to withstand the challenging rigors to which he has been subjected. It is worth noting the simple yet effective layout: each element stands alone, relatively straight, with minimal overlap; the composition, with its three focal points of teepees, youth with his dog, and horse arrayed against a setting of four trees each, creates a full yet uncrowded effect.

Kay soon became able to concentrate much more fully on purely visual aspects of the horse. In a pair drawn in April 1976 we find smoother and more contoured bodies and bent legs, as well as an effort to show one animal physically dominating another (138). A drawing one month later represents a concentrated effort to produce a convincing likeness of a few particular aspects of the horse

137

138

139

141

(139): its head, its facial features, and its neck. In the precision of line—the carefully drawn nose, eyes, mane, ears, and surrounding background—this drawing represents a considerable advance. (The attempt to depict features and to sign the drawing in a "cute" manner are equally noteworthy.)

Even as the horses gained in schematic subtlety, further scenic variations were also attempted. Thus in a sketch of October 1976 Kay again confronts a horse with an Indian, this time a young princess (140). Dramatic effects are more successfully secured as the princess faces the horse, and a branch on a tree stretches across the sky as if casting its spell over the protagonists.

But by 1977, when Kay had turned eight, a subtle change began to mark her drawings. The horses themselves become more stylized. They tend to appear in a graceful walking or jumping position, their profiles now regularly arrayed to their right (141). Their manes and tales are smoothly groomed; they exhibit carefully placed features; every hair and limb seems precisely in place. Sometimes they are placed in a scene with a rider (142); sometimes they are depicted alone; sometimes they occur in an organized composition where they are surrounded by carefully colored flowers and a sun with numerous rays of different hues

142

(143). But even as this increase in precision, and, if you will, photographic realism, can be discerned, a muting of creative originality also seems evident. Dramatic scenes give way to placid bucolic compositions; adventurousness in depiction gives rise to an elegant but essentially static composition which becomes wholly predictable. Kay herself told me that her drawings were not as good as they were two years before, and, at least in certain respects, I agreed with her. The age of artistic expressiveness, or at least its original flowering, seemed at an end.

143

We have now had a chance to consider some representative efforts of children's art—works which, I must stress, are in no way remarkable for children of this age. There is little doubt that these works have a certain power and charm. But we must now recoup our original question and assess the extent to which such efforts merit an honorific characterization as "artwork." Certainly the care taken by the children in making these drawings, their own pleasure in producing them, and the potent effects they can sometimes exert on others make suspect any simple dismissal of these drawings. Surely these drawings are not just happy accidents; too much attention and caring surrounds them to permit them to be discarded out of hand. Indeed, one confronts inescapable parallels between such works and those by contemporary artists like Helen Frankenthaler (144, 145), Adolph Gottlieb (146, 147), and Willem de Kooning (148, 149). And yet, can we adduce more powerful evidence in favor of the artistic status of these single works and our collected renditions of space-people and horses?

To answer this, we require some kind of working definition of a work of art. Two criteria that have often been proposed turn out to be deficient. One criterion, much honored in the psychological literature, is the degree of realism in a work. In this view, if a work is realistic, it earns high marks for artistry. The history of art in the twentieth century, however, so clearly refutes this point of view that it is difficult to take it seriously any longer, except perhaps for certain limited experimental purposes. A second criterion is also flawed—the criterion of excellence. Not only is it extremely difficult to find standards of judgment that represent a genuine consensus over a significant period of time, but quite possibly something prepared by accident could be judged as excellent (for example, the random marks of a chimp which happened to resemble an abstract

144

145

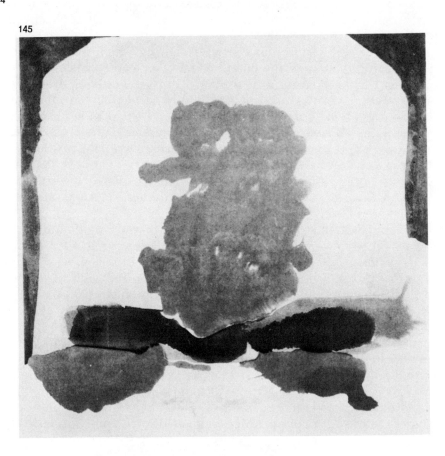

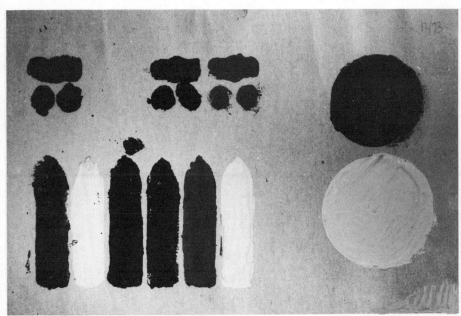

146

147

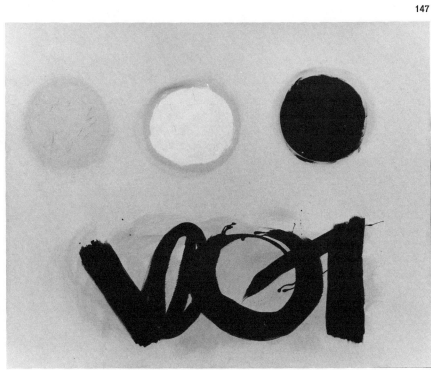

148

149

creation), as even a carefully conceived effort by a master might, for one or another reason, be judged as deficient in artistic quality.

For such reasons it has become crucial to find aesthetic criteria that are less chimerical and less fragile. Some effective candidates have been proposed by the philosopher Nelson Goodman. Proceeding from the observation that artworks are symbols which function in certain kinds of ways, Goodman has suggested that the "art" quality of a work be judged by the extent to which the work exhibits those properties of symbols which are considered aesthetic. Despite appearances, this definition is not circular, for Goodman has specified what he means by aesthetic. And while it is not possible for me to rehearse his analysis in detail, I can indicate two criteria that he stresses.

The first is the inclusion of *expressiveness* in one's artistic symbols. If a child uses the materials of a medium in such a way as to make a drawing that is "lively," "sad," "angry," or "powerful," he has provided one sign that he can fashion a work of art. A second criterion, termed *repleteness*, again involves the way in which the properties of the medium are exploited. If the child can use materials—for instance, the lines of a medium—in such a way that several aspects of that material are significant, he is again demonstrating his capacity to use symbols in an artistic way. In other words, if in his drawings the thickness, shape, shading, and uniformity of line contribute to the work's effect, the child is exhibiting a command over repleteness. If, on the other hand, variations in line (if any) prove immaterial to the impact (and import) of the drawing, then he is not using symbols in a replete manner.

Such definitions form a useful starting point for contemplating whether works produced by a child are actually functioning as artistic works. Yet an individual assessment remains a highly subjective matter: one judge might feel that a child's work is highly expressive and uses lines in a replete manner; a second judge might give the child low marks for expressiveness and repleteness; and a third judge might think that the work conveys a different expression or a different type of repleteness. Such a lack of consensus would constitute a poor recommendation for an artist.

At a premium, then, is a more reliable way of determining the extent to which a child's works really exhibit such "symptoms of the aesthetic." And here is where an ingenious study by Thomas Carothers, who worked with me some years ago when he was a Harvard student, merits attention. Carothers exposed youngsters to drawings that were identical to one another save in the kind of artistic symptom they possessed. As a means of testing sensitivity to expressiveness, subjects were shown one drawing of a scene that was expressively happy (150) and another that was equally unhappy (151).

150   151

In another set designed to test sensitivity to repleteness, one drawing contained lines that were all thin (152), while the other

152   153

drawing featured lines that were all thick (153). In each case the subject was told that the paired drawings had been begun by two different artists. Then the subject was asked to note differences between the drawings and to complete the drawings in a way that the artist himself would probably have done. If the child included those features that counted for a certain expression or repleteness, he gained credit for artistic competence; if, however, he ignored these hints and instead approached all the completions in the same way, he was judged incapable of artistic performance.

Carothers found a remarkably regular sequence of behaviors in his tests. Children at the first-grade level—aged seven—showed little or no artistic sensitivity in any of the tests. Irrespective of the "set" created by the incomplete drawings, the child finished both of the drawings in the same way (154). Sad and happy scenes, thick-

and thin-lined drawings—all were completed in identical fashion. Sixth graders, on the other hand, found the task quite easy; in nearly all cases they fashioned completions that "picked up" on the differences suggested in the initial drawings (155–157). Happy drawings achieved happy endings; sad drawings were so completed; and thick- and thin-lined versions were completed in a similarly consistent fashion. While the age varies, depending on the particular "artistic" symptom under examination, children apparently ac-

154

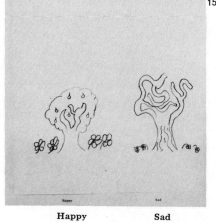

Happy   Sad

155

Happy   Sad

156

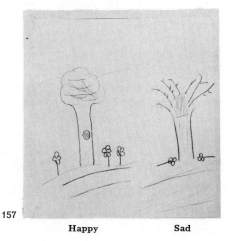

Happy   Sad

157

Happy   Sad

quire aesthetic sensitivity sometime during the middle years of
school.

It might be objected, of course, that the child saw the differences but just could not capture them in his drawings. To see
whether this might in fact be the case, Carothers also presented to
the youngsters sample endings for the drawings and asked which of
them went with each drawing. Sample completions for an expressive set have been reproduced in figure 158; sample completions for
a replete set have been reproduced in figure 159. Though he found

158   159

improvement in the children's performance when they were simply
asked to choose, Carothers basically replicated his initial results: a
minimum artistic sensitivity in the early years of school, gradually
supplanted by firm control of the artistic media in the years preceding adolescence.

This line of evidence certainly counsels against an uncritical
assumption that the preschooler's attractive drawings are adequate
from an artistic point of view. Pleasing and expressive to us, perhaps, yet quite likely these effects were not deliberately sought by
the child. After all, if the child saw no alternatives to the way he
achieved his drawing, if he was simply obeying the edicts of some
internal master, then one does not want to credit him with much
artistic understanding (at least no more than one wants to conclude that the entertaining dog or the cooing infant deems himself
cute).

It is, however, risky to draw a strong inference from this single
study which, moreover, represents an artificial experimental situation. Another relevant line of evidence is thus wanted. And just
such supplementary evidence comes from a dissertation by Diana

Korzenik, an art educator currently at the Massachusetts College of Art.

Korzenik reasoned that if a child is to be considered in control of his artistic capacities, he must possess some awareness of how a work looks to others. After all, should he prove completely oblivious to its effects and to possible interpretations (or misinterpretations), he can hardly be considered the master of his medium. On the other hand, should the child seem aware of how the work looks to others, should he exhibit the capacity to see through the eyes of another person, then it seems reasonable to attribute to him some control over his artistry.

Once again a somewhat indirect route to this issue presented itself. Korzenik asked her subject to draw an object in such a way that a child seated in an isolated chamber, who could see only the drawing, would still be able to recognize its subject—in the case shown in figures 160*a*–*b*, "jumping." The drawer was allowed to hear the guesses made by the isolated viewer and then to revise his drawing in order to make it more recognizable or "readable." If the child proved able to alter his drawing so that it could be identified, this flexibility would suggest that "dissolution of egocentrism" which figures crucially in any artist's repertoire.

Once again the youngest subjects, this time about five years old, proved quite oblivious to the eyes (and views) of others (160*a*). They rarely altered their drawings from one trial to another, blithely expecting that the drawings would "speak for themselves"; they confused intent for achievement, simply blaming the other player when he or she failed to guess correctly. By the age of seven or eight, however, the child was becoming quite sensitive to the demands of the other individual (160*b*); he sought initially to make drawings that were identifiable, and, more importantly, al-

160*a* 160*b*

tered each revision until the partner could guess what was intended.

Here then is evidence that, by the start of school, the child is
already gaining some kind of control over the medium. He may not
be able to handle its purely aesthetic aspects, such as expressiveness or repleteness, but he can at least increase the legibility of
what he is doing and appreciate that others may not see his drawing in the way that he does.

Nonetheless, such experimental evidence calls into doubt the
easy assumption that the young child is an artist, at least in the sense
that we apply the term to the mature artist. Certainly the artists
honored in our culture can use line expressively and repletely; certainly they are aware of how things might look to others and are
constantly making adjustments so that their vision can be more
successfully expressed or apprehended. Certainly they would have
passed with ease the kinds of tasks posed by Carothers and Korzenik
(assuming, of course, that they were willing to play the game).

But what of some art produced in the twentieth century by

161   Pablo Picasso. *Study for the Horse.* Composition study for *Guernica.* 1 May 1937. Pencil on blue paper, 8¼″ x 10½″. On extended loan
to The Museum of Modern Art, New York, from the artist's estate.

162

certain great masters—in particular, art that is characterized by childlike features? What, for instance, of Picasso's simple sketches of horses (161)? Do not their directness and clarity, their lack of spatial sophistication, their use of broad simple lines (which rarely vary in thickness), all bespeak a consciousness very much like that of a child? And if there are few demonstrable differences between their works and those produced by children, then why not equate the two groups of art objects?

We can perhaps make an initial inroad by considering a painting made by a twenty-year-old artist (162). As part of an exercise, this painter wanted to create the effects of the works produced by a young child, and indeed her effort captured the basic forms exploited by the child—the simple stick figures, the limbs protruding from the torso, the elementary colors, the wide spaces between forms, and the direct statement of ideas, which in some ways was very reminiscent of how a five-year-old would portray a simple scene.

Yet even a few moments' examination makes it apparent that quite different processes are at work. We have here a mimetic attempt, one that is perhaps charming but essentially unsuccessful. The forms are far too regular, finished, and measured. The contours

are studied, not free; the facial expressions are cultivated and contrived, not genuine; the spatial arrangements are measured, not
haphazard. There is no trace of motion, spirit, dynamic tension.
Like a mediocre fake, this drawing bears superficial similarities to a
work by a child but does not witstand scrutiny. It is at most a kind
of pleasant joke.

Such indictments do not apply to the works of Klee, Picasso, or
Miró, for their paintings are not in any simple sense copies of children's works. There are no compulsive attempts to reproduce the
forms and the characteristic proportions of a typical five-year-old's
work. Rather, to the extent that these works resemble what is produced by children, such parallels inhere in their explorations of
basic elements. What these twentieth-century masters are doing, I
think, is reducing their artwork to the simplest possible forms—to
lines, triangles, enclosures—and exploring the numerous ways in
which they can be combined for specific expressive ends. If they
embody a certain expression—say that of calm or lightheartedness
—it is because that is what *they* sought to express and not because
these properties happen to recur in children's drawings. If they
perseverate with a single thickness of line, it is because they want
this uniformity to come through.

But what leads the young child to make drawings akin to those
of twentieth-century masters? Is it simply a happy accident, a by-
product of the way he happens to feel, the production of lines and
forms over which he has little choice? Perhaps in the early years of
drawing, say the age of three or four, this description makes sense.
But with children of a somewhat older age, I think that something
quite different is going on.

By the age of five or six, children already have mastered the
basic vocabulary of schemas which enables them to portray the
world. Having the basic "moves," they can produce pretty much
what they want where they want it to be. They are aware of the
properties of the paper, how to fill it, how to leave it blank, and
how to distribute elements across its expanse. More important, they
now sense some of the standards of their society: they are becoming aware of how to draw figures realistically, how to feature symmetry, how, by planning ahead, to avoid crowding or leaving too
many blank spaces. These goals had in fact excessively affected the
twenty-year-old child-mimic introduced earlier.

But while these goals are already perceived by the child of five
or six, they are not yet all-powerful. The child may attempt to
achieve them but he does not care that much if he fails. Or, to put
it another way, he may indeed strive to achieve these goals and yet
regularly fall short of them. At an earlier period, or in the light of
different standards, this failure could be taken at face value. But to

our contemporary eyes this failure ends up by producing a kind of charming approximation, a near hit, a "first draft" of higher forms of art. In striving for symmetry, the child instead achieves balance. In attempting to place the right number of objects on a page and to give each its own boundary and base line, he achieves harmonious composition. In striving for realism, he achieves charming, recognizable deviations from a photographic likeness. The child himself is not bothered by these deviations—the effort to achieve these ends suffices for him. And by the same token, those of us who have tired of high realism and who have learned that deviations exert their own charm, find ourselves strongly and legitimately attracted to these rougher youthful products.

We cannot forget that the adult artist achieves these results by quite different means. He is purposefully turning his back on all the intricate forms he can produce and the variety of moods he can convey in favor of self-consciously and deliberately capturing forms and sensibilities that are often (and perhaps too swiftly) associated with children. Part of what we admire in his work, indeed, is his capacity apparently to suppress what he knows and to achieve a fresh simplicity.* But in this very opting for elements, the artist is making a far more complex statement—one confronting the possibility of innocence despite one's maturity, the use of great powers in the service of simplicity. The young child, in turn, is simply exemplifying that vaunted innocence.

It is possible that I have done an injustice to the child. Children know a range of moods, and, at least overall, they may be capable of more expressiveness and repleteness than I have suggested. Moreover—and herein lies the lesson of Kay's and Jerry's drawings—artistic media provide a special, even unique, avenue for grappling with issues of importance and complexity which do not, however, lend themselves to verbal discussion at this age. It is too simple to say, with Malraux, that "[The child's] gift controls him; not he his gift." As we have seen in the Korzenik study and in the drawings by my own children, there exists some awareness of alternatives, some possibilities for achieving different ends, even in the child at the threshold of school. But at any moment in time the options that can be seized seem severely, perhaps even fatally, limited.

Indeed it may be this paradoxical, ambiguous quality which, more than anything else, conveys the special power and fascination in the drawings of the young child. Were the child as aware of the

---

* Recall Picasso's words: "Once I drew like Raphael, but it has taken me a whole lifetime to learn how to draw like children."

potentials of the medium and the range of alternatives as the adult artist is, he would in fact *be* that adult—he would have already passed through and beyond the special worlds of childhood. If, on the other hand, he were completely oblivious of alternatives, completely a servant of his momentary mood, he would be unable to produce that sustained body of works which is the legacy of so many young schoolchildren, and equally incapable of producing individual works that repay revisiting and re-examination. We can perhaps say that the child is aware of practices, canons, standards, and options, but they do not dominate his thought and action: he can take or leave them. Indeed it seems more accurate to say that the child is in *partial* control of his gift: partial both in the sense that he can sometimes (but not always) achieve what he wants and in the sense that he sometimes (but not always) is actually pursuing explicit ends. Even as the line between reality and fantasy already exists but must constantly be checked and reaffirmed by the young child, so too the line between "directed artistry" and "pleasure in the simple act of producing" is also being constantly crossed at this age by the child. And so it seems proper to speak of "first-draft" artistry in the child.

The flowering of child art is real and powerful but, like other flora, it is seasonal. The magic years, which confer such a treasured quality upon the child's songs, language, and drawings, do not last —indeed they begin to evaporate almost as soon as school begins. To attribute this waning to school is too simple; it probably also occurs in the absence of schooling, and it may well serve positive as well as lamentable ends. But the fact that the child's goals and orientation change fundamentally after the age of flowering seems indisputable—and with effects that are all too clear. For it is pursuit of the realistic and the literally true which casts its spell on the individual in middle childhood.

CHAPTER 6

The Reach toward Realism

"I used to draw much better. My drawings were more interesting. But my perspective is 3000 times better now."

Kay, age 9

WHEN drawings made by eight- or nine-year-olds are juxtaposed to those produced by younger children, a striking contrast emerges. There is little doubt about which came from which group: works by the older children feature a kind of precision, a concern for detail, a command of geometrical form which are lacking in the attempts by younger artists. Schemas for familiar objects are readily recognized, and attempts at rendering less familiar objects can initially be decoded. And yet one hesitates to call the drawings by the older children "better"—indeed most observers, and sometimes even the youngsters themselves, feel that something vital which is present at the age of six or seven has disappeared from the drawings by the older children. A certain freedom, flexibility, *joie de vivre*, and a special fresh exploratory flavor which mark the childlike drawings of the six-year-old are gone; and instead of being replaced by adult mastery, this loss has merely been supplanted by a product that is at once more carefully wrought yet also more wooden and lifeless.

Some documentation of this intriguing trend is in order. Consider, first, a drawing made by an eight-year-old boy (163). A portrait of Christmas morning, it features a perfectly triangular tree with regular rectangular packages arrayed in a straightforward fashion underneath. The five-year-old brother of this child looked at the picture and, as younger siblings are wont to do, made his own attempt shortly thereafter (164). His copy can be faulted in

143

163

164

terms of its relative irregularity and sloppiness, the rough lines surrounding the Christmas tree, the motley packages strewn below. Yet the price paid for regularity, precision, and linearity may be excessively high: in fact, one might even comment that the spirit of fun and exuberance associated with Christmas is absent from the attempt by the older youngster. Even if the younger child's drawing represents, in part, a failed attempt to match the geometric accuracy of his brother, the delightful Fauve quality of his effort cannot be ignored.

Even more arresting evidence of this trend comes from drawings made by the same children over a period of several years. In one study, my colleagues and I have revisited the same youngsters as they proceeded from kindergarten through the early primary grades (165–174). Time and again we find the drawings by the

165 Drawing by Nancy in the first grade.

166 Drawing by Nancy in the second grade.

167 Drawing by Bill in the third grade.

168 Drawing by Bill in the fourth grade.

169 Drawing by Bill in the fifth grade.

170   Drawing by Susan in the first grade.   171   Drawing by Susan in the third grade.

172   Drawing by Peter in the third grade.   173   Drawing by Peter in the fourth grade.

174   Drawing by Peter in the fifth grade.

older children increasingly regular, increasingly faithful to their target, increasingly neatly colored in. But by the same token the sense of life, power, and vitality and the delight in color and form for their own sake, which are so characteristic of the drawings by the younger children, also wane. Indeed this finding has been captured in a rating scale: while *technical competence* is found to improve steadily with age, *flavorfulness*—the extent to which drawings incorporate individualizing features—reaches its apogee in first grade and then steadily recedes thereafter. This discovery suggests that the drawings of the younger children are not merely failed literal attempts; they display virtues that reflect the fresh mental state of the young schoolchild. Whereas the literally oriented child is intent on getting every detail correct and will therefore dispense with a "sense of the whole," the child of five or six has an intuitive sense of what an organized picture should be like—a sense which is, at the very least, submerged during the subsequent period.

Even as they agree on this trend in middle childhood toward a different approach to drawing, experts differ widely as to its significance. For most, the shift is a thing to be regretted. Children are seen as sinking into the doldrums of *literalism*: a pedantic preoccupation with the photographic aspect of drawings undermines the child's involvement in the expressive genius of the graphic medium. In such a Rousseauian view, literalism should be avoided at all costs; or failing that, this stage should be postponed as long as possible or negotiated as quickly and painlessly as possible. The seduction into literalism is blamed on an interfering and manipulative social system; left to her own devices, the child's natural genius should preserve her expressive flair and buttress her against the perilous seductions of photographic likenesses.

This view is not unanimous, however. A thoughtful minority, while conceding and even admiring the charm of earlier drawings, feels that they achieve their appeal through extraneous factors and reflect little genuine gift on the child's part. For these conservative commentators it is this "mere unfolding" which should be aborted, so that the more serious business of genuine artistic tutelage and production can commence. In their view the child's increasing care in making drawings, her obsession with realism, her concern to render spatial relations accurately, represent a beneficent turn of events. These authorities argue that the child still can, if so urged, draw in the "freer" style of former times: it is her deliberate (and wise) choice to go another way. Only to the extent that the child is willing and able to master the nature of the medium and to exploit its resources so as to achieve explicit representational goals, only to this extent can she be considered a serious and genuine participant in the process of the arts.

Adjudicating between these contrasting positions proves a most ticklish matter. Much of what is valued—or devalued—turns on matters of taste, which can yield judgments that, in another century, might well have gone in the other direction. The very disdain for realism which grips our "sophisticated" age would, a hundred years ago, have been replaced by a pleasurable response to faithfully realistic renditions. Indeed, what seems to us to be a decline in the degree of artistry may simply be a peculiar artifact of life in Western culture. Perhaps elsewhere, perhaps even here in a time of different values, one might not witness this alleged dip in artistic worth during the early years of school.

Before reaching any closure about this trend, it seems prudent to examine it more closely and to consider its positive as well as its negative aspects. One must affirm at the outset that at least in certain respects the apparent decline in activity is a genuine phenomenon. Whereas drawing, painting, and other graphic activities are "the thing" in the preschool years, they become less central and less common as the school years pass. Less variability and less idiosyncracy mark older children's drawings: stock characters, stock styles, stock themes gain the ascendancy. And, as noted, neutral judges concur that later drawings exhibit less flavor and increasingly taste the same. The sameness is propelled chiefly by a desire to produce pictures that are realistic: at premium are works that follow the canons of classical Western drawing, ones that strive to resemble photographs, ones that seek to capture in as faithful form as possible the colors, forms, sizes, and surface appearances of entities in the world. Even as the realistic drawing comes to be prized above impressionistic or abstract art, so too in her own artistry the child seeks to fashion drawings that could "pass for" photographic works and to seek out those individuals or books that can reveal the road to realistic effects.

Nor is this heightened interest in realism an exclusive preserve of the visual arts. In nearly every sphere of life the child is increasingly intent (if not "hung up") on getting things just right, on treating things "just the way they *really* are." Words, for example, are to be used in the way that they are meant to be—no more or no less. Figurative language is despised and spurned—a person should not be called *sour*, a tie dare not be termed *loud*. In the area of social activity, games are judged and played solely in terms of their rules; these are to be stated with precision and adhered to without modification. Attempts to ignore a rule lead as rapidly to rejection as does the coining of a metaphor or the production of an abstract design.

As this interest in accuracy overwhelms the child's behavior, she pays homage to those symbol systems and those sets of ideas that lend themselves to precise rendering. It is for this reason, I think, that the child of eight, nine, or ten comes to pay increasing attention to language and to rely increasingly upon it. Up to then, words were still an unreliable means of expressing feelings: drawings (be they of horses or Star Warriors), as a relatively accessible means of exploring complex thoughts and feelings, bore a special responsibility—and furnished a special opportunity. But by the school years, it is language that holds the key to genuine precision: one can tell others what one wants to have done, one can criticize things one does not like, one can explore one's feelings of love, fear, or sadness, and one can introduce subtle ethical distinctions with the promise of being understood and obtaining results. This power of words constitutes a principal reason that most children come to favor language rather than drawing as a means of self-expression— even as it explains why language must at this age be uttered with nary a tinge of ambiguity.

The gaining of knowledge and the desire to be "right" about things are of great importance during this stage of life—and particularly so in our society. What was only intimated beforehand becomes stated explicitly in school: rewards greet those who know the right answer and can issue it quickly and clearly. Moron jokes pepper playground conversation, a telltale if wry sign that it is good to be smart, ridiculous to be in error. For the first time, a child in the midst of singing or drawing will nervously ask, "Is this right?" Such trends are epitomized in the ubiquitous IQ test, a measure that rewards rapid performance and fosters the notion that she who can get the most right answers most quickly is the most intelligent.

Remarkably, among the more popular means of assessing intelligence at this age are various draw-a-person or draw-a-man tests, in which the child is asked to draw an individual in as complete a fashion as possible. An intricate scoring system is based roughly on the assumption that the more features included, the brighter the drawer. While such a test may well serve certain clinical and assessment purposes, it exists in fundamental tension with artistic criteria. For the very impulses that culminate in a high score on this test—a compulsive inclusion of every feature—have little to do with what bestows value on a work of art, and may even preclude the child's attainment of expressive power. Paradoxically, however, the test fits in neatly with the values held by children of this age: both children and testers concur that a drawing ought to resemble its referent as slavishly as possible.

In describing trends in the art of Western schoolchildren, I have already suggested some of the reasons for the decline in artistic practice. The mores of the school, the general bent toward literalism, the premium on "getting things right," and the heightened reliance on linguistic resources all encourage the profile of this period. Some other culprits can be nominated. There is the role of peer or social pressures at the hands of others who are already "there": if other youngsters ruthlessly pursue realism, it is not surprising that drawings of a photographic ilk are fostered and esteemed. A rise in the child's critical faculties may also figure. In earlier years the child drew what she wished, apparently without caring whether her work conformed to some external standard of acceptability or excellence. Now, however, closely tuned to the standards embraced by the wider culture (and, except among a small élite, these tend to be realistic ones), a child's critical faculties engender production of artwork that passes the test of realism. And by the same token, the child is likely to become dismayed if her own performance does not honor sufficiently the rigorous rules for realism.

A more speculative explanation, one that has gained popularity of late, traces properties of this period directly to changes in the child's nervous system. By the start of school, the achievement of brain dominance (typically by the left hemisphere) is essentially complete. And the chief consequence of this dominance is that the child's linguistic capacities (which are "localized" in that region of the brain) are now unambiguously established and increasingly dominant over the child's behavior. By implication, then, those capacities that depend upon right-hemisphere dominance—generally considered to be those involving visual and spatial functions—are already beginning to take a back seat in the vehicle of cognition. Intriguing support for this hypothesis comes from the recurrent (though still anecdotal) finding that children with learning difficulties—and specifically those with reading problems—tend to have late-occurring or "mixed" dominance; significantly, these same children are often tapped by observers as having an especially deep and abiding involvement with graphic expression. It certainly makes sense to suggest that drawing will continue to hold special attraction for those youngsters who, for one or another reason, evince trouble in expressing themselves in what has become the chief symbol system of the culture.

A final hunch worthy of mention takes as its cue the affective tone of the schoolchild's life. Following Freud's account, the early school years are widely viewed as the *latency* period—a time when, in the wake of a resolution of the Oedipal crisis, the child's feelings and energies are relatively quiescent, a lull before the *Sturm und Drang* of adolescence. I have suggested that drawing serves in early life as a crucial means whereby the child can express her deepest and most potent feelings, anxieties, wishes, particularly during those periods when other means are not available or not as well developed. Accordingly, the widely observed decline in graphic activity during the school years might also be linked to a lessening of desire to express strong moods and, correlatively, the emergence of diverse means for expressing these concerns.

There is yet another possibility—children may simply conclude that their feelings can no longer be captured graphically or that drawing is no longer a suitable means for confronting one's own feelings. Commenting on the widespread decline in expression during this period, Rose Alschuler and LaBerta Hattwick, authors of the massive study *Painting and Personality*, suggest:

> By the time the children are nine or ten years of age they have, as a rule, been so thoroughly infused with the need for reproducing exactly what they see that their own natural modes of self-expression have been blocked off and the earlier impulse to paint and express themselves from within have very largely been stifled.

It may be, then, that expressive drawing is most likely to involve those children whose developmental course has been unusually rocky—those who, owing to personal or family problems, intellectual or social difficulties, have not yet succumbed to the pressures molding other youngsters.

Yet, in truth, it is too simple to suggest that the child stops graphic expression altogether, even as it is misleading to imply that the need for expressing emotions ceases. What seems to happen instead is that the child now has available a number of alternative avenues for such expression, including ones that have not yet been exploited. Within the arts the child now attends to the way in which effects are rendered, and so she can, when asked, produce drawings in a number of different styles. Moreover, even when children in school draw the "approved way," they often will explore quite other subject matters and styles in the locker room, the bus station, or their notebooks. A similar blossoming of options occurs in other media of expression. And it is this blossoming, as much as the more nefarious social and cognitive pressures cited earlier, which may help to account for the child's preoccupations (and omissions) during this period of her life.

As an appealing example of this increase in options, we can contemplate a map of the inside of her head (and her mind) drawn by my daughter Kay when she was comfortably ensconced in the literal stage (175). To begin with, one is struck by the physical accuracy of the proportions and features: the shape of the head is rendered with accuracy (not without erasures, but these naggingly careful erasures are precisely to the point). Next, there is the compulsion to label and classify—to allocate a specific area for each idea

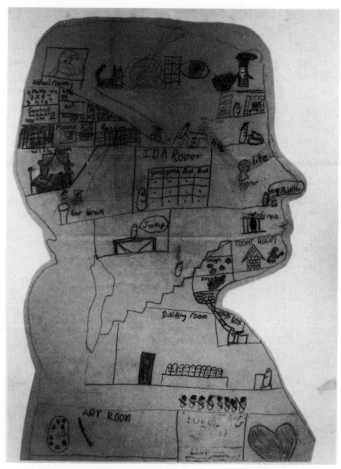

175

of importance. Each of the carefully delineated boxes is duly
marked with its contents: some humorous (a cough and a sneeze
area near the nose); some whimsical (sand source near the eyes);
some faithfully cataloguing school subjects (gym, music, math,
"central" subjects); several reflecting personal values and concerns
—the adored cat atop the skull, the room filled with good and bad
ideas, the "deciding" room, the various ghostly and other wraithlike
figures sprinkled around, the opulently appointed wish-room, and
other such mental accouterments.

But more telling than these precious details of realization is
the whole conception of the drawing. Taking her lead from a lesson
in school, Kay has hit upon a metaphor for her thought processes—
a drawing in which she can depict a treasure-trove of ideas and
feelings that have come to dominate her thinking. And she can use
language to make clear to others precisely what she is alluding to in

her drawing. For in order to share her ideas, she (though not every artist) really requires recourse to words. Here, then, at the hands of a literal child, one finds interesting mixes of graphic and linguistic resources, in the service of a complex conceptualization.

Consider another instance—the illustrated chart of favorite holidays of members of her class, one of a dozen "surveys" conducted during the school year (176). Here we see Kay hitting

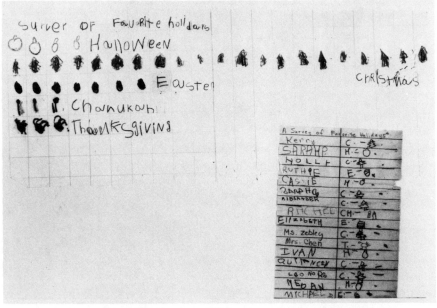

176

upon, and experimenting with, the devising of notation. She creates on the spot a set of symbols that can help her keep in mind her central concern—be it hobbies, chores carried out, the succession of kings in France, the network of islands off the coast of Britain, or, in this case, preferences among holidays. Coalescing in such activities are twin factors: a desire to record events of importance in her life-space, and a sense of enjoyment in the cultivation of tools (of mapping or notation) that can be invoked to aid her in this process.

Not all notations need to be invented ad lib. Many children of this age are beginning to master the number system, musical scoring, and principles of map making, and the energies of applying pencil or marker to paper are to some extent absorbed (some might say dissipated) in the pursuit of these graphic but nonartistic processes. Most decisively, of course, nearly every child in our culture expresses herself in writing—at first simply mastering the formation of letters and familiar logos, later producing whole passages, and eventually harnessing her emerging literary powers to express in figurative language the thoughts, feelings, anxieties, and dreams that occupy her mind.

An interest in writing antedates the school years. As early as the age of two, some children have already cordoned off certain activities (even by name) as writing, and many attempt to copy the peculiar visual properties of cursive script. Indeed such youngsters have come to understand that a certain class of marks corresponds to words, though they do not initially appreciate the equation of specific graphic units with specific sounds. Gradually children do come to acknowledge the equation between written and spoken words. They display this insight through oddly illuminating practices, such as making a mark for each word they utter, or by designating separate strings of letters in a book as they articulate such words as "once upon a time" or "I don't know." And by the age of four, particularly in this Sesame Street culture, youngsters can generally write most letters and a few words as well. Certainly by the time of school there is no confusion on the part of a normal child between the realms of writing and drawing, and there is considerable understanding of the nature of the graphic code.

Yet until she has learned to read and until she can write prose with some fluency, the child is not yet able to marshal her literary resources and to express significant messages with her pen. This process usually takes years. And so until the task of writing has been mastered, the system of drawing is the only one sufficiently elaborated to permit expression of inner life. Once writing mechanics and literary accomplishment have advanced sufficiently (as they ought to have by the age of nine or ten), the possibility of achieving in words what was once attempted in drawings comes alive: the stage is set for the decline—or demise—of graphic expression.

We can see these trends directly in the poignant set of drawings collected by Gertrude Hildreth, a researcher at Teacher's College during the 1930s. Hildreth's young subject, obssessed with trains, drew many hundred such vehicles over a ten-year period. If one looks at the role of writing in these drawings, one can observe a subtle yet ultimately decisive transition in the depiction of the trains: in the preschool years letters and words are used merely as decorations upon the trains (177, 178); but in the years of middle childhood it is the vehicles and tracks that are merely decorative, for the major thrust of the narrative is now carried by verbal means. Indeed in the final drawings (179, 180) the trains are simply illustrations for the stories and poems—emotions are no longer

177

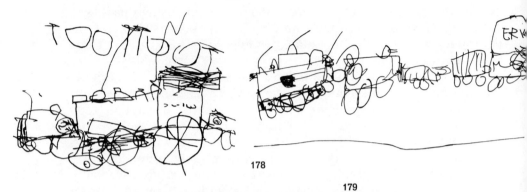

TOOT TOOT

ERV

178

179

TOOT TOOT THE TRAIN IS
MOVEING FAST FASTER AND 1000 MILES
AN HOUR
FASTER AND FASTER AND FASTER
2000000 MILES AN HOUR
4 CARS ON THE TRAIN
WHEN THE TRAIN
WRECKED AT 2000000, MILES
AN HOUR

180

TO GET THERE NO. 1

ANY PLACE
AT THE
AVE ELL

GET
UFF
AT
COAL

ST

75

WEST

ST

GET
TO NO
2 ROW
THE
CARTO
NO. 3
+ UNCH BACK
OR NOTR DAME
NAME
THE
NEXT

1 ST PRIZE 1200
NEXT 10 000 NEXT
NEXT 2000 NEXT
1500 NEXT 1000 NE
750 NEXT 500 NEXT 100
NEXT 300 NEXT 10
705 PRIZES 100 E
50 PRIZES 10 EA
10 CRIZES 5 EA

VIII-7

conveyed by expressive depiction of trains but rather by varying the size of the writing and the pressure of the pencil on the paper.

Knowledge of such notation systems, including writing, exerts still further effects on the child's drawings. She now becomes acutely aware of numerous conventions that can be exploited to achieve effects. Where, earlier, conventions were restricted to a few highly familiar schemas (for example, a circle with radiating lines to depict a sun or a flower), the child now picks up more subtle forms, including ones bearing little visual kinship to the notion being conveyed. And where earlier the child had to invent means for conveying visual information—for example, depicting motion by means of a series of scribbles—she now picks up the tricks of her culture. She comes to know that one can depict motion through the use of a series of lines behind the individual or object; that flying hair stands for the presence of wind; that a character's voice is shown by words in a balloon suspended above the character's mouth, just as a suspended cloud or bubble denotes an idea; that to depict rhythm, a space between dots translates into a period of silence between two impulses. As can be seen in Kay's drawings after the cartoonist Hirschfeld (181), children's attempts to realize these conventions are often humorous and at first only partially succeed; but again the *idea* that one can depict a more abstract conception in such a way that it will be readily accessible or "readable" clearly enters the child's consciousness (and armamentarium) during this period.

Some conventions, including those that crisply express a verbal concept, are picked up readily, indeed effortlessly: once told how to depict someone having an idea, a nine-year-old can invoke the "bubble" convention immediately and effectively. Other conven-

181

tions, however, which require a genuine mastery of the graphic medium, need to be worked out over several years through a careful exploration of line, color, and shading. The capacity to render perspective, to bring out an appropriate blend of brightness, to capture a variety of spatial relations, to master shading or foreshortening—all of these emerge as goals during the early years of schooling, but none can be wholly mastered except through years of practice. Indeed, as we shall see later on, they constitute a compelling agenda for subsequent phases of artistic development.

In considering children's increased preoccupation with the mastery of conventions, the learning of notations, the acquisition of skills of mapping, and the accurate capturing of spatial relations, we have confronted the other face of children's drawings during the early school years. Viewed from the Rousseauian perspective—a perspective that values above all the charm, flavor, and originality of the earlier years—these works are deemed lacking. They are less fun to look at, less lively, less likely to violate sacrosanct conventions, less unpredictable. But they exhibit this greater predictability because, perhaps for the first time, the agenda of the child has come to resemble that adopted by the surrounding culture.

For the child is now intent on mastering the way in which graphic activity unfolds in her milieu. And in so doing, she employs the only way of learning that she knows, which is to pick out specific features of mature adult performance—be it perspective, convention, or notation—and to seek to master the steps involved in achieving these effects. Sometimes autodidactism prevails: the child simply looks at works that have been executed and copies their effects as best she can. But the child may seek direct tutelage from someone more knowledgeable, either in person or through a "How to" book. She now has a fresh and urgent agenda—not merely to let the "natural patterns of artistry" unfold, but rather to master as best she can the skills and techniques of graphic activity which have evolved in the culture she inhabits.

Indeed, while we are pondering the relation between the period of flowering and the stage of literalism, it is appropriate to discern aspects of discontinuity as well as aspects of continuity. In one sense the agendas of the two groups are quite different: the preschool child is pursuing her intuitive sense of an organized work of art, one picked up in a general way from the society but not linked to specific modes of execution. The schoolchild, on the other hand, is intent upon proper behavior and exact rule-following, and so necessarily adopts a more atomistic and literal approach to her work. As an example of the aspects of continuity, even the preschool child has some dim awareness of what procedures are appropriate in her culture. In that sense, she too strives to achieve realism and regularity—her failure to do so produces works that hold charm for us but may well strike her as inadequate efforts to achieve what others about her have already mastered.

In contemplating the contribution of the surrounding culture to the child's graphic agenda, we find ourselves face to face with an even more profound issue. Can we attribute what we have seen at this age to anything other than the effects of life in Western culture? Would we necessarily spot such specific trends as a preoccupation with mastering perspective, or even the more general trends, such as an interest in literalism or realism, in an alien cultural setting? Would we necessarily behold a decline in artistic participation in a culture where most adults practice the arts, where greater license is afforded the child, or, conversely, where there exists but a single, preordained way in which to draw? For perhaps the first time in our inquiry, a question arises which cannot and will not go away: Is our picture of the development of drawing following the initial stages a genuinely general account, or is it rather a caricature obtained through the technologically tinted lens of our own culture?

Would that the question permitted of an easy answer, but it does not. For while drawings have been collected in numerous settings, it has proved astonishingly difficult to obtain information on the way in which developmental progressions are realized in other cultures. Longitudinal studies are few; skilled observers have rarely been "on the scene"; the drawings most likely to be obtained are from families "under the influence" of the West; children from preliterate cultures are understandably shy about sharing their products with Western observers; and in more than a few cultures there are pitifully few, if any, drawings to share.

Recently, however, a very important source of information on this issue has become available. Alexander Alland, a cultural anthropologist at Columbia University, has visited a number of cultures, including ones where children have never drawn. Rather than resorting to the usual ploy of collecting drawings, Alland has actually filmed the child as she is given a marker and asked to draw. In Alland's view the "universal" picture of children's drawings offered by experts like Rhoda Kellogg has been exaggerated. He finds no evidence for such purportedly ubiquitous elements as mandalas and circles: by the same token, the age norms generally reported bear little resemblance to those uncovered on his own expeditions. And, among children who have not drawn until the age of eight or nine, he has seen a series of stages passed through in a matter of half an hour.

While many generalizations about children's art seem suspect, Alland finds strong evidence, even in the earliest drawing, of influ-

182

ences by the culture. Children within specific cultures tend to draw in formally similar ways. In Bali, for example, youngsters are compulsive about filling space; their charming repetitive little forms are drawn separately yet snugly across the page, as if driven by some horror of a void (182). Taiwanese children milk the kinds of "cute" schemas of houses, trucks, and trees found among youngsters in Western society (183). Drawings by Japanese children, produced with sustained concentration and attention, feature simple elements delicately spread across the page and often exhibit beautiful composition (184). These drawings seem to exhibit a rhythm and composition characteristic of other aspects of Eastern culture: one can almost sense a Balinese dance, a Haiku poem, in the works of these youngsters. Unless these observations are off the mark (and there is no reason to suspect that they are), an uncritical chronicling of stages must be placed into question; the contribution to drawing skill made by explicit models and the implicit tempo of the culture must be taken extremely seriously.

What more can be said about the validity of our analysis of drawing? In cultures with strict rules of how to draw and with standards that are supposed to be inculcated in every child, drawing seems to hold up better. More individuals draw and more individuals satisfy the standards of their culture. To be sure, not everyone perseveres. Yet in a locale like Soviet Russia, where drawing is a prescribed part of the curriculum, or in certain South Sea societies, where drawing constitutes an important vein of cultural

183

life, nearly every child manages to obtain and to retain a certain minimal level of competence. Instead of a decline, there is attainment of basic literacy—the kind of skill acquired (admittedly with difficulty) by learning the three R's, the basic skills in our culture. These lines of evidence suggest that if "rendering" were made the fourth R, if it were an endorsed basic skill, we should encounter less of a decline in drawing in our own society. Our ambivalence about whether one should draw and, if so, in what manner, seems responsible in significant measure for the decline in graphic artistry in our culture.

184

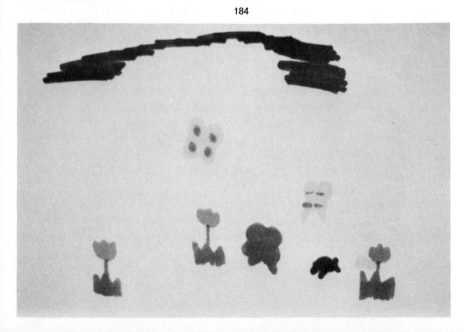

This survey still leaves unresolved another epochal question: whether the kind of pluralism and self-expression cherished in our society can be preserved through the school years. After all, the most powerful examples of a continued artistry stem from cultures where procedures are considerably more rigidly constrained than in our own. My own guess is that this trend toward literalism is a universal one; children will always want to know what the rules are and will attempt to follow them—whether they promote realism or abstraction. In every culture, shortly after the beginning of the school years children may well feel a strong pull to find out how things are done in their surroundings and then go on to learn the process. But this may not be pursued elsewhere with as much vengeance as it is in this country. Nor must a valuing of realism necessarily enforce mechanical stiffness: one can portray reality with vigor and feeling. Nor, finally, must such a shift toward realism be realized in formal schooling; it can occur by observing, by informal tutoring, or by identification with admired masters. After all, in many cultures the request "How did you do that?" elicits a simple repetition of the act itself.

But even if I am right, even if children will always push toward discovering how the culture accomplishes something, pluralism could still be preserved. In other words, if a culture approved of diverse graphic models and cultivated a set of acceptable styles, children might satisfy their need for discovering "the rules" while at the same time the quality and quantity of their works would persist.

Probably the closest thing to an "experiment in nature" comes from progressive schools within our culture, models of alternative education where the values of pluralism are directly promulgated and pursued. Again, these institutions have not been studied with the care that they merit, but it seems that the lure of literalism can at least to some extent be combatted through a culturally approved avoidance of literalism, a flexible interpretation of realism, or, alternatively, a passionate pursuit of pluralism. Even so, it is my impression that the "rule-boundedness" of youngsters of this age cannot be easily silenced. One comes up, therefore, with the paradoxical finding that "it's OK to do things in many ways, or to express colors in funny ways . . . at least it's OK in Ms. Leary's class but don't do it elsewhere." And as Barbara Leondar has pointed out in her sensitive study, "The Arts in Alternative Schools," these communities often end up promoting either a rigid ideology of their own, one that is equally dogmatic as the accepted ideology, or a kind of ritualistic freedom which reduces to repetitive works in the minor crafts and features little of the seriousness traditionally cherished in the arts:

Insofar, then, as the arts demand of their practitioners stern concentration, periodic isolation and withdrawal, even on occasion blind resistance to social proprieties, to that extent they have suffered in alternative schools. Paradoxically they may have suffered most in those schools which are most free—free, that is, of adult authority and externally imposed structure. In such schools new tyrannies, subtler than their predecessors, may breed . . . the freedom of alternative schools can prove to be merely an alternative coercion.

Our survey has documented the complexity of the issues surrounding the school-age child's attraction to realistic modes of depiction. It is far too simple to view this stage as a wholesale rejection of the arts; equally uncritical to see it as a necessary, healthy, and wholly beneficent milestone in the growth of the child. Rather, like developmental phenomena generally, it eludes easy evaluation. Literalism has an aura of necessity about it—it cannot simply be sidestepped or ignored. This phase of growth can, however, be negotiated with greater or less sensitivity, with more or less openness, and the ways in which it is negotiated will probably determine whether, at its conclusion, the child has completely abandoned graphic artistry or has instead added to the emotional openness and exploratory fervor of earlier years and gained the mastery of such essential tools as color, line, and shading.

We have arrived at a point where these issues no longer are—and perhaps no longer can be—left in the hands of the individual child working (or playing) alone at the kitchen table. Influences of the culture lurk everywhere and must be directly confronted. And nowhere is this pressure greater than in the art class or the art school: there the ways in which the later stages of artistic development are negotiated must be directly grappled with and eventually solved. As we learn more about how children develop, these issues become increasingly joined. Supposedly long-buried arguments between the "copyists" and the "spontaneity buffs," the "unfolders" and the "trainers" have again arisen, with greater insistence and force than ever before. Nor is this unreasonable, for the way in such disputes are resolved will influence the artistry of future generations.

CHAPTER 7

To Copy or Not

THE two attempts to draw a rhinoceros shown in figures 185 and 186 certainly seem the products of different hands. The animal on the left is composed of a central oval form, to the bottom of which are attached several stunted rectangles, while a long thin neck at the top culminates in a series of concentric circles which suggest a head. The bulk of the torso indicates a squat animal, but more precise identification proves difficult—one could as well be viewing a cow, an elephant, or perhaps even a cat.

Recognition of the drawing at the right proves far less problematic. The head is carefully formed so that one can readily distinguish an eye, two ears, and an upright horn on the snout. The legs, far more solid and sturdy, emphasize the strength and stability of the animal. The textured lines on the back and sides have been arrayed to indicate the roughness of the skin, while the regular horizontal lines across the body also reveal a measure of elegant control by the artist. Overall, the drawing at the right seems more accomplished and, indeed, bears a certain resemblance to Dürer's famed woodcut of a rhinoceros (187). This is not surprising, because the young artist was actually viewing the Dürer while he completed his rhinoceros. What may be surprising is that the very same child had produced the first drawing just a few moments earlier.

Chris, the eight-year-old who drew both pictures, was a student in the art class of David Pariser, an art teacher working in suburban Boston. At first Pariser simply asked Chris (and his classmates) to draw a rhinoceros. Presumably accustomed to conjuring up such animals on his own (or another's) command, Chris retrieved a tried-and-true schema from his repertoire of animal forms, one that could (as we have seen) pass for any number of vertebrates. Similar requests could have readily evoked a house, a bird, a truck, or indeed several dozen members of each of these cate-

185   186

gories. And in each case the resulting sketch could have been readily decomposed into its component schematic parts and related to
schemas that were favored during earlier stages of drawing.

A few minutes later, however, Pariser posed a radically different task. Placing a reproduction of the Dürer woodcut in front of
the class, the teacher asked Chris and his classmates to look carefully at its contour and then, eying the paper as little as possible, to
trace the contour with pencil on pad. Now, instead of evoking
established schemas and monitoring them to make sure they succeeded one another according to the usual plan for the animal, the
child was encouraged to record "passively" each twist and turn of
the contour, allowing his yoked hand to record his visions. It was as

187

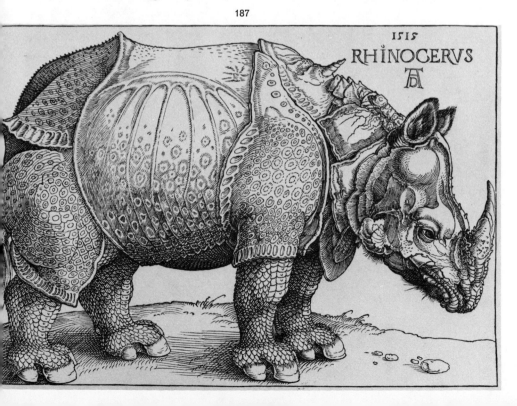

if, like cutting the blank in a key-duplication machine, the lines were being expertly guided by the model into a faithful duplicate of the original. And while the result still retains some traces of the particular young artist who fashioned it, the overall contour of the animal, the delicately wrought texture, and in particular, the realization of detailed features in the region of the head are decidedly more accomplished. Rather than confronting the typical products of a child's clumsy hand, we are viewing a drawing that bears at least a fleeting resemblance to that wrought by a master draughtsman. Nor need the model be of the quality of a Dürer. After spying a simple horse on a calendar, my ten-year-old daughter Kay effortlessly transcended her favorite schema for a horse (188, 189). And

188   Horse drawn free-hand.   189   A copy of a horse.

another of Pariser's students, engaged in an exercise like the one just described, produced the startling set of horses shown in figures 190 and 191 within a few minutes of one another.

But these skilled contoured drawings have been purchased at a cost, a cost found by many to be too severe—the cost of copying. The disparaging way in which such an educational tack has been

190   Horse drawn free-hand.   191   A copy of a horse.

dismissed by most individuals has been well conveyed in an anecdote related by the British art historian Quentin Bell to his colleague Sir Ernst Gombrich:

> I used to teach school children. With me there was a much better teacher . . . One day she came into the room where I had been teaching and found a series of (to my mind) the most surprising and beautiful water colours. "What are these?" said she. I explained that they were copies of Raphael made by eleven and twelve year old children. I would have gone on to explain how interested I was by their resemblance, not to Raphael, but rather to Simone Martini, for they had all the shapes beautifully right but none of the internal drawing or the sentiment, but I was checked by her look of horror.
>
> "You've made them copy from Raphael?" she said. Her expression was exactly that of someone who had been casually informed that I had committed a series of indecent assaults upon the brats. And in fact in subsequent conversation it appeared that this was very nearly what she did feel. For her, what she called "self-expression" was as precious as virginity.
>
> The irony of the thing was that these creative virgins were coming to school with traced drawings of Mickey Mouse and pictures from the lids of cereal packets and had indeed been violated 1000 times over before I ever introduced them to the forbidden delights of the Divine Urbinate, as Claude Phillips used to call him.

Indeed for many years, particularly in European circles, the ideology voiced by Bell's self-righteous colleague has reigned supreme. Artistic development has been viewed as pre-eminently a natural process, one that proceeds optimally when it can unfold with minimal interference from the surrounding environment. And this view seems eminently sensible for at least two reasons. First of all, as we have seen, there exists a regular, spontaneous, and productive sequence through which children naturally pass in the early years of life—one that engenders a flowering of artistry by the time school begins and which seems well worth cherishing and protecting. Second, this antipathy to copying itself emerged as a much-needed reaction to the straitlaced classes of Victorian times, where youngsters were compelled to draw in precisely the same stylized and realistic fashion, and where originality and spontaneity were (by most accounts) effectively strangled.

Nonetheless, no matter how accurate and appropriate this "progressive view" may be for the preschool years, there is no denying that drawing takes a sharply different turn during the years of schooling. No longer does the child continue to follow his own muse, exploring, playing, and creating with little regard for what

others think, see, or do. The child has now become fascinated—
even tyrannized—by the drawings of others in his culture. He
abandons without regret a carefree approach to paint and paper in
favor of a more restricted and controlled orientation, and in its
wake there emerges an increasing preoccupation with depicting a
world in as realistic and literal a manner as possible.

Even as the child's personal agenda changes, so those in the
society concerned with the development of children must address
new questions. Is there a need for this interest in realistic drawing?
Is such a stage obligatory and desirable, or is it a harmful aberra-
tion, which should be rapidly negotiated or even bypassed? Should
the earlier bargain to let the child's natural powers unfold be honored in perpetuity, or is the time at hand for a more aggressive
approach, one that teaches the child how to draw? And if intervention is to be the order of the day, of what sort? Should one aid the
child to do what he wants to do or what seems best to the teacher?
Should he be exposed to a variety of models or simply one kind?
And, perhaps most controversial of all, should he be encouraged, or
even allowed, to copy?

Perhaps at first blush these sound like merely pedagogical
questions, which may be of concern—and of polemical import—to
those who call themselves art educators, but which offer little il-
lumination for dispassionate students of artistic development. In
fact, however, it is impossible to avoid such issues: both the child
and the society insist on them. The child is now actively seeking
aids as he strives to achieve drawings that satisfy his newly acquired standards of realism, or photographic accuracy. And the
society, charged in one or another way with the education of the
child, must also, whether or not it so desires, confront the question
of how best to respond to these needs, while remaining faithful to
its own values. One can no more escape the question of optimal
training during this stage of childhood than one can divorce the
child from all social influences and allow him to develop on his
own, moored on a desert island or set down in a literary Utopia.

And so what seemed to be "merely" an educational dispute
turns out instead to be an intrinsic feature of any portrait of artistic
development. Even if one strives to be purely descriptive, to dwell
only on what happens, one cannot wholly sidestep questions of
prescription and value. All the participants in this discussion harbor strong feelings about what should, and should not, be done,
and their convictions inevitably leave their marks. Moreover, questions concerning artistic training acquire even more centrality once
one recognizes their relevance to the development of the gifted
artist, the child who may one day achieve full mastery of the
medium. It is therefore more than idle curiosity that prompts an

investigation of copying and other forms of modelling: at issue is whether such a practice can help to bring about, or is more likely to undermine, notable artistic accomplishment. At the same time, a discussion of copying may provide insights into the sources of phenomenally precocious realistic efforts, such as those that emerge from the occasional child or the exceptional culture. Accordingly, we will first consider the various forms copying can take and then seek to determine whether any form of copying may actually be essential for the achievement of a high level of representational skill.

The history of attitudes toward copying can best be summed up as the swing of a pendulum. We have already charted one point of the arc. Art classes during the early nineteenth century generally assumed that the proper way to achieve artistic skills was through the careful following of instructions and the faithful representation of appropriately clad models. Nor was this attitude surprising. It reflected concepts of pedagogy of that time, as well as society's desire to train individuals competent in realistic descriptive drawings.

A growing fascination with the nature of the child, a burgeoning interest in various forms of primitive art, and the emerging waves of progressivism in education both here and abroad stimulated a vigorous reaction throughout the first part of this century. As articulated by the Czech educator Franz Cizek and endorsed by the acclaimed Austrian-American art educator Viktor Lowenfeld, the precious content of art was seen as flowing spontaneously from the child's hand, with as little intervention or modeling on the part of the outside world as possible. On this account, the hands of babes were viewed as sacred—any tampering was likely to vitiate the quality of what was produced.

Of late, however, a contrasting approach to art education has been gaining (or regaining) adherents. The ironic comments of Quentin Bell, quoted earlier, found a sympathetic listener in his colleague E. H. Gombrich. Moreover, in his own enormously influential writings, Gombrich has reminded a whole generation of the extent to which all drawings are based upon ones made earlier by other individuals, be they competent peers or acclaimed masters; he questions whether there is such a thing as an innocent eye, a virgin hand. Still more recently, the point of view that endorses tutelage and reserves a privileged place for copying has been taken up with unmuted enthusiasm by two educators at Pennsylvania State University, Brent Wilson and Marjorie Wilson.

According to the Wilsons, copying has always served as a major vehicle whereby a gifted artist has mastered his craft. Not only does this approach have tradition in its favor; it is also, in fact, the appropriate way for art education to proceed. Natural unfolding can guide a child through the first few years of life, and this process should be allowed to follow its irregular but basically progressive curve. Once of school age, however, children will no longer be able to progress on their own. Their own resources are too meager, their own minds increasingly enveloped by what surrounds them. The logical places to locate sources of inspiration for artwork are the cultural media they have come to esteem. No wonder that comic books, television shows, adventure stories, science fiction, and assorted other popular favorites are sought and studied by youngsters who want to draw.

In addition to pleading on common-sense grounds for the importance of images that can be copied, the Wilsons also have sought out empirical support for their point of view. In one study they interviewed 147 high-school and college students about the sources of their images. It turned out that virtually every image drawn by the subjects could be traced to some previously existing graphic source; models ran the gamut from drawings made by family members to images from popular media and illustrations and photographs available at home or in school. Children turned naturally to such sources because they themselves did not know how to render desired effects, nor did they possess any "programs" of their own which they could effectively adapt. Once they located a schema for achieving a certain effect, they would readily and repeatedly introduce minor modifications as a means of achieving more specific graphic effects.

The potential significance of copying is powerfully revealed by those youngsters who have produced a plethora of drawings. Anthony, a youngster studied by the Wilsons, has made about ten thousand pictures in the style of Marvel Comics, depicted from a virtually unlimited number of perspectives and locales (192, 193). According to the Wilsons' analysis, Anthony was able to draw a character in any position he chose by virtue of reviewing all the similar attempts he had made in the past and then "averaging" these configurations in order to fashion a new and desired figure. Like a comedian who can adapt his material for any occasion, Anthony had so well internalized the range of options available for drawing a human figure that he was able with little effort simply to project any new possible configuration he desired. This practice, this *calculating capacity*, differentiates the highly talented artist who seems able to produce seemingly innumerable new visions, from the average child, whose limited set of schemas can rather readily be exhausted.

Another line of evidence on the importance of copying has also

192

193

been proposed. The Wilsons reasoned that if such models stimulate drawings by schoolchildren, then the works by children from a milieu rich in "mediated models" should be more varied and more sophisticated than efforts spawned in a society where only a small set of such models was available. For instance, asked to draw a set of pictures that relate an adventure story, children who come from a richer cultural environment ought to feature more characters with recognizable personalities, a wider range of depicted actions, and a larger number of perspectives from which to view a scene.

The Wilsons had the opportunity to test this hypothesis when they secured two sets of drawings obtained under comparable conditions—one from America, the other from Egypt. Sure enough, the narrative drawings documented the expansive set of "drawing schemas" freely accessible in American society and the relatively restricted set of media sources available for exploitation by Egyptian youths. From one point of view, it can be said that this study merely confirms the obvious. Yet in the Wilsons' judgment, such a result gives the lie to competing camps—to those individuals who vigorously oppose copying as well as those who feel that it accomplishes little.

Other lines of argument can be marshaled in favor of activities of a copying sort. In a recent set of studies undertaken at Stirling University in Great Britain, youngsters were asked to draw perspectival views of cubes, as well as to copy abstract designs that were unlikely to be seen as familiar objects (194). Two unexpected findings emerged. First of all, children were able to draw those pat-

194 Sample stimuli from the Phillips study. Pattern B has the same number of lines and regions as pattern A but lacks dots and does not in any obvious way represent a solid object. Pattern C is identical to A but lacks dots. Pattern D is identical to C but is rotated 45 degrees.

Children were more likely to see A and C as pictures of objects, and B and D as two-dimensional patterns. Children more accurately copied patterns B and D, than patterns A and C. Their copies were also more accurate when they were required to look continuously at the model than when they were allowed to look back and forth between the model and their drawing.

A	B	C	D

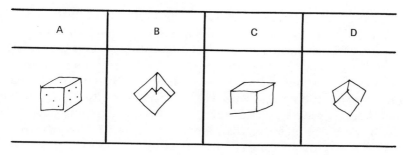

A	B	C	D

195 Examples of drawings which were classified as accurate.

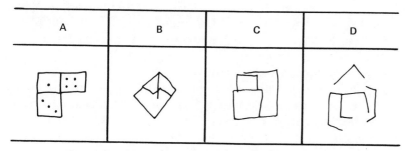

A	B	C	D

196 Examples of drawings which were classified as inaccurate.

terns that could not be construed as objects with greater accuracy than those seen as familiar entities (195, 196). Apparently, in a manner reminiscent of Pariser's classroom demonstration or Kay's two horses, the knowledge of how to draw something, how to exploit one's prior schemas, actually interfered with a perceptually accurate rendition, while the opportunity to draw merely the thing-in-itself stimulated a superior performance.

Second, the experimenters compared copies made by youngsters who were looking continuously at the model and were thus unable to monitor their own efforts, with drawings made by children who were allowed to shoot glances back and forth between the model and their own attempts. Once again the advantage accrued to those children who were able to suppress their own knowledge of the means by which effects are usually rendered and to attend instead, and with their full concentration, to the physical dimension of the model. Such studies suggest that the more one knows about the identity of something, the more likely one is to rely on previously elaborated schemas rather than on actual "retinal" properties. Conversely, attentive copying produces accurate renditions.

Clearly then, some good words can and should be said for copying. Not only do schoolchildren appear to seek out models when they have not been provided, but dire consequences have failed to follow from copying and some benign outcomes may even be anticipated. It seems clear that children are going to look at models, particularly when they want to achieve effects they have not acquired in some "natural" ways and which they are unable to conjure up on their own. And yet, in my view, the Wilsons have rightly been berated because of a failure to confront perils that might accompany a strict regimen of copying. Any program that focuses too exclusively on such activity runs the risk of signaling children that they should subordinate their artwork to what others have done. There is the parallel risk that teachers may provide only one kind of artwork to copy, or that students themselves may gravitate to only one art form—in all likelihood representational realism. Copying is unlikely to convey the full range of means for depicting the real world, not to mention the many ways in which imaginary worlds or fantastic concepts can be portrayed.

Apologias for copying also minimize a distinction of potentially great importance, one that has been articulated by Rudolf Arnheim. Models can in fact serve two radically different purposes. They can be the stimulus for slavish copying, by which one seeks to duplicate, almost in the manner of a forgery, every detail of the model, and in the process suppresses one's own individuality. While such an activity may eventually yield certain tricks and strategies, mechanical tracing has little to do with what is central in artistic expression. And once the model has been removed, the experience gained from such copying efforts is unlikely to carry over to other graphic attempts.

But models can also be used in a much more benign and generative way, as an indication of how things may be done, as a suggestion of ways to proceed, as a guide to solving problems and overcoming obstacles. Viewed as helpful guides rather than dictatorial masters, models can be of great value and have in fact been resorted to spontaneously by artists in every era. They can suggest to novices how to achieve desired effects of texture, shading, or perspective. Models serve in that instance as a means of helping the artist achieve what he himself wants to express, in a way that makes sense to him and to others, rather than as a path toward sterile duplication of what someone else, working for quite different purposes, may have produced. Used effectively, a copy should function like a translation of a poem: it should help one capture in one's own language the essential points of a work, rather than translate every word literally irrespective of the role it happens to have played in the original. And building on the lessons of such copying, artists should be better able in future work to express what they desire in a satisfactory manner.

The positing of two contrasting approaches to copying—copying as a generative means and copying as an end in itself—makes sense. Certainly we recognize the difference in singing between the student who parrots the words and notes of an anthem without understanding them and the student who uses the recording of a gifted singer, or the examples of his voice coach, as a means for training his own voice. Yet before we can fully embrace this distinction, we should consider two further lines of inquiry. On the one hand, it is important to ascertain whether one can in fact distinguish behaviorally between these two kinds of copying. Then, in addition, we need to consider how copying behavior, of whatever sort, may actually figure in the achievement of a high degree of representational skill. Though we will eventually return to the issue of the role of copying in "normal development," it may prove helpful to approach these questions initially by considering a number of highly unusual individuals.

Intriguing evidence for two separable kinds of copying skills comes from an unexpected source—an amateur artist whom my colleagues and I studied some years ago. This seventy-three-year-old man suffered from a form of visual agnosia—a condition in which, following a stroke, he ceased to recognize any objects presented to him visually. Proof that this malady was not simply a language problem came from his ability to name these same objects correctly when they were handed to him for tactile inspection. Correlative evidence that it was not purely a visual disorder came from the fact that he could accurately trace in the air with his hand the outline of a visually perceived object.

When asked to copy drawings or to draw particular objects, the artist in fact demonstrated two approaches. When he did not know what the objects or drawings were, he copied them slavishly. In fact, he could often copy objects nearly perfectly in every particular (while all the time insisting that he did not know what they were [197]). Even when (for other reasons) he failed to include every detail in the correct place, he left little doubt that he was in possession of a superlative slavish copying mechanism (198, 199). When, however, the artist was able to recognize the object visually (as sometimes happened) or when we told him what he was beholding, an entirely different "drawing" program came to the fore. On these occasions he exploited his arsenal of schemas which had evolved over the years. The pictures drawn with the aid of such knowledge included certain features of the particular target object but omitted others (200, 201). They were more characteristic of his earlier style and (to our eyes) more lively and filled with character; yet they were significantly less faithful to the physical parameters of the object-model. "Drawing knowledge" outflanked

197a An original silkscreen of a rooster perched on top of a pot-belly stove.

197b Patient's copy of the silkscreen.

198 Copy of a toy airplane—note the overdrawing of the propellers and the neglect of features such as the nose of the plane.

199 Copy of a Raggedy-ann doll.

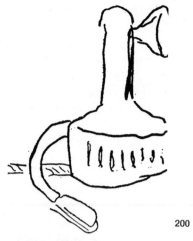

200

"pure (but mindless) recording." Here in a generative type of copying he was skillfully blending his perception of the object with his own well-developed graphic style.

The existence in a *single* individual of different approaches to copying serves as at least an initial documentation of Arnheim's distinction. Moreover, since we know that many artists have in their own training done considerable copying and that one particular artist retained the ability to copy in two manners, it seems legitimate to conclude that copying can play a formative role in the achievement of artistry. But now we need to consider as well a different question: Must artistry build upon copying or is it also possible to achieve artistic heights without a program of copying— in fact, by pursuing a strikingly different route?

To approach this question, I want to review evidence from two quarters which may well never have been juxtaposed before. To my mind, these exemplars raise with equal insistence the question of the origins of superior artistry, and, at least in this sense, they deserve to be yoked. The two sources I have in mind are the works produced by cave artists in prehistoric times and the drawings produced by a single and singular young girl named Nadia.

In the summer of 1940 some young schoolboys were playing in the fields of Montignac in the Dordogne in southern France. While searching for treasure, they stumbled upon a cave and decided to explore inside. Though they had entered such caves before, they uncovered in this one a most astonishing sight: hundreds of carefully executed drawings of animals of various shapes and sizes— bulls, deer, horses—running, jumping, swimming, or engaged in combat, and produced in a variety of styles ranging from naturalistic to fanciful. Returning to their elders, the boys reported their find, which turned out to be no less than the prehistorical graphic treasures gracing the caves of Lascaux.

Archaeologists and anthropologists have now viewed paleolithic art from numerous sites in Europe and northern Africa, from Altamira in Spain, Thayingen in Switzerland, and Otranto in Italy to Mexin in the Ukraine. These drawings differ from one another in many ways: some are done completely in black; others feature a combination of browns, reds, and yellows; some include numerous details and varied actions, while others amount to simple outlines of animals in profile. There are also telling similarities: humans are rarely depicted (though one fascinating set of faces was discovered

202

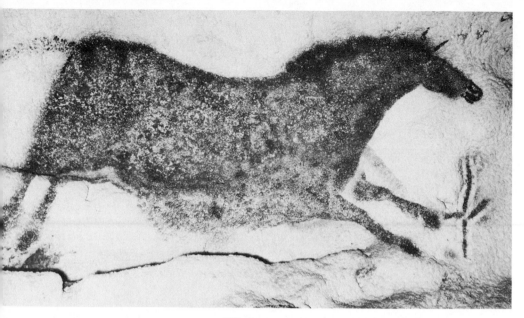

203

in the Dordogne in 1976); there is little identification of sex and infrequent sexual activity; the relative sizes of animals are generally ignored; and the depictions predominate in deep and apparently inaccessible areas of the caves. But what has most struck diverse observers is that the best of these drawings feature a clear command of the artistic medium by those individuals selected to decorate these places of significance in the life of their culture (202, 203, 204). By no stretch of the imagination could they be

204

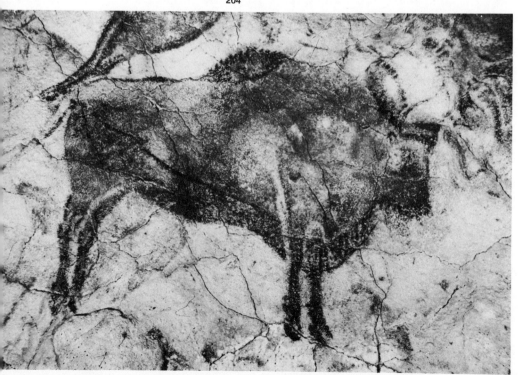

casual or unplanned occurrences. As Alexander Marshack, the chief contemporary student of this artwork has concluded, "The ice artists at their best produced masterpieces equal to almost any from any period since."

Just how artistry of this skill—reflecting virtuosity and planning of the highest order—could have emerged at this time of simple hunting and gathering, with no alphabet and only elementary tools, has intrigued (and befuddled) scholars. It could be, of course, that these cave artists arrived at their skilled contour drawings by passing through the same lengthy evolutionary processes that we have observed in children of contemporary Western culture. Such an evolution might have occurred either gradually across generations (and we happen to have access only to the heights of this achievement) or in the lifetime of every child, or of some very special children, in the way we anticipate now with a highly gifted child. But it is also possible that cave artists were drawing in ways quite distinct from contemporary artists, that they arrived at their powerful works by a very different route.

Even to suggest that cave artists achieved *their* mastery by an alternative route—perhaps, for example, by seeing the animals in their mind's eyes and simply "copying" the record onto the cave wall—is tantamount to heresy. Having patiently made the case that individuals pass at a predictable rate through the same regularly programed sequence of stages, with ample opportunity (and perhaps need) for copying, we risk undoing our whole argument by this mere suggestion. It flies directly in the face of the view of development presented here: the gradual and careful elaboration of schemas, their increasingly flexible use, a lengthy trajectory from total reliance on rigid schemas to an ability to render faithfully the details of specific entities. Is it really possible for individuals—now or then—somehow to short-circuit this process, to achieve the fluidity of natural contours by some special route?

A surprising and possibly decisive *yes* can now be proposed to this question. In 1977 a case study was published of a five-year-old child named Nadia, who was making drawings every bit as impressive (and enigmatic) as those of Pariser's copiers and the draughtsmen of Lascaux. Moreover, Nadia was by no means a genius who had simply raced through the stages of drawing and was now performing "across the board" at the intellectual level of a ten- or twenty-year-old. Quite the reverse—Nadia suffered from the severe disturbance known as infantile autism.

First described in the early 1940s by a Baltimore pediatrician named Leo Kanner (just about the time the French youths were discovering the caves of Lascaux), infantile autism is a condition in which children are cut off psychologically from the world of human beings. Owing either to some genetic disorder or to extremely bizarre pressures in their early environment (experts dispute which is the case), a tiny minority of youngsters remain unable to relate to other persons. Such children avert eye contact with others; they neither respond to other persons nor use language to communicate their wants, needs, or fears. Instead, they are locked into their own world, often reduced to banging their heads against surfaces, rocking compulsively back and forth, spending their days and nights exploring physical objects, repeating meaningless sounds, or staring vacantly into space.

While autistic children are clearly retarded in certain areas and exhibit profound emotional disturbances, they can be distinguished from children with general mental retardation, as well as from youngsters with a childhood psychosis. Symptomatic (and even diagnostic) of these hapless children is their striking preservation of certain islands of skill. There have been reports describing autistic youngsters who can recognize, remember, and reproduce hundreds of melodies; sing entire operas at the age of one and a half; assemble and disassemble complex objects while in their preschool years; carry out lengthy arithmetical calculations at computerlike speed; and read texts aloud at the age of two (without, however, appearing to comprehend the very words they are decoding and mouthing).

Authorities have generally treated these bizarre preserves as evidence that certain "mental computers" can unfold in children even in the absence of that social and affective support which typically is forthcoming in the first years of life. The ability to recognize and re-create certain regular patterns—the kinds honored by the musical system, the mathematical system, and certain syntactic and orthographic aspects of the language system—may be found even in an individual who is otherwise isolated from the rest of society. (Indeed, most human prodigies have appeared in just these intellectual domains where rapid progress is possible despite scant intercourse with, or understanding of, other persons.) But until the publication of *Nadia*, there was little reason to suspect that the same kind of "pure unfolding" of skills might also prove possible in the realm of graphic depiction.

Nadia was born in Nottingham, England, of Ukrainian *émigré* parents, in October 1967. The second of three children, she seemed at first to develop in a relatively normal way, but the few words she knew dropped out at the end of her first year, and she thereafter became increasingly autistic. By the age of three her developmental profile was already markedly impaired: motor development was slow; she neither understood the language of others nor was she able to communicate her own thoughts through the usual channels of language, gesture, or music. In fact, underlining her woeful deficiencies in the symbolic realm, she did not engage in any pretend play.

At the age of three and a half Nadia, otherwise a lethargic child, suddenly displayed an extraordinary capacity to draw. Using her favored left hand, she began to draw animals, particularly horses, in a way more reminiscent of a skilled adolescent or adult artist than of a young child, let alone a young child with devastating cognitive and emotional deficits (205). Running directly

205

counter to all previous descriptions of the origins of graphic symbolization, she apparently skipped the various scribbling, schematic, and tadpole stages. Nor, when producing figures, did she rehearse the usual schemas composed of simple geometric forms juxtaposed together. Rather, apparently without any need to practice, her drawings showed a remarkable fidelity to the contours of the depicted object; moreover, and again running counter to every existing account of the development of drawing skills, Nadia's works exhibited skill with perspective, foreshortening, and other tricks of the artist's trade, ones usually acquired only after years of patient drill and evolution of the "natural" drawing capacity (206, 207).

How Nadia drew was as amazing as what she drew. She did not draw from a model. While her drawings were often inspired by pictures she had once seen, in most cases she had not seen the picture recently. Instead, using such pictures merely as points of departure, she varied her versions almost at will, experimenting with different forms until she hit upon a finished product that satisfied her own exacting standards. Often her final drawings appeared to be composites of numbers of works seen before. More tellingly, she did not seem to need to draw details in any particular order or even to juxtapose features next to one another: she was able to place one

206

207

detail in one spot on the paper, another detail in another spot, and then join them at a later moment, sublimely secure that the composite parts would fit together. Indeed she did not even need to look at the lines she had drawn; for instance, in drawing a horse, she first sketched a neck and then positioned the ears so that they were in correct spatial relation, while the outline of the head remained to be drawn. Her overall approach was as different as conceivable from that of most child artists: whereas children her age compulsively repeat the same schema and are discombobulated by a request to alter the usual sequence of lines, Nadia drew very quickly and could return, even after considerable interruption, to the exact point where she had ceased drawing.

> She was rather like a sophisticated adult artist in that one couldn't see how the picture was going to come out. She would draw a little bit here, a little bit there, in fact bits seemed to come in from all over the place. She would then economically put in the strokes that were needed to pull it all together.

Because Nadia's overall performance was so extraordinary—one of her therapists, Lorna Selfe, aptly calls it "unbelievable"—and ran counter to every report about both normal and abnormal children, any attempt to explain her gift must necessarily be speculative. This youngster seems miraculously to have wed preschool expressiveness with school-age mastery of realism. Her therapists toy with the idea that, as a brain-damaged child, she longs for some avenue of expression, and that nature in its wisdom guided her toward the graphic realm. To my own mind, however, this explanation seems neither necessary nor sufficient. Certainly there is no link between brain damage and heightened capacities—after all, most brain-damaged children produce drawings as primitive as their performances in other realms. To be sure, some anomalous form of brain damage, which thwarted Nadia from using the more usual avenues of communication, may possibly have pushed her toward the graphic sphere; and in fact there have been a few other autistic youngsters who have gravitated toward the arts. Yet this explanation gives not the slightest indication of why she should have produced such precocious drawings in so virtuosic a manner.

Some clues come from Nadia's performance on other tasks. Several aspects of her behavior suggest that she possessed eidetic imagery, the capacity to see vividly in her mind's eye scenes she had previously seen in the real world. She passed the most rigorous test of eidetic imagery by recognizing the contents of a composite image which could only be constructed by juxtaposing in her mind two images presented at different times. She performed better on tasks in which she had to recognize the forms of a puzzle than on any other tasks posed for her. She was skilled at matching pictures to their silhouettes; and when a drawing she was copying was covered, she was still able to complete the copy. As further evidence that she was guided by an image, Nadia often continued to draw right off the edge of the page as if compelled by the shape she was trying to realize; and unlike most young drawers, who correct automatically for the dramatic increase in size of objects projecting directly at them, Nadia drew such extended objects in accurate retinal dimensions.

In sharp contrast to this set of imaging characteristics, Nadia was very poor at seeing drawings as meaningful entities. When she was asked to form classes out of pictures or to categorize pictures on the basis of the *meaning* of what was represented, she generally failed. Apparently, while Nadia could retain in her mind the purely visual aspects of objects and displays, she was generally unable to categorize them. Since it has been shown that the mental image tends to disappear when the eidetic individual is required to classify or otherwise label the object, Nadia's inability to classify (a consequence of her brain damage) stands as suggestive evidence that, even if not in possession of eidetic imagery, she had very powerful retentive capacities.

However, even as brain damage seems an insufficient explanation of Nadia's performance, the eidetic interpretation is similarly lacking. After all, there are numerous eidetic individuals (perhaps 10 percent of the child population), and generally they do not draw in a special, or specially gifted, way. Seeing is a prerequisite for drawing, but by no means can most people (eidetic or not) effortlessly draw what they see. Nadia had in some way to realize through fine motor patterns those forms that were so vividly impressed in her mental imagery.

Here, I think, we find a suggestive link to the exercises in contour drawing described previously, and perhaps also to the stunning achievements in the paleolithic caves. Posit, to begin with, an individual with extremely powerful and vivid visual imagery. Suppose further that this person is cut off from the rest of the social world so that he has little contact with what others do and how they do it; yet at the same time he retains a profound need to make some sense out of experience, by virtue of those few avenue of conceptualization that remain relatively spared. It is at least conceivable—just conceivable—that this combination of elements might give rise to a unique set of performances, which, when they come together, allow an individual to achieve a set of behaviors which are almost always reached by a different route. Like the *idiot savant* who plays chess or solves arithmetical problems at the level of a talented adult, Nadia may have been operating with a high-

208

209

210

powered mental computational device—one seldom, if ever, exploited by others but perhaps available to at least a sample of the human species. Possibly this computer exists in others but has never been noticed; or possibly, when it occurs in a normal child, that youngster reaches the literal stage so rapidly that his remarkable powers are missed.

Just what might the nature of this computer be? Even as the ordinary child can readily explore a tactile shape by passing his hands over the surface, Nadia may have been able to capture and explore the shapes etched on her mind's eye by moving her hands in a parallel way. Her hands were locked to her eyes much as Pariser's students' hands mimicked the contours of a model. Certainly she had to have had the advantage of viewing Western perspectival representation—and we know that she did. Indeed, Lorna Selfe reports that Nadia often studied a drawing for several weeks before she herself produced a version of that drawing (208) and one can see that at least some of her initial efforts were virtual duplicates of the model (209, 210). But Nadia had many opportunities to re-create these patterns, and it was natural that accidental variations and deviations in such copies would eventually lead to schemas that seemed more original and more powerful. Thus when we consider these opportunities, together with a strong motivation to achieve competence and virtually no other options for realizing her communication needs, we begin to appreciate why unique artistic genius might appear.

There remains the question of whether Nadia may in fact have passed through the normal stages of development, either in her drawings or in her mental imagery, before the age at which she was first studied. We simply lack information to answer this question. Yet at least a few early drawings done at age three and four feature a dim reminder of the simple schemas we have come to expect in the drawings of preschool children (211, 212, 213). It thus remains

211

possible that Nadia realized the same developmental sequence as normal youngsters but did so at an unbelievably rapid rate.

In considering the paleolithic artists and young Nadia, we appear to have moved quite far from the topic at hand. The practices of classroom teachers would seem to have little connection with cavemen of thousands of years ago, who (at least at first) had no ready stock of completed works from which to draw; or with one hapless young girl, who achieved her most remarkable artistry before going to school and who, in fact, nearly ceased drawing once she had begun to attend a regular school. Slavish copying seems precluded, and even "intelligent copying" seems at best to have played only a supporting role in these staggering achievements.

Yet the exotic can sometimes provide clues about the prosaic.

212

213

Even as we have turned to a brain-damaged artist and prehistoric cavemen for evidence about kinds of copying, we can consult such sources for clues about the options available to the artist-in-training. We note, to begin with, the extreme accomplishment of both the cavemen and Nadia. In neither case does the individual seem restricted to a single way of rendering. At the very least, these artists possess extremely supple schemas, ones that can be adapted to serve a variety of purposes and ones that seem to be genuinely expressive, capturing those details of motion, mood, and individuality which mark the active artistic enterprise. We can assume, I think, capacities to look very carefully at objects, to remember their appearance but also to go beyond what was seen before—in life or in books—and to combine these capacities in ways suited to one's own purposes.

The existence of such individual cases, no matter how rare, infirms a strong version of the thesis in favor of copying. It does not seem essential to spend lengthy hours copying the works of others in a slavish way in order eventually to arrive at a more individualistic and expressive means of rendering. Such copying activity can in fact take place and may even be helpful, but it seems, at least in principle, possible "to go it alone" and "to go beyond the model."

To offer a positive characterization of the capacities that enable a paleolithic artist or a young autistic child to fashion drawings of such skill and expressivity proves a more daunting challenge. It would be safe to say, and most difficult to disprove, that these individuals are simply more gifted and more precocious than others; they may simply pass through the same stages as other individuals at a more rapid tempo. And this may indeed be the case.

And yet I must voice my hunch that something else was going on. Given adequate genetic potential, it is obviously possible for individuals to develop to the point where they can readily draw as convincingly as the cavemen or Nadia did. After all, this is just what gifted artists do. It seems to me at least conceivable that certain individuals may be born with an extremely highly developed or prepotent talent in this area. Thus, like the child who learns to speak in a manner of months, such persons become able to draw objects in a realistic and convincing manner with relatively little drill or tutelage. Their computer is so highly articulated to begin with and so primed to "take off" that it needs only the most meager impetus to realize its full potential. Even such geniuses as Picasso or Klee realized their potential only after many years. What we all do in language, and a handful do in music or chess, one or two can perhaps achieve in the graphic sphere.

The localizing of this capacity in the brain is not a high priority in our inquiry, but it may be worth a whispered speculation that such visual-spatial skill may be a function of the right hemisphere. Should this be the case, it would then make sense if this capacity achieved outstanding proportions in a left-handed girl who was completely devastated in language and who possibly had little use of left-hemisphere tissue. And perhaps at a time before written language, with high mentation already achieved, there may have been a group of individuals who also exploited their right hemisphere to a much greater extent than is done today. One evolutionary price we may have paid for the adoption of a highly verbal style is a "selection" away from individuals of this sort, with the exception of a few talented artists.

But while the easy flowering of this capacity may be lost for nearly all contemporay individuals, its eventual achievement is not. Evolution has not occurred with such rapidity as to preclude the attainment of skilled drawing by many of us. I see the early years as setting the groundwork for eventual achievement in drawing within the context of overall cognitive and emotional development; and the years of middle childhood as a time when we can (ordinarily through training) realize a high degree of realistic accuracy in the visual-graphic domain. Actually most of us do not (and perhaps do not want to) achieve such skill; but this latency phase of middle childhood has been awarded to us by nature as a period in which we can "make up" for the time and skill lost between Nadia and ourselves.

Viewed in this admittedly speculative way, the discussion of copying takes on another shading. Children confront at this time the challenges of gaining skill in the analysis of the objects of the world and then of capturing the fruits of this analysis with some fidelity in their own graphic activity. Some achieve this with little strain, while for others it represents a major achievement. And some train vigorously in an effort to make this come about more readily. The painter William Hogarth, for example, tried to train a faithful memory:

> I therefore endeavored to habituate myself to the exercise of a sort of technical memory; and by repeating in my own mind the parts of which objects were composed, I could by degrees combine and put them down with my pencil. Thus, I had one material advantage over my competitors, viz., the early habit I thus acquired of retaining in my mind's eye, without coldly copying it on the spot, whatever I intended to imitate.

It is time for a final assessment of copying. We have seen that for individuals in our society the achievement of accurate representational skills is at a premium during the years of schooling. Copying presents itself as an obvious means for attaining such skill, and we can expect youngsters to gravitate toward it with or without support from others in their society. But the extent to which children will copy and the kind of copying in which they engage will clearly vary as a consequence of the child's own powers and inclinations, as well as the models, suggestions, and pressures put forth by teachers and others charged with guiding of children.

So much for the typical trajectory during middle childhood. But what of the gifted youngsters? Those individuals endowed with the strongest computational capacities will have passed through the early stages of development with great rapidity. They then have the option during their school years of engaging in informed copying of models in their midst or, in the manner of Nadia and the cavemen, of pursuing more personalized exploration of the medium itself. They are unlikely to embrace slavish copying, and even if they do, it is unlikely to yield much profit for their subsequence artistic activity. Indeed in the most gifted—be they autistic children, prehistoric individuals, or future artists—the graphic computer is so highly articulated that copying in the presence of a physical model proves unnecessary, and copying an internal image gives way quickly to active experimentation and invention. Provided they arrive at the point where they can readily produce acceptable likenesses and make countless variations on them, they are likely in the years of adolescence to transcend such realism and to formulate personal graphic statements of power and expressiveness.

THIRD INTERLUDE

Forming Artistic Characters

THE three creatures and one corpse, clad in mock medieval garb, form but a small part of a pictorial menagerie created by eleven-year-old Stuart Carter (214). Since the age of seven, inspired by such sagas as Tolkien's *Lord of the Rings*, Stuart has invented dozens of characters who become involved in various adventures, who possess distinctive personalities, and who reflect the imaginative life of their creator (215). Stuart takes counsel with these charac-

215

ters nearly every day, for he draws whenever he has the opportunity—in school during class, at home in front of television, on
weekends at his desk. Even as the characters gain their life and
energy from Stuart's graphic efforts, he draws inspiration and sustenance from the adventures they launch.

While Stuart has no trouble swelling this Hobbitlike population, his drawings are not restricted to creatures of this style. Some
of his characters have a distinctly contemporary appearance. For
example, he has depicted a football player, triumphant, as he is
about to get socked in the head with a football (216). He has
limned collections of sheriffs, desperadoes, and an Indian
chief (217). And he has sketched a number of half-clad divers being
propelled through the air (218). These characters assume various
poses, bear diverse expressions, and are engaged in different activities. Stuart has indeed mastered at least the preliminaries of the art
of caricature, or, as he prefers to call it, cartooning.

Yet Stuart himself concedes that his artistry is very limited. He
wants to be able to draw in a realistic fashion, to make things look
the way they appear in the world, but he feels that he has not
succeeded in doing so. He speaks with awe of a friend who can
draw convincingly from "real life." Stuart himself takes his inspiration from comic strips, from cards with monsters on them, from
illustrations in books. He also watches television avidly and tries, in
effect, to freeze characters so that he can capture in memory their
most characteristic poses and grimaces. But he is only at ease when

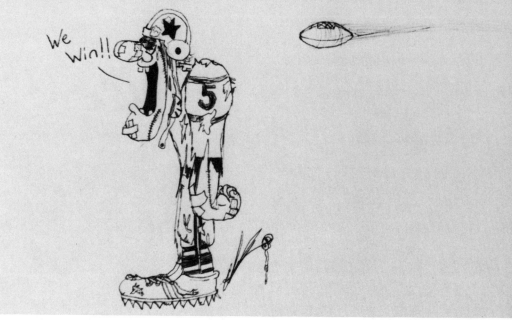

216

217

he undertakes caricatures, because these leave him a degree of freedom. No one can tell whether he has completed a character in just the way that he intended, and so no one can mock his drawings as inadequate. Cartooning represents a compromise between a desire to draw really well, to capture the precise expressions he sees in his mind's eye, and his anxiety lest he fail to render something in a convincing manner.

A budding artist for many years, Stuart was already making such cartoons when he was much younger. His mother has saved some earlier creatures contrived when he was about seven (219). Characters of that time are still only minor revisions of canonical human figures, with just a few features exaggerated. Their poses are also highly canonical: directly facing forward or in simple profile, they rarely suggest movement; when attempts are made to depict a less typical pose, the results have the charm of childish approximations. Only the humor seems firmly established. What Stuart has accomplished in the intervening years is to convert his budding set of monstrous characters into supple schemas, which he can produce as readily as he once evoked a tadpole or a stick figure. And he has learned how to represent certain actions, mo-

219

tions, and poses with sufficient fluency so that any of his characters can be rendered crawling or flying, laughing or sighing.

Stuart is basically self-educated. He sometimes draws with a
friend but for the most part he has picked up strategies on his own.
Countless cartoons and a single drawing book have been the major
cultural sources. Occasionally Stuart has self-consciously sought to
master certain effects. For example, dissatisfied with the way he
was rendering hands, he pored over a few books and eventually hit
upon a procedure that satisfied him (220). For the time being, hands

220

will be drawn in this way, at least until he encounters another inadequacy that must be combatted.

Stuart is a reasonably good student in school, an enthusiastic athlete, and quite popular with his classmates. All the same, he is a quiet and somewhat withdrawn fellow, dislikes certain school subjects, and seems most at ease and most content when he can be drawing alone. He speaks quite seriously about becoming a cartoonist: his current goal is to become a political cartoonist like the *Boston Globe*'s Paul Szep, and he treasures an autographed picture sent to him by this artist. Stuart seems only dimly aware of the demands of this role, however, asserting that all he must do to attain the rank of political cartoonist is to learn how to draw a few more forms and features.

Or is he perhaps more aware than he seems? Stuart tells me that he feels he has gone about as far as he can on his own and really needs some guidance if he wants to draw well. He complains that he does not know how to use color appropriately (though he seems to feel much of his problem lies simply in not being able to color forms properly within their boundaries. At the same time, however, he seems reluctant to accept help. Possibly he dislikes the social aspects of a drawing class, but possibly he also fears that a teacher will look askance at his gallery of rogues and try to instill in him some graphic values he does not like—for example, those of contemptible "modern art."

I asked Stuart to draw some common objects in the room (221). We were both struck by how average these renderings were,

 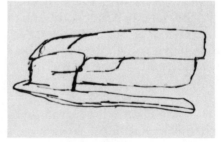

 221a   221b

reflecting little of the verve or flavor that enlivens his caricatures. Lacking generalized schemas which can be adapted to all subject matter, or a sufficient supply of specific schemas, Stuart was reduced to amateurish copying. Only in animating his own world is he able to create a variety of moods and scenes, depicting characters at rest, at play, involved in arguments, flying through space, descending upon a ranch, occupying a stool at McDonald's Restaurant. It is through these characters and encounters that Stuart explores various facets of his own life. The same young man who has difficulty in rendering a convincing stapler can with virtually no effort produce pleased, worried, and disgruntled variants of one of his characters (222). In each case the basic components emerge in

222

identical form in a matter of seconds, while variations in shape of mouth, orientation of eye, and play of the hair confer the desired expressiveness.

Clearly, Stuart's métier consists of re-creating again and again various episodes in the lives of his group of characters. He draws in a vein quite outside trends of contemporary art. He rarely goes to a museum, has no use for contemporary art movements, and in fact ridicules abstract works as stupid. He saves his regard for those who can execute representations (including caricatures) more effectively than he and hopes some day to be able to equal their achievements. In the meantime he continues to draw daily, whenever he gets a chance, and to hope that somehow, either by his own efforts or through some acceptable form of tutoring, he will be able to achieve those effects that he considers essential to artistry. Like a true primitive, he strives to epitomize the one style that matters to him.

In her attitude toward the contemporary art scene, eleven-year-old Alison Franklin virtually echoes her counterpart Stuart Carter. She too finds little use for the more radical of contemporary artists and feels that representation is the core of artistry. "Any two-year-old can make an abstract picture," she dismissively declares. She also displays marked ambivalence about formal art training, apparently sharing Stuart's belief that something valuable, even precious, may be lost through such intervention. Yet, like Stuart, she too has become keenly aware of her limitations and searches for some kind of alternative regimen or aid which can more fully align her skills with her ambitions.

Alison's inspiration also stems largely from the world of cartooning, but her imagination and style have assumed another but equally intriguing form. In one drawing (223), she has assembled a fantastic set of characters, each with his own description and story. But the way in which she has proceeded in this drawing seems much less organized, much more tied to the moment, far less "conscious" than the path followed by Stuart and his "regulars." Let Alison describe this elaborate collage in her own words:

> The first thing I did was this thin lady. She's the cashier. She's making Christmas exchanges. That woman on the stool is her opposite. One is long, the other short, one is fat, the other is thin. It didn't work exactly. Next I made a two-headed lady with her eyes bulging out. Then you see those little weird worms. They are stacking worms which I took from the Dr. Seuss books. Next I made a tennis ball man. There are spider webs connecting his arms. He's Mr. Cool, with teeth that are sparkling, with boots, rollerskates, and things. Above him is a Navajo bird—the designs on his tail are Navajo. The dripping guy is the kind you think of when you have a cold—he's all drippy.
>
> Now there are the Chinese people. I got the idea on the way to my choir lessons. There were windshield wipers which made

forms like Chinese people. The windshield wipers then erased the form so I wrote them down so that I could save them. I often do that.

Next I made the basketball player. He has little bulges like his sister. Next to him you can see that his facial features have all spilled out, like his eyes are at the end of his neck. He's smoking a cigarette. The shoe is now made of snakes, the purses are out of alligators—it's a protest against killing animals.

Then we've got this weird "joker" guy. The big guy is a woman and a man, with hands in the pockets—a combination of different people. Also there are the Arab-type people with turbans and weird shoes, long puffy noses, and snakes for tongues. Next to the one Arab guy, waving bye, is another Arab. I started to make a fat lady, but she became two men, and then she became Arabs. My drawings never turn out exactly the way I wanted them to do.

This young artist lets herself begin by simply scribbling and thereby spawning a raft of geometric froms. One form or shape leads to another, and (like Leonardo peering at shapes lurking in the midst of the rocks in the mountain), Alison begins to perceive a representation concealed therein. Then she amplifies these shapes, erasing if necessary, until she arrives at a character or object that strikes her fancy. She rarely uses a model and rarely relies on her visual memory, though years ago she did try to re-create characters that she had drawn before. Only infrequently does the character come out with the shape or expression that she expected but, again, that does not matter. Indeed she seems to relish following the unconscious play of her hands and her mind, exploiting the opportunities that come up, creating a fantastic hybrid which brings about personal delight even as it evokes appreciative smiles from those around her.

Compared with Stuart, Alison seems to have a more casual, less compulsive approach to artistry. Though she draws often, it is not a daily activity. In fact she sometimes lets weeks pass without any drawing. Nor does she watch television or read books for ideas, preferring (as she puts it) to let "nature take its course." She has a wide variety of interests, ranging from writing, to playing the piano. She is also an inveterate collector of objects—glass figures, shells, knick-knacks: these she uses to create her own living environment, which she arranges and rearranges for hours on end. One of the very best students in her class, Alison is considering a number of careers in addition to being an artist.

Though most of her drawings now are representational, Alison has in the past produced numerous nonrepresentational pictures. She once favored richly colored designs, replete with various shapes, line configurations, intricately balanced forms, and the like.

The pair of drawings reproduced here are but two of dozens completed years ago (224, 225). It seems that her admirable sense of form—no longer exhibited as pure design—has been incorporated into her narrative representations (226). Like Stuart, she began

224

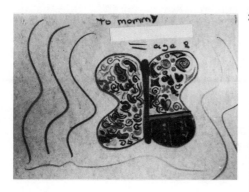

225

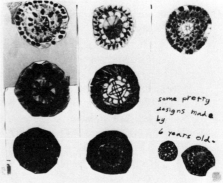

226

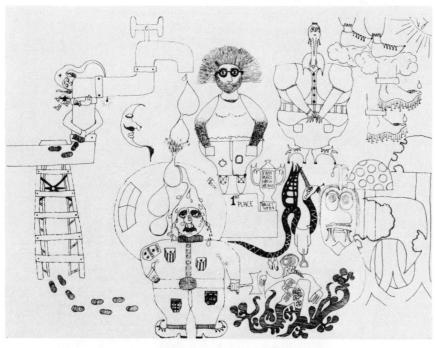

some years ago to portray a phalanx of characters, and though earlier groups were not as fantastic or compelling as recent efforts, they were from the beginning marked by graceful humor and a sense of the macabre.

Consistent with her "multi-media" orientation, Alison has illustrated her writing. Some of this has appeared in a newspaper that she issues with a friend. A recent poem about babysitting and the accompanying illustration (227) express both humorous subject matter and chaotic spirit.

Injustice (to be read fast)

My little brother jumps on my head
He punches his sister who bled and bled
The supper is burning
The whole house is churning
The baby's a screaming
The water's a steaming
Mother's away
And father can't stay
The furniture's ripped
My brother has tripped
My hair is on fire
And I'm beginning to tire
Of this rowdy time.
And I think it's a crime
To have any child to babysit.

227

Alison's versatility comes through as we examine other drawings. For instance, consider the careful way in which she draws a house, displaying a sure sense of specific textures within an integrated and well-proportioned composition (228). And as a contrast, note the quite unique and charming creature she created just after her tenth birthday (229).

This impressive variety raises again the question of whether Alison's drawing is really as unpremeditated as she claims. For instance, when requested to re-create the drawings she made of the Arabs, she readily succeeds in doing so, both in a direct copy (230) and from memory (231). Nor is she totally immune from cultural influences. She tries sometimes to copy items—note, for example, her charming portrait after Edward VI by Holbein (232).

Still, like Stuart, Alison is, and indeed prefers to think of herself as being, a naïve artist. She contrasts things she can draw

228

229

230

232

231

well—leaves, vines, trees, feathers—with entities that pose difficulty—people in funny positions and animals. She disdains formal
drawings and formal perspective, saying that it may be OK for
some people but that it is very different from what she wants to
achieve. In fact she insists rather indignantly (and rather sophisti-
catedly), "The Egyptians had their own perspective and many
people think it's just as good as ours."

Yet despite her doubts about the way of art today, Alison exhibits considerable sensitivity to the impulse underlying any aesthetic activity. She says that she likes drawing, first of all, because,
like writing, it gives her a sense of accomplishment. She goes on to
point out that it is a means of showing how you feel. And she insists
that people who *know how to look at drawings* can see, by looking
at your drawing, the way you are feeling. Further, she feels she
would draw even if no one could see it—so important is this activity to her. And indeed in her notebooks she sometimes makes drawings just for herself, even as she often discards drawings she has
made. Although uncertain herself about a career as an artist, Alison
reveals that she already is sensitive to many of the factors that
motivate, indeed impel, artists.

Like other gifted eleven-year-old artists who are essentially
self-taught, Stuart and Alison exhibit marked similarities. The kinds
of subject matter that engage them, their profiles of capacities and
lacks, and their suspicion of formal training and of the world of art
link them not only with one another but also with that cadre of preadolescents who continue to gain pleasure and sustenance from their
drawings. They are best at drawing what they like to draw—creating imaginative characters, bestowing upon them experiences that
matter and expressions that fit—and are far less distinguished at
the kinds of assignments an art teacher (or a psychologist) is likely
to contrive. And, aware that their goals are not necessarily the same
as those of adults who profess an interest in the arts, they insistently express their desire to pursue their own course. Indeed, as if
to underscore the important part played by drawing in their own
lives, both children can instantly recognize and re-create the occasions that inspired each of the scores of drawings we reviewed
together. Still, both of them voice regret that they cannot achieve
certain effects they would like to attain, and both seem to have
come to the reluctant conclusion that they are unlikely ever to
succeed in these pursuits if they remain entirely on their own.

It is difficult to know how much importance to attach to the
various differences between our two young artists. Does Stuart really plan his drawings to a significantly greater extent than Alison,
or is it more a difference in the rhetoric of self-report? Is Alison
genuinely more versatile than Stuart or simply more willing to

undertake something new? Is Stuart more serious in his artistry, since he draws every day and even in school? Or is it merely that he gains greater sustenance from, and is thus more reliant upon, his graphic activity? Will Stuart, with his more well-articulated goal of political cartooning, soon surpass Alison in drawing, in view of her less focused mission? Or will one or both young artists, like so many other preadolescents, soon retire their pencils as they find alternative and perhaps less isolating means of self-expression?

This last question is probably the key one in the life of the young "pre-artist." What unites Alison and Stuart, and already distinguishes them from many of their contemporaries, is the fact that both still draw and that both seem to gain real strength and genuine solace from graphic activity. Alison is perhaps more articulate about it; Stuart perhaps exemplifies this trait more in his daily existence. Yet my interactions with them have strongly suggested that both are working out important parts of their own existence through their artwork. Stuart has a need for a community with which he feels comfortable, in order to deal with various strains and tensions in his own family, and he does so in large part by a regular, serious, almost monkish dedication to this drawing. Alison is an individual of versatile talents, gifted with an imagination so keen that it might well get her into trouble if it were expressed too directly and too insistently to more suppressed individuals. Like a ventriloquist or puppeteer, she is able to harness and channel considerable energy and wit through her drawings, thereby investing a significant part of herself in what she makes; as she herself notes, others are then free to extract from her products those aspects and traits of herself which she has invested in them, and which they can comfortably acknowledge.

Because these youngsters live in a culture replete with examples of artistry, because they have the opportunity to draw at home and in their schools, because they have peers and parents who are willing to look at and enjoy what they do, they have been able to continue to draw and to make steady, sometimes even notable, progress. Both have on their own hit upon the solutions adopted by most young artists in our culture: the exploitation of the caricatured world of the media. In so doing, they have avoided the feared tedium of formal art classes while basically satisfying the twin needs of realistic rendition and a sense of accomplishment. Moreover, both seem to have found an outlet for seminal but potentially troublesome facets of their personalities.

Whether they will continue and further deepen their involvement in the arts may depend upon several factors. To begin with, as they both recognize, the amount of self-education they can pursue is limited. Unless they are extraordinarily skillful at sifting lessons from their culture,theywill at some point need some formal art training. They must take care, however, that the genuine original-ity they have evinced will not be destroyed or undermined by the rival values and structures of the formal art world. They must, moreover, continue to generate ideas and feelings that they wish to express and to share with others—something that is difficult (at least for them) to put in words or in some other communicative medium, but which lends itself to satisfactory and satisfying ex-pression in the graphic medium. This medium will have to allow them to express the bodily sensations, the emotions, the tensions, the goals, and the aspirations which will come to populate their lives as adolescents. Others about them will have to continue to value their output and to make them feel that life as an artist is an acceptable, possibly even an honorable, calling. Perhaps most elu-sively, and yet most crucially, they must continue to develop into whole, interesting persons who have messages to communicate which will matter to others. Stuart's compulsiveness, drive, and sense of mission must be wed to the imaginativeness and explora-tory zeal displayed by Alison. Without such methods, and without such messages, they may continue to amuse or to divert, but they will not speak profoundly to other persons.

CHAPTER 8

Personal Perspectives

AT the very end of the fifteenth century Leonardo da Vinci completed his *Last Supper* (233). This work is not only a treasured masterpiece by a uniquely gifted Renaissance artist; it also represents the culmination of several currents of Western art which had coalesced in the work and the person of Leonardo. There had been numerous "Last Suppers" before (234), but none could compare to the wall painting at the Santa Maria della Grazie in Milan. For in one massive composition Leonardo had captured as never before the excitement, the drama, and the religious significance of the most pivotal moment in all of Christendom—that terrifying instant when Jesus declared that one of his disciples would betray him.

Leonardo's work has been so often reproduced and so often dissected in detail that we do not find it easy to view it with a fresh eye. Perhaps some steps toward such an innocent appraisal are possible if we contrast Leonardo's achievement with the attainments of his predecessors: such a discussion will at the same time serve to introduce our later treatment of certain milestones achieved by adolescent artists in our own society. Where earlier "Suppers" had been laid out in a relatively flat arrangement, Leonardo's work is consummated in sharp perspective, with the room having a clear shape and depth and ultimately opening onto a view of the world beyond. Where earlier "Suppers" featured the disciples simply aligned from left to right, Leonardo painted each with clear traits of personality, definite facial expressions, unambiguous individual activity—talking, gesticulating, eying one another, reflecting the drama of the moment. Indeed, the very fact that a *moment* is being depicted, that Jesus has just made his pronouncement and thereby instigated diverse reactions on the part of his brethren is itself an innovation: rather than painting a posed portrait that could have been done at any time during the Passover ceremony, Leonardo is clearly capturing an instant of peak dramatic tension.

233 *The Last Supper* Leonardo da Vinci c. 1495–1498.

234 *The Last Supper* Andrea del Castagno c. 1445–1450.

Many other factors differentiate this work from its predecessors. Its composition is a marvel—with the apostles in trios, linked in each case by gestures and movements; the arrangement about Christ who, while clearly the cynosure, yet remains in his sacred isolation. The treacherous Judas too, while not segregated from the group, seems isolated, for he alone neither gesticulates nor questions. The shadowing and shading, the use of muted colors, the play of light, the emotional expressions of each personage—all contribute to the power of the work; at the same time, these qualities highlight the ways in which paintings of the Renaissance, and the works of this Renaissance master in particular, stand apart from achievements of earlier times.

Another comparison also presents itself. Just as Leonardo's work differs in many profound ways from those of pre-Renaissance painters, so too it features a number of characteristics that are absent from works by preadolescent youngsters. At least in a loose sense we can note unmistakable parallels between the pre-Renaissance artist and the preadolescent child. Neither has yet mastered principles of perspective; of portraying movements; of using the tools of light, shading, color, and chiaroscuro with finesse and expressivity; or of capturing the drama of a historical event within the constraints of a two-dimensional medium. Leonardo would spend days staring at his incompleted work, without painting a stroke; and perhaps it was this infinite time and care, as well as his genius, that made possible these unique results. It is also possible, however, that only in the wake of the scientific, technological, and conceptual breakthroughs of the Renaissance could such a work have been successfully consummated.

Leonardo was not only an incomparable artist; he was also the most profound student of painting of his time, and quite possibly of all times. His notebooks and comments on painting are still consulted by students as well as scholars. In them he reveals the concerns that exercised him and the more farsighted of his peers, and the insights he gained as he reflected upon his artistic activity. His system of values is conveyed by his stress on accurate depiction of depth relations. "Perspective," he declared, "must be preferred to all the discourses and systems of human learning." He examines the principles by which light functions and the attributes of the eye, and then deduces that "every object sends its image to the eye by a pyramid of lines; and bodies of equal size will result in a pyramid of larger or smaller size, according to all the differences in their distance, from one to another." Practice must be founded on sound theory; "Perspective is the guide and the gateway; and without this nothing can be done well in the matter of drawing."

Nearly all of Leonardo's breakthroughs can be detected in the notebooks. Leonardo concerns himself with the theory of colors, with aerial perspective, with the depiction of the human figure, with the portrayal of emotions, folds in draperies, shadows, and with overall principles of composition. His most passionate passages treat of the depiction of individuals: old people, little children, grotesque persons. He indicates the eleven kinds of noses, the ones that can be depicted full face, and the ways that one should remember them. A pithy passage unveils the means for portraying an angry man:

> You must make an angry person holding someone by the hair, wrenching his head against the ground, and with one knee on his ribs; his right arm and fist raised on high. His hair must be thrown up, his brow downcast and knit, his teeth clenched, and the two corners of his mouth grimly set: his neck swelled and bent forward as he leans over his foe, and full of furrows.

Steps for achieving the skills of painting are carefully laid out: "The youth should first learn perspective, then the proportion of objects. Then he may copy from some good master, to accustom himself to fine forms. Then from nature, to confirm by practice the rules he has learned. Then see for a time the works of various masters. Then get the habit of putting his art into practice and work." Advice is dispensed on how to live in the country while painting, on the advantages of painting with companions, on the importance of painting and studying nature.

Leonardo's notebooks even aid us in approaching *The Last Supper*. Thus we read of "one who was drinking and left the glass in its position and turned his head toward the speaker . . . Another, speaking into his neighbor's ear and he, as he listens to him, turns toward him to lend an ear, while he holds a knife in one hand, and in the other the loaf half cut through by the knife." Notes on how to depict groups of individuals can also be found:

> As you go, observe, note, and consider the circumstances and behaviors of men in talking, quarreling, or laughing, or fighting together; the actions of the men themselves and the actions of the bystanders, who spear them on or who look on. And take note of them with slight strokes, thus, in a little book, which you should always carry with you.

Indeed, the notebooks give us unequaled insights about the ways in which one Renaissance master viewed various works, including his Christian masterpiece.

Of course Leonardo's comments should not imply that great work results from mastering a set of principles in a guidebook (one must know when to violate them as well), nor should they imply that works like *The Last Supper* can be reduced to a few verbal formulas. The existence of a verbal account does not ensure achievement, nor does the absence of such notebooks foreshadow inferior artistic practice. Nonetheless, as we consider the artistry of Leonardo's time, we encounter a more ambitious agenda than had been set forth in earlier times, as well as a greater self-consciousness about what one wishes to achieve and how to realize this goal. Indeed the very range of concerns that stood out in Leonardo's time is the same one that normal young artists within our community are confronting as they approach adolescence. But it is not as paradoxical as it may seem for normal youths to be attempting today what only the greatest master could achieve some five hundred years ago. For in every area of life—ranging from the understanding of basic philosophical concepts to the mastery of the principles of physics, astronomy, or chemistry—the most innovative ideas of one generation pass gradually into the public domain in the following generations, thus permitting youngsters to acquire them quite easily and in a more "natural way." It is incomparably easier to assimilate an idea that is in the air and that has been generally accepted by one's elders, than it is to be the first to conceive of the idea: that is why we continue to honor Socrates, Aristotle, Kant, Newton, Darwin, and Einstein.

How, then, to contrast the youth of thirteen, fifteen, or eighteen years with the child of eight or ten, whose activities have preoccupied us in earlier sections? We have come to understand that the adolescent, over and above her clear physical and physiological differences from younger children, is already beginning to think about the world in new ways and to entertain new concerns. At earlier stages of life she had come to know the world directly through her physical actions upon the world and through sensory organs. This was the time when she began to scribble and to gain pleasure from the simple marks left on the page. Soon she acquired the capacity to think of the world in terms of symbols; and as a consequence she could "read" marks made by others and, ultimately, contrive marks that themselves depicted objects in the world.

To join the symbolic realm with the world of her physical and sensory experience was the major challenge facing the child at the beginning of the school years. More often than not a solution was reflected in a growing desire to fashion works of art that looked just like the real world, as well as an impatience with graphic efforts that countenanced too great a disjunction between the world around her and the world on her drawing pad. Yet at this time the child was still limited to the use of language, pictures, and other symbols as a means of characterizing the physical world as directly as possible.

With the cognitive breakthroughs of adolescence, the child (who is no longer a child) comes to think of the world in a far more sophisticated manner. She is now able to conceive of and reason about the world through the juxtaposition and comparison of statements about the world. The youth can describe a state of affairs, or even a world, and then consider, transform, modify, or revise the description—all exclusively on the plane of words. She becomes able to theorize, to deduce, to conceptualize a whole range of possibilities, and to decide which one makes more sense, without the exigency of trying things out in the physical world. And at the same time there is a dramatic rise in critical acumen. The youth can more rigorously criticize her own works and the works of others. Naturally this heightened ability exerts a crucial influence on her own artistic output; for if at such a time of critical scrupulousness one's own artistry is found wanting, the pressures to cease may prove irresistible.

Ushered in with these fundamental conceptual breakthroughs are dramatic alterations in the youth's *personal* and *social concerns*. While in the first year she was oriented chiefly toward family members and then, somewhat later, toward peers of her own sex, her circle now widens and deepens. Her interest in other persons gains in emotional significance as she enters into fuller and more abiding relations, eventually including intimate relations with members of the opposite sex. At the same time, she also becomes increasingly occupied with herself. Once the sense of self is developed, she thinks of herself as an object apart: she is concerned with the goals she has set for herself, her success in achieving them, and the ways in which others think of her. There is the emergence of a sense of identity—a preoccupation with the way in which the various roles one has been experimenting with come together to form a coalesced and balanced whole. There is as well clear peril should such a synthesis of personal aims, motives, and history fail to come about.

The capacity to consider various intellectual and social possibilities confers fresh power upon an individual's artistry. No longer anchored to realistic portraits of one's surroundings, the youth can venture forth along at least two different paths: she can depict items in ways that make personal sense, even if they fail to satisfy canons of realism; and by the same token she can draw objects or events that do not exist, and even ones that have never existed.

Moreover, building upon the ability to contemplate the way a picture has been rendered, the adolescent now has the power to consider the most sophisticated aspects of depiction; the ones pondered by Leonardo: how best to depict motion, perspective, character, personality, and conflicts. And not merely restricted to seeing these features and reflecting upon their achievement, and less tied to compulsive conformity, youngsters can now actually ferret out principles, articulate them, try them out, revise them: in short, apply methods of the experimental scientist to the practice of artistry. For these reasons the adolescent can master shading, movement, proportion, perspective. She has the cognitive equipment to track down the methods and the pertinacity to master them.

The youngster also becomes capable of an expanded approach to color. Whereas in early childhood she displayed a strong attraction to bright and primary colors, and in middle childhood strove to bestow every object with its "true-life" hue, the adolescent is able to exploit color to a much finer degree. She is sensitive to the effects wrought by the juxtaposition of colors: she will experiment with mixtures and arrangements until she achieves a sought-after tone or mood; and she can (and will) use color to achieve expressive and emotional effects, even when these run counter to the canonical coloring of objects.

Subtler but equally important, the adolescent captures—or perhaps recaptures—the ability to portray objects and events within a totality. Pictures and paintings are no longer mere conglomerations of individual elements; the possibility of fitting them together so that they constitute an organized and integrated entity has arrived in a much more self-conscious and controlled way than ever before. This sensitivity to an organized whole confers upon the individual far greater ability to comprehend and to criticize the great works of the past, even as it unleashes the potential to produce (though it by no means assures the achievement of) works that are themselves informed by such an integrated intelligence. At the same time, in the wake of this enhanced sense of organization, the production of works that themselves presuppose another genre —parodies, ironies, caricatures, satires, and other "take-offs" or "put-ons"—becomes a live option, a kind of wry testimony to the youth's enhanced capacity to conceive of an artistic symbol as an integrated (though revisable) whole.

In all aspects of the adolescent's life one can discern reverberations of this fresh synthesizing capacity. As part of the search for a coherent and acceptable identity, the adolescent develops, perhaps for the first time, a recognized personal style or *way of being*, one that cuts across various dimensions of her existence and, if all goes well, infuses her artistic products as well. The full-blown achievement of a style—be it a personal or an artistic one—takes many years and may (perhaps fortunately) never be completed. Nor can it be consciously achieved: a genuine and sincere (as opposed to a contrived) style must follow naturally from one's experiences in the world and one's productions in the symbolic realm. However, the *possibility* of such an informing coherence clearly comes to the fore during adolescence; increasingly an individual in her own right, the person has a chance to make herself into a work of art, to create a *person* who will be known by others directly as well as through her works. Artists may begin this process at a far earlier time than other persons.

An intriguing strand of support for these contentions emerged in an exhibit at the Israel National Museum during the winter of 1978–1979. Assembled in a special exhibition hall were paintings by some of Israel's major artists—works which were done when they were still youths. In most cases it was possible to look at works produced by the same child at various ages. While there were of course individual differences across artists, some general patterns could be discerned. The drawings by the young children were usually quite precocious: their use of line and color, their sense of composition, and their skill at representation were very impressive. Formal art instruction usually commenced at the age of ten or eleven, quite possibly because it was at this time that the artists (or their families) felt the need for some skilled guidance. During these preadolescent years, the artists often demonstrated astonishing technical facility—indeed some of the children were actually virtuosos of the brush by the age of twelve or thirteen. But only during the middle years of adolescence did evidence emerge of a person behind the drawing—an individual voice or style—which informed the whole canvas and gave it an emotional power. To be sure, signs of artistry, such as the skilled use of properties of line or sensitivity to expressive moods, could be detected earlier. But it was only among the drawings of the artists as adolescents that one had the feeling that these individuals had the inspired talent that would permit a life productive in the arts. Some of the drawings by these adolescents, but none of the drawings of the preadolescents, could have gained entry into a museum on their own merits.

It seems clear from the preceding considerations that the events of the later years of childhood come to exert a profound and far-reaching impact on the artistry of individuals—at least those who continue to participate in the arts. Indeed the examination of artistry in adolescence entails a study of each of these epochal changes. Accordingly, in what follows we will glimpse such youngsters as they attempt to master the various challenges of these years: the achievement of pictorial effects that depend on an informed spatial intelligence; the capacity, equally formidable, to convey personality and expressiveness in one's artistic works; and the achievement through training and natural growth of a special personality, one that enlivens the possibility that one will become an artist.

The undertaking of graphic activity is easy and natural for the young child. She enjoys making marks and dotes on their effects, but she is unlikely to pose existential questions about the nature of this activity. Asked to depict a given object, she throws out a glance (and often hardly more) and then marks down her graphic equivalent for that entity. Indeed, if asked to draw a set of objects, she draws them in the same general way, whether she is simply given a list, shown a picture, or instructed to portray a live array exactly as she sees it. But with age, children come to realize some of the complexity entailed in such instructions. They appreciate the variety of ways in which to portray something; and they themselves confront the possibilities of succeeding or failing in each.

Nowhere does the perpetual tension between the agenda provided by the culture and the child's own developing skill come forth with greater clarity than in the child's efforts to master the principles of perspective. Nearly every child within Western culture is exposed to standard perspective and sooner or later comes to understand that special techniques are necessary to depict objects that lie further away in the distance. And most children attempt on their own to achieve such perspectival effects. To observe how children approach perspective turns out to be very informative: one has the opportunity to determine whether perspective can be acquired by simple imitation, whether it may be acquired even in the absence of appropriate models, or whether it follows some other kind of developmental trajectory.

The British psychologist John Willats asked children of different ages to draw a simple (though highly pregnant) scene: a rectangular table with a few household objects laid out upon it (235). Children were seated so that they faced one of the long sides of the table. Thus all subjects had to attempt a task that, in a humble way, resembled the one undertaken in his mind's eye by Leonardo some five hundred years ago. The resulting drawings were divided into six groups, each of which represents a step in the process of achieving perspective. A study of these steps can give us insight not only into the normal developmental course of rendering perspective but perhaps also into the history of depictive attempts that antedated the achievements of the Renaissance.

As can be seen in the figures, the youngest subjects, aged about six or seven, made a rectangular box for the table top and simply drew the desired objects above it (236). For them there was no problem, and hence no attempts at perspective. Those in a sec-

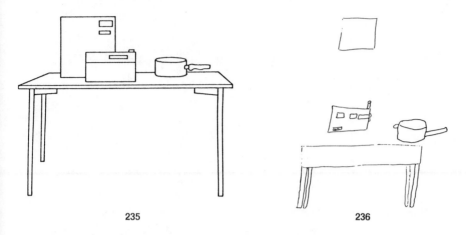

235   236

ond group (237) made a single straight line (reminiscent of the base line) for the table top and placed the objects from left to right atop that line. Once again, concern about perspective was minimal. A third group of subjects (238) also portrayed the table top as a

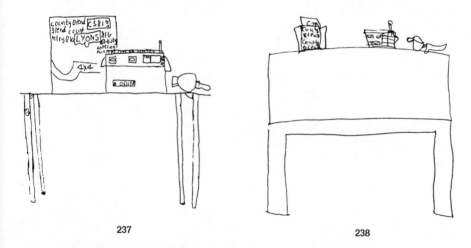

237   238

rectangle but this time featured objects placed above it in approximately the correct topological relationships. Here for the first time there was discernible concern with capturing on the canvas itself something of the geometrical relations among objects.

Genuine attempts to portray the table top in correct perspective are seen only in the fourth, fifth, and sixth sets of attempts, and each set corresponds to a different form of perspective. In the fourth set (239) we see an example of oblique projection: here the two short sides of the table are drawn in isometric perspective rather than in converging form. Front-to-back relationships in real

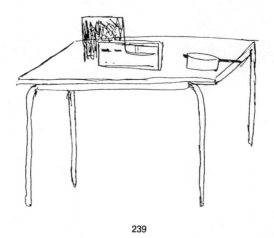

239

life are represented on the picture surface by oblique relations, making the overall table a parallelogram.

The drawings in the last two sets rise to the challenge of central perspective; each documents that the table is rectangular but that the far side appears smaller to a measuring glance than the close side. Drawings of the fifth type (240) feature "naïve perspective": the artist has the idea that the two sides of the table should differ in length and the two legs in extent, but does not carry these ideas through with geometric accuracy—the results are approximate rather than exact. In contrast, drawings of the sixth type (241), considered to be "genuinely perspectival," feature accurate convergence. One might say that in the fifth stage the child has learned the rule that orthogonals converge but has not yet learned to apply the rule in order to convey the actual appearance

240   241

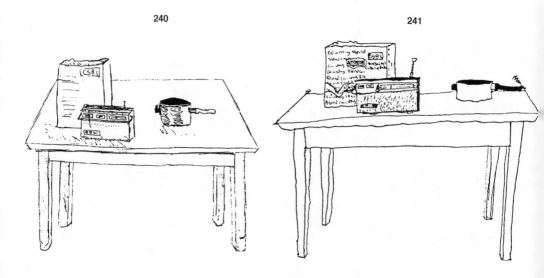

of the scene; she is still to some extent obeying the rule "blindly." In the sixth stage, however, the child has learned to coordinate her own framework of reference with that of the perceived scene; and so she draws upon the tools of perspective to draw a scene that captures what she sees and produces the same visual effect upon others.

As Willats pointedly remarks, the actual steps taken by children as they attack perspective challenge any simple-minded account of how graphic skills are acquired. If perspective could be attained by slavish imitation—be it of nature or of drawings—there would be no need for such a lengthy process. Nor could there be any accounting for the various intermediate steps—the objects lined up in a straight array, the peculiarities of oblique projection: after all, none of these is widely available as a model in the culture. At the same time it is equally misleading to say that each child invents the solutions of perspective simply by herself. If she did, then perspective would have been devised far earlier in Western history and would be far more pervasive throughout the world. Moreover, there would be no reason for children to be impelled to continue until they reached stage six and then stop. An adequate explanation for the achievement of perspective must, accordingly, be more complex. Like other aspects of drawing considered in these pages, the course reflects an interaction of the child's own evolving skills and view of the world with the kinds of models and examples she encounters. Achievements by Leonardo do not ensure that every child will master perspective: but with those achievements in the background, there is a far greater chance that the average youngster can convert her naturally evolving skills into correct perspectival renditions.

And so, we see the child working out through the graphic medium the rendering of the world in a pleasing and geometrically impeccable manner. The story can be told again and again, as one considers how the child learns to portray motion; how she masters bodily proportions; how she converts single canonical version of an object into a flexible schema. In each case we encounter a single, relatively inflexible solution at the beginning. Interesting, even amusing, hybrid attempts follow, as the child seeks to transcend her schemas: witness the depiction of a running person with one foot stuck out in the air, a bending person with one limb much longer than another, a profile of a dog with a face contorted into a full-face view. And finally the child arrives at a higher level of solution where an adequate version of the desired concept—be it motion, perspective, or shading—has been attained.

Whether the individual transcends her various compromise efforts—which preserve the basic schema while making a "gesture" in the right direction—depends on many factors. Certainly tutelage and the availability of models cannot be underestimated. The child's own willingness to experiment, to look carefully at other works, and to reflect upon her own percepts make an appreciable difference. The particular drawing tasks in which she is involved and the importance she places on achieving desirable effects are further components of the equation. But in any case, and by whatever means, the more successful child eventually develops schemas for introducing variety in her work—limbs that bend, faces that bear different expressions, objects that correctly overlap one another, entities that are far away, and the like.

Once armed with this range of schemas, the child is in a favorable position to extrapolate: to examine almost any new scene and to conjure up a solution that is located, conceptually and perceptually, somewhere (hopefully at the right distance) between the two most neighboring schemas. Such compromises do not always work, to be sure; indeed one frequently encounters efforts to interpolate between two views (say, running and walking, or sad and depressed) which succeed in capturing neither view, or even a third view, but rather culminate in something bizarre or grotesque. Fascinating discoveries can come, however, from these apparent misses, providing the youngster is alert to what she has done, is willing to learn what it really looks like, and is ready to incorporate it in her canon for the time when it might be exploited. As the cartoonist Rodolphe Töpffer knew, nearly every variant of the human eye or the human mouth simply provides *another* face that can be seen in the world; and by the same token, nearly every variation of a drawing from real objects finds some correspondence in the everyday world of the person (242). If not, it can always offer itself as a depiction of the fantastic or the grotesque.

So far we have considered the developmental steps through which the normal preadolescent passes. But since the normal preadolescent is unlikely to become an artist and may, in fact, draw less as time goes on, we must ask whether our typical developmental picture encompasses gifted children. As our Interludes suggest, gifted youngsters are no exception. They, too, show a concern with literally accurate depiction and are disappointed when they cannot achieve it; they often revert to a stylized form of drawing, partly as a defense against their difficulties with accurate realism; and with every passing year they set themselves more ambitious tasks in the realm of spatial and expressive effects.

But what of even more gifted individuals, and in particular what of those preadolescents who will one day be artistic masters? This question can be asked most pointedly with reference to those contemporary artists who ultimately spurned the goal of realism

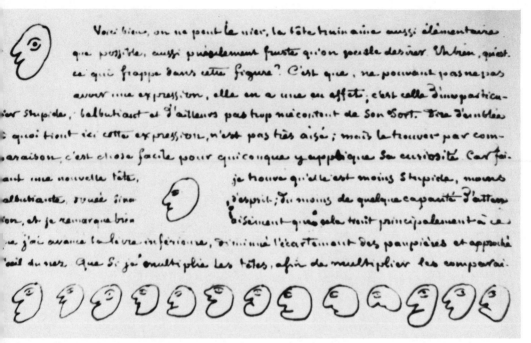

242

and instead produced works of a more abstract, or more "primitive," nature. When one examines the youthful work of Pablo Picasso (243–250) and Paul Klee (251–257), the answer comes through very clearly. As youngsters, these future masters passed through the same stages as did the normal and the talented children represented here. To be sure, they did so at a more rapid rate and with a kind of profundity and sensitivity seldom encountered in the typical household. Yet up to their teen-age years, despite the fact that Impressionism and post-Impressionism were already on the scene, they were still producing works of a highly realistic flavor—of picture-postcard accuracy and fidelity. One might say that they were literal-minded with a vengeance. Somewhat later they began to copy works by acknowledged masters. Here they often attempted to mimic the style, even when it was nonrealistic, but the kind of compulsive precision of their attempts seems an even stronger confirmation of literalistic tendencies. Only when they were well into adolescence did their own graphic approach—at first a hybrid of the most influential styles about them—begin to come through. And it was still a matter of years before they hit upon the personal modes of expression for which they are justifiably renowned today.

Thus we find that, even among the most talented of young artists, efforts are devoted to the drawing of the world as it actually looks. The inventions and advances of the Renaissance were simply

243 *Bullfight scene and doves*, Malaga, 1890 (age 9)

244 *Page of notebooks with dogs*, 1893 (age 12)

245 *Portrait of old man Corunna*, 1895 (age 14)

246 *Study of hands*, Barcelona, 1895–1897 (age 14–16)

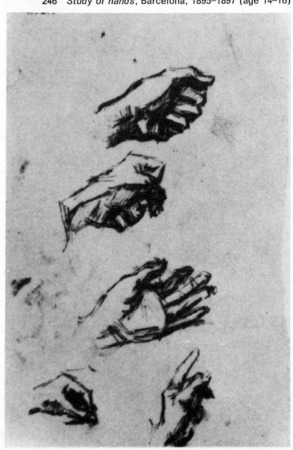

247 *Bust of woman in profile*, Barcelona, 1896 (age 15)

248 *Copy of Velasquez portrait of Philip IV*, 1897–1898 (age 16–17)

249 *Various sketches*, Madrid, 1897–1898 (age 16–17)

250 *Menu for Els 4 gats*, Barcelona, 1889–1900 (age 18–19)

251   *Man, ?, chair, rabbit*, 1884 (age 5)

252   *Horse, sleigh and two ladies*, 1884 (age 5)

253   *Lady with parasol*, 1883–1885 (age 4–6)

254   *Two moving figures*, 1885 (age 6)

255   *Country home in Bern in the Länggasse*, 1888 (age 9)

256   *View of Berner Matte as seen from Kirchenfeld*, 1890 (age 11)

257   *Bell tower in Bern*, 1892 (age 13)

more powerful tools for making increasingly veridical drawings—
so much so that the camera added comparatively little to the
armamentarium of the most realist artists. However, there is yet a
further agenda that every young artist confronts at this time of her
life—the challenge of using her tools to make a drawing that bears
significance for her.

It is here that alertness to possibility becomes so important.
The adolescent artist has available to her not merely an arsenal of
tools—perspective, proportion, personality, expressions—for drawing the world in a realistic way; she also has a new set of concerns
which preoccupy her, which enrich her social and emotional life,
and which offer themselves as possible subjects for treatment. No
longer is the youth constrained to draw the world as it looks to the
camera, or the allegedly innocent eye. She can begin as well to
explore the worlds of thought, of emotion, of form, of design. And
she can do so in a way that makes sense to her, that captures on a
piece of paper her innermost and greatest concerns. The relation to
other humans, which was all-important in the first years of life,
once again moves center stage.

The desire to express these thoughts in her artwork is probably
a principal way in which the youth differs from her younger coun-
terparts. But the manner in which this orientation beyond the realistic comes to be expressed varies greatly from one person to
another. Sometimes it can be seen in the way the adolescent por-
trays the real world. The colors selected no longer simply ape the
natural colors in the world; rather the artist chooses color, at least
in part, with an eye toward the mood it is likely to evoke in others.
The shape and thickness of line become another means of capturing on paper the nature of one's feelings. And of course the subject matter itself can be a powerful clue to the concerns of the
individual.

An orientation toward portraiture often emerges at this time.
While the human figure has always been a favorite of youthful
artists, the adolescent now approaches the human body and face in
a highly charged frame of mind (258, 259). There is a heightened
concern with the sexual characteristics of one's subjects: an emphasis of the secondary sexual characteristics—particularly in depicting individuals of the opposite sex—and an experimentation with
the range of physical possibilities in one's own sex. Sensuality flows
in these works. Much effort is exerted on portraits—especially likenesses of those one loves, admires, or fears. Not only are there fresh
attempts to achieve likenesses, but once again a premium is placed
on capturing the mood, character traits, and personality of the subject. It is not enough that the portrait look like its subject—it must
"feel" like its subject as well. And perhaps if it feels sufficiently like
its subject, it will come to resemble the person.

258

259

„Demon"

260

Experimentation with abstract art forms has become common among adolescent artists. In the wake of the breakthroughs by Picasso, Mondrian, and Braque, as well as the more radical movements associated with the New York School, youths find license—if not encouragement—to experiment with pure forms. (By the same token, more recent developments, such as Pop Art, Op Art, and the New Realism, also find ready echoes in the experiments by young adolescents.)

A burgeoning concern with abstract forms can also be seen in a long-standing yet curious phenomenon—the doodle (260). Nearly everywhere that markers are available, the youth can be counted upon to doodle—to ornament the words (and pictures) in her notebook with repeated line configurations, to embroider pages everywhere with intersecting lines, forms, and shapes, to fill whole pages with intricate filigree, ornamentations, and other extrarealistic and surrealistic forms.

Various factors seem to prompt doodles. Sometimes the child simply has excess energy to use up; sometimes the doodle—like a figured bass in a concerto—accompanies a daydream or fantasy; at other times there is a concentrated effort to experiment with forms and shapes for their own sake. But what is most intriguing about these supposedly meaningless forms is that they remind us of the scribbles, forms, and designs of the prerepresentational child. These doodles document that, for the first time in a decade, the individual is free of the tyranny of representationality. And they also suggest that the youth is giving fuller rein than previously to the operation of unconscious processes, to the kind of experimentation with pure form and shape which may constitute crucial unconscious input to artistic creativity. In the geometric marginalia and whorls of preschool children, adolescents, and experimenting artists, one encounters the most direct manifestation of the graphic imagination at work—perhaps even the keys to creative breakthrough. And if this is indeed the function doodles serve, they should prove of considerable aid to the youngster as she attempts to find a form and a format, that will enable her most effectively to express her concerns, feelings, fears, and aspirations.

For it is only if the arts continue to provide for the child an outlet for her strongest concerns that they retain any hope of surviving within her daily repertoire. The pressures against involvement in the arts as a profession are sufficiently stringent, and, paradoxically, the competition sufficiently rigorous, to require that an individual possess tremendously powerful motivation if she is to remain a practicing artist. In all probability the factors that inspire a lifetime devotion to art are as varied as are the cultures and the epochs in the world. Within our own culture it does seem, however, that those individuals likely to select themselves as artists and likely to be tapped by the society as having something to contribute to its cultural life are those for whom the graphic domain provides a unique outlet—a means of expression which no other avenue can supply and which serves as a tremendous "release" function for the individual.

Some suggestive evidence supports these speculations. Two educational psychologists, Jacob Getzels and Mihaly Csikszentmihalyi, studied a cadre of art students at the School of the Art Institute in Chicago in the hope of determining why each had chosen a career in art and which ones would ultimately achieve success in it. The biographies of the aspiring artists reveal a number of intriguing and telling similarities. While there were no unambiguous signs early in life that these students would become artists, those who eventually chose such a calling had been characteristically successful in art in school, were consistently rewarded for their gifts, and were unlikely to have excelled to an equivalent extent in anything else. Notwithstanding their success in this realm, these individuals had tended during adolescence to be lonely and to experience feelings of inferiority; they sometimes combatted these feelings by drawing, often in an unflattering way, those individuals who tormented them.

Their artistry also came to fulfill more positive functions. It became more expressive, and less purely defensive, as the artists attempted, within the lines, forms, shapes, and colors of their works, to negotiate their way among the various tensions and pressures in their lives. Seldom would these conflicts be acted—or sketched—out directly. A hostile father need not be so presented in living color. But the feelings of tension, rejection, and hostility were revealed in the expressiveness of the paintings, whether they were rendered in representational or abstract form. And the more successful of these youngsters became able to capture their conflicts successfully and consistently, so that they were now controlling them—at least in the visual graphic modality. Getzels and Csikszentmihalyi describe this pattern:

> As [young artists] develop the means for exploring the most ambiguous and intimate experiences, they uncover new contradictions, new questions, new problems. In this sense the predicament of the young artist is similar to that of a scientist who, while studying a hitherto undetected virus, becomes infected with an unknown disease and must find a cure that will save his life. The artist projects on the canvas a visual expression of the experiences that trouble him. In working with these elements, he discovers the shape of his problem, a problem with no known solution. Now he must find a way out of this bind.

A similar line of reasoning foretells which artists will achieve the greatest success after the completion of school. On this account, it is the ability to discover problems in one's own artwork, and then to use the means at one's disposal to solve the problems, which comes to mark the most successful artist. Getzels and Csikszentmihalyi were able to furnish novel empirical support for this claim. After providing all their students with a set of objects and asking them to deploy the objects as they chose within a painting, they found that those individuals who were able to *find problems* immanent in the array and then to solve these problems through their artistry were the ones who subsequently achieved the greatest success. In the view of these researchers, the successful artist is the individual who experiences a conflict in her own life; formulates a problem that articulates this conflict; expresses the problem in visual form; succeeds in resolving the conflict through symbolic means; and thereby achieves a new emotional and cognitive balance.

I find this formula seductive but perhaps a little too neat. Indeed, probably any formulation that attempts to *explain* the mysteries of artistic creativity—including Freud's famous dissection of Leonardo's genius—is likely to be insufficient and even to sound hollow. Fortunately, a bracing corrective to such a highly particularistic view of artistic achievement can be found in the work of another psychoanalyst, Otto Rank, who wrote particularly of the artists who lived in Western society after the Renaissance.

Rank saw the period of adolescence—the very time of attainment of various technical and expressive skills—as a crucial period for the person who will become the artist. For in Rank's view what is quintessential to the achievement of great artistry, above and beyond the conquest of technical means, is the ability to attain the personality of the artist—to become a person who feels special and is regarded by others as special, to achieve a personality or style that marks one off as being different, extraordinary, capable of fashioning works that will matter not only to oneself but to the world in which one lives. The future artist must be driven to execute something of importance: to become a figure of transcendence, one must possess a set of traits and an emotional makeup that can be captured and expressed within an artistic medium, and the energy and strength to devote all of one's powers to the achievement of one of the few possible forms of immortality. By definition, only a few individuals will succeed in making their lives such a work of art—and of course in the absence of technical skill such an individual will scarcely become a major creative figure. And yet it is telling to consider Rank's reversal of the usual equation: rather than finding greatness and individuality emerging from the work, Rank sees the future artist as one who first becomes a distinctive personality. Only then can the artist utilize skills in a sufficiently potent yet subtle way to become a master who matters.

Given the generally precarious position in which artists are placed and the various pressures that militate against such a life, it is difficult to remain involved in the arts in our society. It does not suffice to want to be an artist: society ultimately exercises the determining vote. To become a practicing artist is in itself an achievement, even as the attainment of great artistry is a rare and perhaps inherently unpredictable process. A confluence of factors—embracing early gifts, excellent tutelage, command of the medium, connections within the world of art, a special driving energy, and perhaps in most cases a conflict-ridden personal history—may all be necessary ingredients of success. Only individuals who are capable of (and intent upon) realizing a range of possibilities, who seek to capture moods in their works, who themselves are developing into significant personalities—only those individuals seem to stand a reasonable chance of breaking into the charmed circle of artistic accomplishment.

The achievement of a Leonardo stands apart from that of other mortals, and the effects he wrought in his *Last Supper* lie beyond the ken of even the most gifted adolescent today. Yet the kinds of personality traits that were "selected out" by the Renaissance—the drivingly ambitious, creative, and vigorous person, the concern with rendering every feature exactly correct, the desire to synthesize all knowledge and to capture all feelings, the motivation to surpass all one's peers (or to fail magnificently in the attempt)—these remain at a premium in our adolescence of today. It is difficult to escape the analogy between the achievements of the adolescent in our time, and the milestones that marked Western art during the *quattrocento*. Yet in voicing this point, we are moving onto dangerous developmental ground: for while it makes reasonable sense to speak of individual development and to chart its course, the perils of characterizing the art of an entire civilization are far more pronounced. Still, any developmental treatment of the arts needs to consider such historical issues. And so we must turn our attention to the question of whether there can be progress in art.

FOURTH INTERLUDE

Portraits of an Adolescent Artist

I T IS HARD to imagine a living space more cluttered than Gabriel Foreman's bedroom (261). From floor to ceiling, across each wall, and throughout the central area the room is laden with an amazing assortment of stimulation—a mélange of colors, forms, objects, and sounds culled from every aspect of one sixteen-year-old boy's existence. Moreover, Gabriel assures me, "Everything in this room has a story connected with it . . . Not that I want to make a big deal about it, but I wouldn't just put any old thing in it."

261

Despite its superficial grandiosity, Gabriel's claim has a convincing ring to it. This highly imaginative youngster does seem involved with each of the multifarious cultural artifacts present in his room. His engagement with the popular culture is underscored by the posters of singers, comedians, and other stars, the decals, posters, and neon signs from various commercial establishments, the television set and the radio (blaring forth rock music), the pages torn from pop magazines. His serious interest in the fine arts is reflected in a poster of a portrait by El Greco, as well as the numerous pieces of sculpture and drawings he himself has fashioned. His preoccupation with his own experiences comes across in the many photographs and drawings of himself, including a remarkable series of snapshots taken each year since early childhood and aligned in annual order in one niche of his room. His immersion in adolescence is reflected in the various drawings connected with sex ("Keep on Trucking"), the magic-marker graffiti that adorn virtually every inch of unfinished wood in the room, the collection of license plates near the bed, and the pinball machine which, when not in operation, is covered by a hill of papers, books, magic tricks, funny books, old clothing, wine bottles, junk, and memorabilia from scores of experiences he wants to remember and cherish.

Not that memory poses any problem at all for Gabriel, at least in the visual sphere. As he pores over scores of his drawings created over the past dozen years, Gabriel is never at a loss for the story behind the drawing, the experience that prompted it, the techniques used, his (and others') initial reaction to the work, and his current critique of it. His mind appears to be an endlessly rich repository of visual images—together with the graphic moves necessary to re-create these images in drawing: he can at will retrieve any one of them, combine them together, revise as he likes, or conjure up fresh and hitherto unimagined combinations. The spaces we design for living are an intimation of the kinds of experiences with which we have an elective affinity—those things we value, those things that hold moment for us. There is much creative chaos in Gabriel's mind but there is also order and organization, and we can glimpse at least a hint of that order as we behold the jam-packed corners, the object-laden crevices, and the richly furnished central spaces of his room.

Though but a junior in high school, Gabriel has a clear sense of who he is. His confidence, as well as his considerable capacity for self-advertisement, came through when I asked him whether he wants to become an artist. "I am already one," he shot back immediately, "I can't help it." And indeed in a number of ways Gabriel has earned that title. He has been drawing regularly and with increasingly impressive skill since the age of two. He has achieved remarkable products in a range of artistic media, ranging from film to sculpture. He is intensely and perpetually involved in the arts. He has cultivated an artistic mien—a sensitive face, flowing locks of hair, and graceful movement. How he thinks of himself—serious, somber, deep, sensitive, graceful—comes across in his self-portraits, and it is not widely at variance with how others perceive him (262).

Gabriel comes from an environment tailormade to spawn a talented artist. Both his parents are painters who have exhibited widely and who make their living in the graphic arts. An intelligent, articulate, and caring couple, they have strongly supported the artistic efforts of Gabriel and his talented older brother D.L. They are readily available to demonstrate artistic techniques; they have lavished artistic supplies upon their sons; and they have provided a household in which art objects are prominently displayed and lived with: Perhaps most importantly, they have, through example, made it clear to their sons that it is permissible, acceptable, and even admirable to follow the calling of an artist.

262

263

264

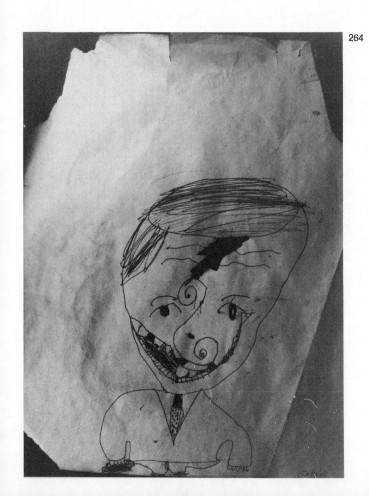

This hospitable atmosphere bore early fruit in the case of Gabriel Foreman. As a preschooler he swiftly passed through the prerepresentational stage and by the age of three or four was already painting persons and scenes that went well beyond the simple schemas usually found at that age. Confronted at age five with a photograph of himself and his two brothers, he proceeded to draw in pastels a remarkable likeness of the three children, one reminiscent of waifs drawn by the early Picasso or the hagard figures sketched by the contemporary French artist Jean Léon Jansem (263). Other drawings from the same period—for example, the head and the cat in figures 264 and 265—underscore his versatility with figure drawing.

During his early school years, Gabriel was already exhibiting a strong penchant toward the drawing of portraits—pictures of individuals familiar to him, figures seen in other paintings, or personalities in the public eye. We see his developing capacity to capture a likeness in his copies of Frans Hals's portrait of Claes D. van Voorhout (266) and of the Mona Lisa (267)—both at age eight—and also in a self-portrait (268) at the age of ten. But Gabriel was also strongly influenced at this time by more popular modes of character depiction. He copied with amazing accuracy a series of caricatures by R. Crumb (which he wryly attributed to R. Crumble) (269), as well as a set of skillful adaptations of the work of *Mad Magazine* artist Don Martin (270). During this period Gabriel's own flair for producing grotesque forms emerged, as exemplified in the picture of a pathetic wall-eyed creature done at the age of eleven (271).

Because he has become fascinated by new media for expression—the playing of the violin, the making of films (he and his

265

AGE 10
self portrait

270

271

brother have made nearly a hundred home movies, ranging in
length from three minutes to a half hour), various kinds of sculpture, and the building of a moped bike—Gabriel has been unable to
concentrate fully on graphic artistry. Nonetheless, his ability to
capture likenesses continues to improve, and his skill in portraying
character and personality has deepened substantially. Moved by a
visit to an old-age home, he drew a set of elderly persons aligned
lugubriously in a row (272). A rabbi of his acquaintance posed for

272

a portrait, yielding another remarkably sensitive study (273). And
as a comparison with a similar work done at age ten (274) makes
clear, Gabriel has advanced significantly in his own self-portrai-
ture. He now has recourse to symbolism—via the cracked mirror—
and is able to convey a mood of deep seriousness and foreboding.

    This progress has occurred quickly and with relatively little
self-consciousness. Gabriel was already achieving quite effective
results at an age when other children are still struggling to transcend the most elementary schemas. His parents could show him
how to render desired effects, though that was not always necessary; for instance, by the end of the primary grades he had ferreted
out the principles of perspective on his own. Gabriel was also rewarded early in life for his drawing skills. Recognized by his peers
and teachers as a child with special drawing ability, he even had
the drawings he made in second grade featured in an art-education
textbook.

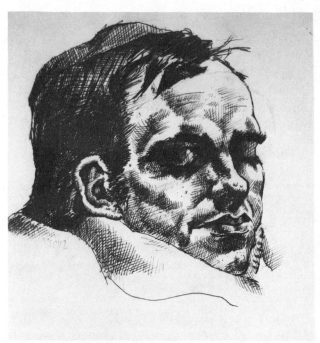

273

274

At age sixteen Gabriel has a full and reasonably valid view of himself, his abilities, his aspirations, his techniques, and his limitations. He feels he can handle most challenges of representational drawing. Having thousands of faces in his mind's eye and at his graphic fingertips, he can evoke them readily and fashion nearly any combination, inspired equally by what he sees and what he imagines. He enjoys the feel of a pencil in his hand, and he cultivates the habit of observing the reactions of an audience to what he does. He does not worry when he cannot achieve something graphically—indeed he welcomes this impasse, because he then has the opportunity to be inventive, to conjure up a solution, and ultimately to absorb it into his artistic armamentarium.

Gabriel is very ambitious. He wants to be successful and famous, though he does not yet know (and he does not seem to care) whether this acclaim will be achieved through commercial art, acting, directing films, illustrating books, or following his parents into "straight" artistry. With his engaging personality, he eagerly sells himself and exhibits a perhaps excessive curiosity about what steps he can take to gain recognition for himself and for his works. Yet he is not immersed in the "world of art," as he calls it, rarely visiting museums and holding little brief for contemporary abstract works. And like nearly all other youngsters his age, he seems leery of formal art lessons.

This suspicion of formal instruction is a curious phenomenon, one I've encountered in several preadolescents and adolescents. Ostensibly, these youngsters oppose being told what to do and would rather "feel out" their artistic destiny on their own. This view seems at least partially valid, particularly since much of their teaching has been of indifferent quality and may actually have discouraged rather than elightened them. Moreover, in the case of Gabriel, who has had considerable informal teaching at the skilled hands of his parents, the need for formal teaching is obviously attenuated.

Yet there may also be a less rational aspect to this attitude. Most talented youngsters have for several years been considered special—by their friends, their parents, their teachers. They possess a gift they want to protect. To be sure, they fear that this gift may be destroyed or damaged by formal instruction, but I think they fear, too, the loss of their special status. After all, in an art school they will be surrounded by many others as talented as they and so will no longer stand out. They will also discover many things they cannot do and things that may even pose formidable difficulties for them. Most threateningly, they may encounter others more gifted; they may even discover that they are not good enough to "make it." All of these prospects are disconcerting. And so, even though in

their own mind they may realize the need for—and even crave—
some tutelage, they are wary of the vulnerability that such an opportunity may expose.

The only time Gabriel is willing to concede weaknesses in his
own work is when he talks of his older brother D.L., now eighteen.
The siblings have a curious and special relationship. Each is extremely ambitious for himself in the arts but not, it would appear,
at the expense of the other. They have collaborated together not
only on films but even on drawings. They speak well of one another, and Gabriel envies D.L.'s ability at cartooning, his capacity

275

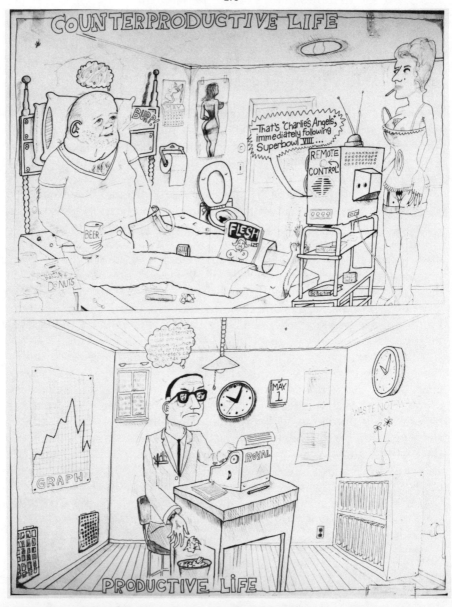

to capture a face in one line, and his verbal talent (he can
write stories and poems and has even composed a 10,000-word
palindrome!).

A comparison of the brothers is instructive. Both raised in the
same environment, they have both drawn skillfully from an early
age. Each has been potently influenced by the popular media, and
each can draw in the style of notable cartoonists and caricaturists.
Given his literary bent, D.L.'s picturing is less purely visual. Usually it has a theme and a title, and often it constitutes an effort to
vivify an abstract concept or an autobiographical motif. D.L. has
been criticized for leaving school at an early age, for being somewhat dour in temperament, and for not using his time wisely. Re-
sponding to these wounds through his talent, he has poked
somewhat bitter fun at these characterizations in his drawings of
Productivity and Happiness (275, 276). His striking mastery of a
cartoon form and content is exhibited in a sixty-frame cartoon
which is not only witty and pungent in itself but also doubles as a

277

278

statement on the nature and ultimate significance of the cartooning medium (in the last frame, the cartoon itself disintegrates) (277). D.L. is capable of faithful portraiture (278), but, even more so than Gabriel, he indulges a penchant for drawing the grotesque, the vulgar, and the ludicrous in somber browns, grays, and blues (279). His room is at last as idiosyncratic and bizarre as Gabriel's, though quite different and equally distinctly his own. Even in the way in which they live and rebel against the rules of society, the two boys exhibit a significant kinship.

In many ways the Foreman boys exemplify the traits I have encountered time and again in talented adolescent artists. They have for many years been working at their artistry, steadily and with little letup (though sometimes through different media). They are comfortable, and probably happiest, when at their easels or their desks. They compulsively collect objects and then create an environment out of these treasures. They crave access to the models of their culture, particularly the popular models, and they assiduously copy them and learn from them. They do not hesitate to express their feelings in their drawings, even (or perhaps especially) when these entail some obscenity or grotesqueness. And they hold little brief for "fine arts" museums, or the abstract art that has been so touted in our time.

But the Foreman brothers also diverge in several ways from

279

other gifted adolescent artists. Perhaps most importantly, they have had the opportunity—like young Mozarts or Picassos—to develop in a spontaneous way, secure in an environment where artistry was the most natural thing to do—indeed *the* thing that one did. In contrast, other promising young artists have had to contend with greater odds—not necessarily a hostile environment (though that sometimes exists) but often a noncomprehending environment, or an environment that signals its ambivalence about the value of sustained artistic activity.

Accordingly, the latter young artists are more likely to have been discovered by teachers who have told them that they are special and who have championed their causes and encouraged them to study art, to participate in contests, to pursue art lessons, to contemplate a life in art. To sustain these youngsters within a hostile, or at least noncomprehending, social context, there must be positive factors such as rewards in artistry, a feeling of enjoyment, and the rapid gaining of skills. And quite possibly some negative factors may also play a role. I have in mind the fact that many talented adolescent artists are individuals who prove ordinary in other areas of life—in personality, in scholastic matters, in athletics; it is in opposition to these traits, and by virtue of their extraordinary artistry, that they stand out.

For the Foreman youths the arts provide an avenue for expressing deep feelings, as well as a way of eventually earning a living, if not making a killing. I have found many adolescent artists who have an even greater emotional stake in their artwork, seeing it as a way of grappling with and coming to master their strongest feelings—for example, their religious convictions, their political ideas, their emerging ideological stands, their still germinating understanding of complex philosophical concepts. Here again the arts constitute a means whereby an individual can articulate to himself and others those feelings and concepts that are of great importance to him, and to which he cannot effectively gain access in any other way. In addition, in cases where young artists are confronting deep personal problems—family crises, delicate sexual decisions, conflicting pressures about school matters or career options—one often can see reverberations of these tensions throughout their artistic work.

For such youngsters, work in the arts acquires a special status. Whereas the Foremans are interested in publicizing and selling their art—they protested when I told them I preferred to protect their and their family's identity in this book—other adolescent artists prove to be more private, protective, ambivalent, even shameful. They have rejected offers, including sizable fees, for their artwork. They keep at least some of their work secret. And they are at best ambivalent about "cashing in" and exploiting what they have produced at considerably psychic cost to themselves.

In earlier times there existed established ways for entering into the fellowship, or the community, of artists. One enrolled at an atelier, assisted a master, passed through a prescribed series of steps, and eventually, if these were successfully negotiated, one became a full-fledged artist. Now the status of artist is far more ambiguous and fluid and there is no road map available for every would-be artist. This state of affairs is reflected in the range of attitudes among youthful artists—from the cocky confidence and occasional braggadocio one encounters in the Foreman children, to the excessive secretiveness and sensitivity that sometimes predominate in other adolescent artists. No doubt the decidedly mixed signals issued by our society toward those who would devote their lives to an artistic career help to fuel these flames of ambivalence.

Nonetheless, we stand in no danger of a society without artists. In Boston, a city of less than a million, with a metropolitan area of perhaps twice that figure, more than a thousand individuals belong to an artist's union and many times that number consider and call themselves artists. In nearly every school I have visited, some youngsters term themselves artists, and some (not always the same ones) are considered as future artists by their instructors.

Whether Gabriel and D.L. will eventually choose that calling and whether they will in turn be seen by their community as successful artists cannot be foretold. On the one hand, few youngsters in our society have had a better preparation. Nearly every relevant factor has been in their favor. They talk, they think, they act, they even look like artists. Their work is certainly comparable in quality to the best examples of other adolescents and is at times reminiscent of the efforts of individuals who in later years went on to become masters. Yet it takes more than opportunity and desire to become a successful artist—it involves tenacity, the willingness to overcome obstacles, the drive to succeed. More especially, it requires not only the ability to say something in one's own voice but the reality of having something to express—something, moreover, that will move the rest of the community. Hints of this capacity can already be discerned in some of the drawings collected in this book. Yet on these issues the fates have yet to display their full hand.

CHAPTER 9

Developments

WHETHER it be within the life of the individual, the group, or a whole culture, the realm of the arts is never completely static. Even as the scribbles of the child give rise to geometric forms, and eventually to realistic ones, so, too, the progression of art in every society evolves, if sometimes more slowly and uncertainly, over the centuries. It almost seems as if there are forces at work—perhaps Hegelian or Darwinian in spirit—which guide the course of artistic output and, by extension, the hands of the artists who produce it.

No one has put forth this thesis more boldly nor defended it with more vigor than Suzi Gablik, a contemporary painter and commentator on the art scene. Gablik's epiphanous insight came after she had read the writings of Jean Piaget and pondered the finding that every normal child passes through a number of qualitatively different mental stages: the *preoperational period*, where the child is incapable of following through a single, consistent line of thought; the *concrete operational stage*, where the child can reason systematically in terms of physical objects and relate them to one another; and the crowning *formal operational stage*, where the grown individual can execute a logical train of thought solely on the level of verbal propositions. Moreover, she learned from her studies that this general trajectory of mental development can be seen at work in specific domains—for instance, within the realm of spatial intelligence: the preschool child makes simple forms which have unregulated relationships to one another; the schoolchild can organize forms so that they roughly duplicate the physical arrangements in the world; and the preadolescent can master principles of perspective, rendering a scene as it appears to an individual situated at a specific location.

Gablik made the crucial leap of applying Piaget's analysis to the history of Western art; she concluded that, just as there is progress in the mind of the child, so, too, there is progress in the history of Western art. "The thesis I am putting forth for examination," she announced, "is that art has evolved through a sequence of cognitive stages and may be viewed as a series of transformations in modes of thinking; and I shall argue that the dynamics of stylistic change can be explained, at least in part, by patterns of cognitive growth . . . progress in art is not made, as was once thought, by the accumulation of knowledge within existing systems; it is made by leaps into new categories of systems."

Far from launching a simple analogy, in which certain broad parallels between "early child art" and "early Western art" are duly noted, Gablik has worked out her brief in detail. As she sees it, the work of artists until the Renaissance is best thought of as preoperational. Artists did not—because they lacked the necessary conceptual apparatus—present scenes that were organized in a systematic and coherent way. Like the youngsters asked by Piaget to draw objects placed in front of them, these early artists simply laid out the objects in a rough-and-ready fashion, thus making it impossible for the viewer to know "just how things actually look."

The great breakthrough by Leonardo and other artists during the Renaissance was the discovery and perfection of the principles of perspective. Once artists could draw from a particular point of view and apply geometric principles throughout the execution of their works, they had collectively advanced a full Piagetian stage. Such artists, in Gablik's view, had now achieved concrete operations in their work. They were able to capture their knowledge of the world in the particulars of a given drawing: like the realist child we have described, they could portray the world as it looked. But they were still tied to representational art and to the particular static view of a single observer.

The gift of formal operations enables an individual to deal with all logical possibilities. Given any set of tools and any set of premises, one can work through all logical conclusions and implications. Cubism served as a harbinger of this capacity, for the Cubist artist was no longer restricted to a single point of view; rather he attempted in his works to offer the range of views of an object. Yet even he remained tied to the concrete or immediate physical reality. It is the conceptual artist—for instance, one who devises algorithms or computer programs as a means of exploring all possible permutations and combinations—who has unambiguously achieved formal operational thought. Indeed the work itself is almost an afterthought; the crucial mental exercise involves figuring out the full range of possibilities governing any given form—be it a square, a series of dots, or a set of converging lines—and then presenting this essentially mathematical conclusion within the garb of a particular work of art. In contemporary art "systems are carried out by formal deduction, independent of their application to concrete perceptual objects and they are expressed in propositional language . . . the modern paradigm is characterized by its openness and by the infinite number of possibilities and positions which can be taken." While seemingly simpler than Renaissance painting, contemporary art is really more complex; for where perspective was a single, simple, closed logical system, the modern paradigm is open and can take an infinite number of possibilities into account.

The radical thrust of Gablik's thesis should be evident. With a single phrase she sweeps aside all of the works of art before the twentieth century as reflections of a mentality no more advanced than that of the average eleven-year-old today. While making no claims to judge aesthetic merit, she is clearly evaluating the minds behind these works of art: and in terms of her criteria of Piagetian conceptualization, such masters as Rembrandt and Leonardo, not to mention Cimabue or Giotto, are relegated to a primitive stage of mentation in their creations. In her view, the art of contemporary painters "comes from a differently-directed mentality and from a different mode of thinking."

Whatever the ultimate merit of Gablik's bold thesis, it clearly represents an effort to take developmental principles seriously and to apply them in opulent fashion to the history of art. In brief, she is rehearsing one of the favorite saws of the nineteenth century: that ontogeny (in the instance of the child's own drawing) is recapitulating phylogeny in the cultural realm (namely, the history of the evolution of Western art). Hers is not, however, the only effort to universalize principles of development. Quite another, and equally bold, point of view has been put forth by the art historian and psychologist Henry Schaefer-Simmern.

Schaefer-Simmern's point of departure, like Gablik's, is the natural course of drawing in the child. This authority argues that, left untrammeled by the forces of society, each child will pass through a preordained evolution in his drawing. Moreover, Schaefer-Simmern attributes little of this development to reasoning or to cultural factors. In his view, it is largely a consequence of perceptual growth, a progression that will necessarily come to pass if the child is simply given the opportunity to draw, and thence to examine the results of his graphic explorations. As Schaefer-Simmern puts it, "the visual configuration may be considered the result of an autonomous mental activity, a mental digestion and transformation of sensory experience into a newly created visual entity. It should be emphasized . . . that this activity is independent of conceptual intellectual calculation and that it takes place solely within the realm of visual experience."

So far so good, and in itself not notably controversial. We have already encountered a number of authorities—such as Rhoda Kellogg and Rudolf Arnheim—who concur that the young child is simply following his own genius in realizing stages of development. But Schaefer-Simmern is in fact defending a much broader and much bolder thesis, one of Rousseauian proportions. He feels that the course of development in drawing is so compelling and so inevitable that it will—it *must*—come to pass whenever any human being undertakes a series of drawings. In other words, these stages are not directly dependent on the age of the individual, his mental status, his motivation, the attitude of the community, or any critical period of growth: they are essentially the consequences of any sustained attempt to draw. And Schaefer-Simmern searches for support of this theory by enlisting naïve individuals of all ages and backgrounds—ranging from normal housewives to psychotic individuals and elderly businessmen—and simply asking them to draw.

Just what is this progression of stages like? All individuals begin with simple outlined figures, such as circles and rectangles, which emerge as figures against grounds. Then they shift to figures whose structures are ordered in terms of maximum contrast (280) —that is, all parts in these figures are laid out so as to highlight the distinction between horizontal and vertical planes: every part of the figures must be maximally discriminable from every other. The

280

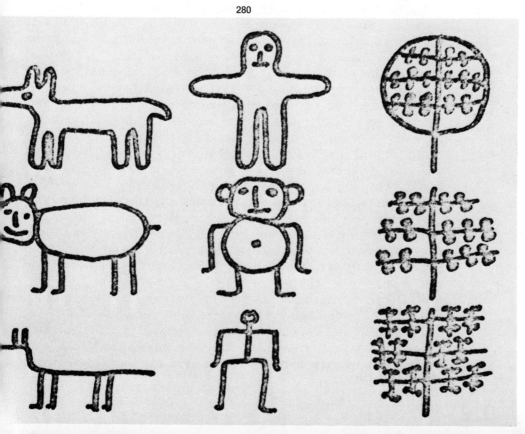

most stringent Gestalt principles are at work at this point: if any changes are made in a balanced form, supplementary changes must be made to compensate.

Up to this point in development, the drawing arrays are static, and these schematic figures can stand for any member of their respective class. But a stage of variability then ensues. Now objects become differentiated into parts: for example, a schematic tree comes to bear a number of smaller branches, which are attached to one another at similar angles. The figure also becomes more vital. Note, however, that this is no mere imitation of nature; rather, this greater vitality is a result of forms featuring greater differentiation and more varied configurations.

Subsequent stages can also be specified. Eventually the individual becomes able to organize a larger picture format, displaying more comprehensive and intricate balance. Eventually, too, he masters more specific features of representation, such as the use of shading and lighting and of colors; and instead of continuing to separate figures maximally from one another, he learns to let them blend smoothly, or revealingly, into one another. These late changes, however, are more likely to emerge at the behest of formal tutoring than on their own. Hence they may not qualify as instances of genuine artistic unfolding.

In his own way, Schaefer-Simmern has developed a thesis as far-reaching, overarching, and problematic as Gablik's. Where Gablik sees a parallel between what normal children do and the periods of "childhood" in our culture, Schaefer-Simmern sees the actual structure of the drawing medium as a key determinant of all artistic growth. It matters not a whit whether one begins to draw at age two or at age twenty-two; whether one is ignorant of the word *perspective* or a master of geometry; whether one exhibits a strong emotional temperament or an exceedingly rational outlook. Given that one has the opportunity to draw and is not artificially pushed into one or another direction or camp, each person's sequence of drawings will look remarkably similar. Schaefer-Simmern goes on to suggest that this sequence can be found as well in the history of art the world over; his major published work is replete with examples of Indian miniature paintings, Chinese works of the Sung period, Flemish tapestry of the Renaissance, and Grecian heads from the sixth century B.C.—each exemplifying one or another of the stages of artistic unfolding. Once again, a developmental progression has been universalized in such a manner as to account for every conceivable (or, better, every perceivable) drawing.

Even as we are impressed by the sweep and grandeur of such pronouncements, and even if we, too, see some of the parallels so artfully drawn by these synthesizers, most of us (particularly those of an Anglo-American temperament) are made uncomfortable by such theories. They are too grand and at the same time too pat. They smack of the kinds of "closed systems" Karl Popper has so vociferously criticized, those attempts to occlude the open sweep of history and undermine the possibility of new discoveries in favor of a ponderous Hegelian spirit, an unseen hand that controls history, what others have done, what we have done, and what we will do. One wonders—sometimes with justification—about the choice of examples. Could another set of examples have supported another view—say, the position that the history of drawing exemplified the stages of Sigmund Freud? Could yet another set have contradicted the stages of Piaget—say, by showing that modern art is influenced by topological arrangements, those forms of geometric reasoning which happen to emerge *first* in the Piagetian orthodoxy? And one has the suspicion—perhaps also with justification—that the authors were initially armed with their theories (Gablik could have taken hers from the art historian Alois Riegl, and Schaefer-Simmern his from his teacher Gustaf Britsch) and then simply searched for corroborating evidence. And to pose the most painful, if most telling, scientific question of all, one wonders what kind of evidence would refute these positions and, if confronted with apparent disproof, whether their proponents would nonetheless continue to embrace them out of misplaced ideological fervor.

Such principled objections can be compounded by further disturbing questions. Does Gablik really wish to go on record as saying that the greatest of premodern artists proceeded in a way fundamentally different from our contemporaries? Does it really matter that Leonardo tried out hundreds of alternatives in his sketchbook, while the contemporary artist Don Judd computes them on a pocket calculator? Does this difference in method touch the heartland of art? Does Schaefer-Simmern want to ignore the vast individual differences between a normal child and a psychotic adult and claim that the same processes, as well as the same behavior, necessarily characterize both individuals? Does he wish, too, to overlook the massive differences in time frames—the fact that what develops over many years in the drawing of a child may be realized by a bright young adult in a matter of weeks or even days? Does he want to withhold from such savvy adults any tricks of the trade, special strategies, superior understanding of principles of light, shading, and perspective, and instead assume that they are constrained to construct these forms of knowledge for themselves in the same painstaking and boot-strap manner as the young child? Would he reject the evidence from other cultures which suggests that older children who have never before drawn fail to exhibit the usual sequence of works? And to tar him with the brush that we have applied to Gablik, does he really feel that resemblances in surface features of works of art produced in millennia past in entirely different cultural settings must necessarily reflect the same factors as those produced today by the students in his own classes? Is it not equally parsimonious to assume that apparent similarities may reflect the fact that *any* set of works must have certain properties in common, rather than to assert a "preset harmony" between the hands, eyes, and minds of artists everywhere?

If so disposed, one clearly can expose limitations in these universalists. Such ambitious formulas should at least be greeted with honest skepticism. But after all, there is little to be gained by simply disproving these positions through the scoring of debating points. There are indeed some beguiling, even insistent connections and reverberations among the stages, sequences, and processes that I have described in this book—and which many others have also described—and the events and processes one observes in other realms of graphic art. Is it not more important to view these theories with some sympathy, to see what validity they might possess, as well as to determine where they may have overstepped their authority or evidence, than to dismiss them summarily and thereby to ignore those insistent parallels between individual and group, child and adult, ontogeny and phylogeny which have struck more than a few unjaundiced eyes?

My own view is that our "universalists" are on to something, but it is not necessarily what they would most wish to acknowledge. They have encountered the phenomena of development—which are real, and genuine, and important—but they have tried to apply them to the arts in too broad and uncritical a fashion. Children pass through stages of development, as do normal adults, skilled artists, and perhaps even whole cultures. Each stage has a structure to it, one that can be set out in formal terms; and every stage has built into it certain opportunities as well as certain limitations. The task of the developmentalist is to discover the particular stage of the individual, group, or culture, to unravel and describe its form, and then to consider the options available at this point of growth. It is not part of this task, however, to invoke a Procrustean schema that preordains the nature of the following stages.

Let me be more concrete. We have seen repeatedly in this book how the drawing of a child at every point serves certain purposes and reflects specifiable cognitive and motor forces. Moreover, we have noted how future events, immanent at that stage, are likely to unfold in the light of further environmental, peer, or personal stimulation, even as certain other options are most unlikely to emerge at this time.

Assume, then, that a similar state of affairs obtains when one casts an eye at other developing systems. Within any culture the artwork will come to exhibit certain features and not others. Most individuals working within that setting will, consciously or not, epitomize the features of that epoch and that milieu. A few—the most advanced, or precocious, or troubled—will come to see the world with an innocent eye, to think of the medium in somewhat different ways, and hence to effect breakthroughs to fresh views, unanticipated graphic ploys, and even new stages.

As a well-documented instance of this phenomenon, consider the state of Western art in the middle of the nineteeth century. Representational art had reached a zenith of faithful realism. Little could be done to enhance further the literal fidelity of works of art. A decisive blow was supplied by the invention of the camera, a machine that produced effects which certainly could not be surpassed by any mortal. The strain on the current "state of art" was hence extreme. From a developmental perspective, a qualitative change in the works of arts was clearly imminent. Yet it seems equally clear that the exact form of the change could not be predicted. Whether Impressionism, or Cubism, or abstract expressionism would come to the fore was, at least in some respects, a matter of historical accident. In retrospect one can of course rationalize the particular sequence that happened to occur, but there seems to be little in either individual or cultural make-up that would make possible a prediction of *the* form of the next artistic stage. At best, one can only indicate which possibilities are more likely and which less likely to ensue.

Or consider as another possibility the turn of events that occurs when one culture, with an entrenched artistic form, abuts another embracing a radically different set of standards. The clash of contemporary Western art with the artwork of tribal African society is one such example. Quite clearly, the works of our own masters have often incorporated features of the sculpture and personal decorations used in African societies. By the same token, syncretic versions of art in these cultures have often exploited both technical equipment and thematic preferences of Western art. Again, some stage sequence seems inevitable, but the exact form, nature, and extent of that evolution cannot be foretold in the given instance.

One does not need to invoke an invisible spirit to account for changes in the drawings of individuals or societies. Drawings can be characterized as reflecting a certain level of sophistication, and this level in turn entails within it certain concerns and options rather than others. It is to Gablik's and Schaefer-Simmern's considerable credit that they realize this possiblity, less estimable that they have been blind to the open-ended (and often unpredictable) nature of this process. For their blindness has prevented them from providing information on the questions that lurk most tellingly in any inquiry of this type: *where* do the creative breakthroughs take place, and *what* is the source of that work of art which truly opens up new vistas—in other words, how do novelty and individual achievement emerge against the background of universal patterns of drawing?

Here, I think, we must confront human development in its deepest and, let us admit, its most myserious and forbidding guise. No creation, no novelty ever arises *ab ovo*—any act of imagination must always reflect processes of development which have unfolded over a lengthy period of time. At the same time, however, there must be some thing—and perhaps many things—in the developmental trajectories of certain individuals working at certain periods of time under certain conditions which gives rise to extraordinary achievements and thereby undermines any glib universalist account of human creative activity.

In my own view, in any effort to locate the seeds of innovative creation we cannot do better than to begin by revisiting the earliest moments of development. For one thing, it is the youngest child who proceeds most identifiably on the basis of his own inherent tendencies and who is least influenced (and hence least molded) by his surrounding culture. Short of the obvious equipping of the child with tools and the general encouragement necessary to foster any youthful activity, we encounter in the area of drawing a period of several years in which processes unfold essentially at their own pace and in their own way. We have seen that the general results of this early exploration are quite similar across populations. What is less widely appreciated is that the child during this period is developing many of the behaviors—the endless repetition, the exploration of schemes, the experimentation with various shapes, the production of forms that produce pleasure in him and in others—which constitute the raw material on which any artistic achievement of later times must be based. During this early period there is a genuine, crucial motor to development—a mechanism of growth and timing which leads the child at his own pace through the early stages. Indeed, as the architect Christopher Alexander has suggested, the very tendencies toward repetition, random variation, and the leveling and sharpening of forms in the course of such variation, suffice to account in large measure for the developmental stages discernible in the production of every child. Balanced forms will inevitably emerge, they will appeal to the child, "and the process in which forms are distinguished from one another as strongly and powerfully as possible is . . . precisely the center of what we mean by the creative power to make order. . . . The source of creative talent can be fully understood in terms of the child's developing ability to force the forms apart from one another."

An equally important ingredient of ultimate artistic attainment crystallizes during the years from five to seven when the child is able for the first time to produce works that in themselves exhibit internal organization and coherence. I have questioned whether the child is fully aware of what he is doing, whether he can be considered in control of this production. Yet even if this tendency to produce a balanced and composed work is in part the result of unconscious processes, ones only partially visible to the child, or of a failed attempt to produce a perfectly symmetrical work, its significance cannot be overemphasized. For even as the scribbling and exploring of earliest life serve as models for the experimentation that is the lifeblood of mature artistry, so too the vision of a balanced graphic symbol constitutes an unequivocally central aspect of any aesthetic achievement.

It may be useful in this connection to recall the notion of a U-shaped curve in development—the view that some important aspects of artistry emerge early in the life of the child, only to "go underground" during a period of middle childhood. Certainly the burden of the evidence that we have reviewed concerning drawing in middle childhood indicates that some of the magical aspects of early drawing—the free exploration, the sense of form unwedded to specific content, the willingness to flaunt conventional practices—disappear from the works of most children. Indeed it seems permissible to say that, even as every toddler displays linguistic genius, every youngster is touched by the spark of creativity in the graphic arts. Still it is during the period of middle childhood that decisions are made, by the individual and by the culture, about which youngsters are likely to go on to produce works of originality and merit.

Be assured, the period of middle childhood is scarcely a time of stagnation in the arts. Or, more accurately, it need not be such. It is then that the child develops particular technical skills; it is then that he is suceptible to (and eager for) training; it is then that he becomes able to plan his work with some thoroughness and accuracy; it is then that he can intentionally place in his own work those features of the aesthetic that figure crucially in later production—such as telltale details, subtle variation of color, and expressiveness of line. And perhaps most crucially, it is at this time that the child undertakes to solve problems within the graphic realm—problems of a visual-spatial nature (such as rendering accurate perspective) and problems too of a personal or emotional nature (such as sorting out his feelings about an individual, a situation, or an ideology).

Some of these aspects are rightly considered technical. Not that this fact makes them in any sense unimportant: indeed, as the masters of Renaissance ateliers well knew, they form the necessary proscenium on which eventually artistic mastery must be performed. Indeed such acknowledged masters as Picasso and Klee passed through such a literal stage with a special vengeance. Yet we could perhaps say that at least some skills involve the harnessing of *computational capacities* within the sphere of normal children. In other words, given enough training and attention, most children can learn to effect a realistic rendering, to master perspective, to plan their drawings, even to include within them more than a modicum of expressiveness and repleteness. And some blessed children may be able to attain these skills rapidly and on their own.

The development of drawing may involve a critical period. Not, to be sure, in the sense that drawing is impossible if one fails to reach certain milestones before puberty. But perhaps in the sense that eventual achievement becomes extremely unlikely if the child does not, by the onset of puberty, already possess some mastery of these mechanical or computational aspects. For the truth is, at least within our society, that unless one's own drawings can be viewed by oneself, and by others, as reasonably competent, they are likely to be found distressingly wanting; the youth in turn is likely to cease graphic artistry altogether and to resort to other, less challenging means of communication. If this notion has some validity, it would certainly call into question the claim by Schaefer-Simmern that the development of artistry is the same everywhere, every time.

From one point of view, the foregoing description does not seem controversial. We have rehearsed how drawing develops in normal children—the needs and forces reflected at each stage of development. I dare add that this view makes sense in the light of our current understanding of human nature. But consider the implications of this account for the claim that certain principles of development obtain across all populations, over all eras of history, and all varieties of pathology. If, in fact, the normal development of artistry directly reflects the conditions that operate upon the child, then claims about parallels in the drawings of others would imply that the race, or the group, or all of history may possess deep parallels to the individual child. This claim is so far from having any basis in fact, or intuition, as to make any entertainment of it mere wishful thinking.

I conclude, therefore, that there may well be some similarities in process, and perhaps in outlook, in the various populations studied by Gablik and, in a more empirical manner, by Schaefer-Simmern, but that any attempt to relate the behaviors of these diverse populations to children's normal development, and to imply that they are basically the same, involves a sleight of hand, if not a begging of the principle. Put simply, it is too much to assume that surface similarities invariably reflect underlying homologies in process. Far better to say instead that there are *some* surface and *some* underlying similarities in the drawing processes of diverse groups, but that the case for deeper similarities remains to be proved. Moreover, it is quite likely that the meaning of works differs profoundly among the various individuals and groups, and this too calls into question the universalist view. If the perspective introduced in these pages—the development of drawing as deeply tied to the development of the child—has validity, then these broad individual and cultural parallels are likely to be wrong.

In properly calling attention to the dangers of drawing parallels, I have myself approached a dangerous precipice. I have come close to arguing that the early freedom and exploration of the child resembles that of the adult artist. And I have implied that only those individuals who survive the perils of the latency period retain the potential to become genuinely creative artists. It is now time to step beyond this argument by analogy and to consider directly some activity that is indubitably creative—at the highest levels.

Few works of art in history have immediately commanded such attention or have so strongly captured the imagination of both expert and lay public as Picasso's mural *Guernica*, the artist's vision of the devastation by Fascist pilots of a small town during the Spanish Civil War (281). The innovation and grandeur of this work are rarely disputed, and its claim as an act of inspired crea-

281   Pablo Picasso. *Guernica*. 1937, May–early June. Oil on canvas. 11'51½" x 25'5¾". On extended loan to The Museum of Modern Art, New York, from the artist's estate.

tion by the most remarkable artist of the century is secure. If we
are to draw parallels between the life and mind of the child and the
work of the artistic imagination, *Guernica* provides a formidable
challenge as well as a unique opportunity.

Two years before painting *Guernica*, Picasso commented, "It
would be very interesting to preserve photographically, not the
stages, but the metamorphoses of a picture. Possibly one might
discover the path followed by the brain in materializing a dream.
But there is one very odd thing—to notice that basically a picture
doesn't change, that the first vision remains almost intact, in spite
of appearances." Whether Picasso bore this phrase in mind is not
known, but he did in fact save scores of sketches made in preparation for *Guernica*, often with the date and order of the sketch noted
directly on the paper. Rudolf Arnheim has written a masterly book
on *Guernica*, in which he presents many of these sketches and
offers a coherent and convincing account of how Picasso proceeded
from opening sketch to the final product.

This is one of those times—not infrequent—in the writing of a
book when one wishes that one could insert a gigantic parenthesis
and invite a lengthy pause. One would like to allow an evening or
two in which the reader could consult the Arnheim book and the
Picasso sketches and thereby consider the evidence germane to the
argument proposed here. Such an intermission is not readily
granted, however. And so, with the hope that readers will accept
my summary and return later to the evidence itself, I offer a few
comments on the genesis of Picasso's remarkable work.

Picasso's own performance bears out the thrust of the statement quoted above. As Arnheim describes it, "Picasso's first sketch
for *Guernica* contains much of the final basic form; the small drawing on a piece of blue paper certainly comes closer to the composition of the mural than anything else the painter put down before he
started on the actual canvas." This statement is particularly astonishing in view of the originality and vigor of the ultimate work.
That Picasso could in a few casual, seemingly unelaborated outlines foreshadow the general structure or format of the work—
whether or not he even knew that he did—is little short of
miraculous.

Much of the final work is indeed immanent in the first sketches
(282). Yet the ensuing efforts were scarcely idle exploration or simple working out of details. Rather, in a manner reminiscent of those
treasure-troves of creative efflorescence—Dostoevsky's notebooks
and Beethoven's sketchbooks—Picasso attempts dozens of variations of the major themes and forms in the work. He concentrates
his energy first on one figure, then on another, in each case trying
out various options of size, scale, relationship, emotional tone, and

the like, before settling, at least tentatively, on one that satisfies him. He changes the media with which he works, the size of the paper, the arrangement among principal elements, and even, on numerous occasions, the identity of the actual elements. Sometimes his work seems highly directed, as he systematically varies the angle of a figure; at other times it is much more accidental, as when the absence of room on the side of a paper causes him to produce a particular shape of a leg, one that in fact finds its place in the final drawing (283).

282   Pablo Picasso. Composition study for *Guernica*. 1 May 1937. Pencil on gesso, on wood, 21⅛″ x 25½″. On extended loan to The Museum of Modern Art, New York, from the artist's estate.

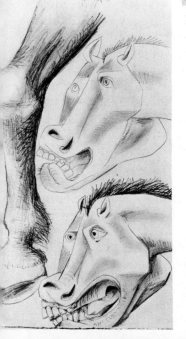

283   Pablo Picasso. *Studies for Horse.* Composition study for *Guernica*. 10 May 1937. Pencil on white paper, 9½″ x 17⅞″. On extended loan to The Museum of Modern Art, New York, from the artist's estate

But even these remarks overstress the rationality and order in Picasso's procedure. There is order, to be sure, but much of it lurks under the surface. Picasso is incessantly exploring in the drawings —with a sense of these explorations being necessary, timely, and helpful but without any apparent definitive sense of just how they will work out. The many sketches and (in Picasso's view) even the final mural are all experiments, part of the science of painting. If these explorations had taken an alternate course— other papers, other accidents, other casual thoughts, other emotional experiences—the final drawing would have turned out differently—perhaps worse, perhaps even more effective, but in any case different.

It is in the process that Picasso (and presumably other creative spirits of the highest order) exemplifies that one encounters undeniable parallels with the work of the child. Here is visual problem-solving—how, for example, to handle a stray arm or to place the tail of a bull—the sort of problem the grade-school child repeatedly engages in. There is the exploitation of accident, which, again, happens routinely in the drawings of the young child. There is much playful experimentation—of the sort that characterizes the scribbles of the toddler as well as the doodles of the adolescent. As Arnheim expresses it, "Pictorial playfulness has always been an important helper of artistic exploration . . . Pictorial playfulness manifests the delight in the variety of visual shape, the elementary affection that every artist has for his medium . . . whether it be rhyming of words or improvising on the piano. Herein lies the oft-noted but nonetheless deep affinity between the exploration of the young child and the experimentation of the artist's conscious and unconscious faculties." Or, as the contemporary artist Saul Steinberg has succinctly put it, "I am among the few who continue to draw after childhood is ended, continuing and perfecting children's drawing . . . The continuous line of my drawing dates from childhood and is probably a way of writing from my illiterate days."

But such similarities in process take place in the midst of profound differences in ability, in training, in outlook. Picasso, after all, was a painting genius from early childhood, able before puberty to so surpass his father that the elder painter laid down his brush forever. Indeed, by the conclusion of the critical period before artistry, he had already attained a master status. He received incomparable training, both at the hands of other masters and by virtue of his own sure eye, memory, and hand. When he painted *Guernica* in 1937 he was nearing the age of sixty, an individual who had created many thousands of masterful works and was possessed of a treasure chest from which he could draw with seeming effortlessness in the service of a new and crucially important commission. And motivationally and emotionally he was deeply involved, a Spaniard contemplating his beloved country on the edge of ruin. Finally, he had evolved a sure sense of form and composition which enabled him, once the opening vision had been expressed, to hold its latent relations in preconscious suspension while working out each of the component parts, and then finally to orchestrate them once more in one of the most complex arrangements ever realized by a visual artist. Comments Arnheim: "The artist is constantly faced with the problem of how to develop the part in terms of the whole . . . The artist works out partial entities, acting upon each other dialectically. An interplay of interferences, modifications, restrictions, and compensations leads gradually to the unity of and complexity of the total composition . . . every addition, refinement or new connection puts a strain on the unity of the work and must be met by a pulling together of the elements, a tightening of the economy. The total result, obtained through successive operations, presents itself as a marvel of organized complexity." Even if we are right in saying that the five-year-old already possesses a basic sense of organization, certainly the gap between the two achievements is more striking than any formal similarity that can be detected.

It would be misleading at best, and more likely the height of irresponsibility, to suggest that any single feature or indeed any group of features can account for the emergence of a Picasso from the ranks of average children, or even from that group of talented young artists who have somehow negotiated the obstacles of pre-adolescence and have embarked on promising careers in the arts. Talent may prove susceptible of generalization, but genius and great creativity elude formula. Moreover, when one attempts to assemble a list of the relevant factors—heredity, opportunity, early training, tremendous energy, social climate, compulsiveness, identification—it smacks of triteness, of Hollywood movies equally germane (and equally uninformative) about achievement in every creative domain. It is as wise to say that every genius differs from others and therein lies his genius, as to introduce the reverse claim that there exists an equation, at least some of whose variables are know, which, if filled in with proper values and provided with the appropriate catalysts, should yield creative works and creating geniuses.

Nonetheless, in contemplating the many features of Picasso which make him (and his work) so different from other artists, we can perhaps gain some final purchase on the major question that has guided this inquiry: the relation between the art of the child and the greatest works of art from adult hands. Certainly we see at work in Picasso a host of factors that separate him from the child: his perfected technical facility, his ability to render almost instantly the exact image he desires, the capacity to plan ahead for long periods of time and to follow through a project over a great period of time. There is also an incomparable store of knowledge of what other artists have done and how they have done it, as well as an intense awareness of the norms and practices that have guided his and other eras. When an artist of Picasso's caliber violates some sort of norm or practice, he is totally aware of this violation and of its consequences. In these as well as other respects, the mature artist stands apart from the young child.

Yet at the same time Picasso also reminds us of the many genuine bonds that link the average, not to say the gifted, child with the heart of artistry. There is the great pleasure, the compulsive satisfaction obtained from a constant involvement in the process of drawing. There is the willingness to disregard what others are doing, to flout convention, and to pursue one's own ideas and goals, however formulated, to their graphic conclusions. There is an intuitive sense of form or balance which almost never fails. At a more profound level, a heightened affective dimension exercises both groups of artists. Even as the young child gains intense affective satisfaction from his involvement in the arts, he also is aided in confronting critical emotional issues—insistent feelings, fears, anxieties, and wishes, which are nowhere so clearly addressed and articulated as in the drawings. Are we not seeing much the same processes at work as Picasso turns to his cherished medium in an effort to make his own feelings—their form no less than their content—clear to himself and to others?

We can in fact propose that creative works are the means, the artist's necessary means, of expressing his being and those feelings that are often inarticulate and inexpressible in other media. He feels constrained to make these thoughts public and to embrace a given medium as the best and possibly the only way of voicing what he feels he must. And it is here that we encounter a direct and genuine link to the young child, for he too, still inarticulate but already harboring many important if ineffable feelings, resorts spontaneously and with deeply felt need to the media at his disposal—most often and most significantly, to drawing.

Having for so many pages "tilted" toward the cognitive dimension of artist, I must now acknowledge that affective matrix of the arts which so powerfully engages both the young child and the gifted master. A grown individual has evolved in a way the child cannot have: he has undergone experiences, crises, and satisfactions which the younger individual cannot even fathom. Hence his drawings can reflect a depth of emotional life and a sense of a person behind that life that remain impossible for even the most precocious child, even that child with full-blown graphic computational skills. We can be delighted, charmed, even thrilled by the drawings of young children, but it is difficult to fathom how we can be deeply moved or profoundly awakened by a work of art from an individual yet to enter his adult years. And, as the writings of Otto Rank remind us, it is that individual with the most developed feeling for life and the richest personality who is most likely to attain the status of artist, most likely to produce works that will speak with significance to a larger community.

A voice that cries to be heard, a measure of technical accomplishment, a developed personality—all these are prerequisites, but none can replace the most central aspect of any artistry—that sense of form within which the feelings and the technical expertise must be wrapped. The greatest works in any medium—by Shakespeare or Milton, by Beethoven or Stravinsky, by Rembrandt or Picasso— are distinguished most remarkably by their sense of organization, that organic sense of form or composition in which the parts truly resonate with and enhance one another. Orchestration, planning, guile, treachery, intelligence, wit, genius—all contribute to this form, and the paradox is that the greater and more formidable the achievement, the more natural and inevitable seems the form when it has finally materialized.

Artists continue to grow and to develop longer than nearly any other group of individuals—like judges and philosophers, their visions usually serve them well until the ends of their lives. The more they work with and explore the medium, the more they intuitively know its possibilities and the more readily and tacitly they can integrate themes and elements which, even in a first sketch, resonate with one another. Just because this sense of organization and form takes so many years to achieve its full fruition, it is inherently a developmental phenomenon and one that cannot be sped up or imposed from without. Indeed, it takes a lifetime to develop. That is why, in the deepest sense, attempts to tease out analogies between the developmental sequences in the child and those characterizing other individuals or supra-individual entities may seem forced. And yet, despite the many intervening years, the analogies between the art of the child and the art of the master seem worth cherishing. For it is in the activity of the young child—his preconscious sense of form, his willingness to explore and to solve problems that arise, his capacity to take risks, his affective needs which must be worked out in a symbolic realm—that we find the crucial seeds of the greatest artistic achievements.

NOTES

PAGE

7–8   Töpffer and Baudelaire are quoted in Meyer Schapiro's essay, "Courbet and popular imagery," reprinted in *Modern Art* (New York: Braziller, 1978), pp. 61–63.

7–9   On the history of interest in children's artworks, see (inter alia) H. Read, *Education through art* (New York: Pantheon, n.d.); L. Chapman, *Approaches to art in education* (New York: Harcourt, Brace, 1978); and L. Chapman, *Children's development in art: A survey* (unpublished manuscript, Cincinnati, Ohio, 1977).

8   Picasso's remark is quoted in F. de Meredieu, *Le dessin d'enfant* (Paris: Editions universitaires Jean-Pierre de Large, 1974), p. 13.

8   Malraux's comments are from *The voices of silence* (Garden City: Doubleday, 1953), pp. 280, 285, 286, and 287.

8   Nancy Smith's comment appears in a paper, "Creativity and aesthetics in the paintings of children and artists," in C. S. Winsor (ed.), *The creative process* (New York: Bank Street College of Education, 1976), p. 44.

8   Montessori's remark is quoted in H. Read, *Education through art* (New York: Pantheon, n.d.), p. 114.

8   Klee's remarks are found in O. K. Werckmeister, *The issue of childhood in the art of Paul Klee*, p. 146.

10   The work of Caroto and the child's slate were brought to my attention in a discussion which appears in B. Lark-Horovitz, H. Lewis, and M. Luca, *Understanding children's art for better teaching*, Second Edition (Columbus, Ohio: Charles F. Merrill, 1973), p. 4.

10   On the general attitude toward children in premodern times, see P. Aries, *Centuries of childhood* (London: Jonathan Cape, 1962).

10   Among the early students of children's drawings were G. Kerchensteiner (1905), C. Ricci (1887), G. Luquet (1913), and F. Cisek (1912).

12   As an example of a completely neutral description of children's drawings, see A. Gesell, *The first five years of life* (New York: Harper & Row, 1940). A strongly affective view is voiced in R. Alschuler and L. Hattwick, *Painting and personality: A study of young children*, revised edition (Chicago: University of Chicago Press, 1969). An analogously cognitive viewpoint appears in the writings of G. Luquet, *Les dessin enfantin* (Paris: Alcan, 1927).

13   The first quotation ("Children's drawing.") comes from J. Goodnow, *Children drawing* (Cambridge: Harvard University Press, 1977). The second quotation ("The child without access . . .") comes from Jean Houston, reported in R. Williams, "Why children should draw," *Saturday Review*, 3 September, 1977, p. 14.

15   On figurative language, see H. Gardner, E. Winner, R. Bechhofer, and D. Wolf, "The development of figurative language," in K. Nelson (ed.), *Children's language* (New York: Gardner Press, 1978), vol. I.

20   On the behavioral repertoire of the human infant, see H. Gardner, *Developmental psychology* (Boston: Little, Brown, 1978), chap. 3.

25   On microgenetic studies, see H. Werner, *Comparative psychology of mental development* (New York: Science Books, 1961).

32   Anthony Weir's monologue appears in R. Weir, *Language in the crib.* (The Hague: Mouton, 1962), pp. 138–39).

40   The dreams of Jung's patient are described in *Psychology and religion* (New Haven: Yale University Press, 1960), pp. 70 and 89. Jung's comments appear on pp. 81, 87–88, and 96.

41   Kellogg's description of children's drawing appears in *Analyzing children's art* (Palo Alto, Calif.: National Press Books, 1969).

43   On the importance of opposites in the child's earliest cognitive activities, see R. Jakobson, *Child language, aphasia, and phonological universals* (The Hague: Mouton, 1968).

PAGE

47   On patterners and dramatists, see D. Wolf and H. Gardner, "Style and
          sequence in symbolic play," in N. Smith and M. Franklin (eds.), *Symbolic
          functioning in childhood* (Hillsdale, N. J.: Erlbaum Press, 1979).

51   Moja's drawings are described in R. A. Gardner and B. T. Gardner, "Com-
          parative psychology and language acquisition," in K. Salzinger and
          F. Denmark (eds.), *Psychology the state of the art*, p. 50.

51   Desmond Morris's remarks appear in *The biology of art* (Chicago: Aldine-
          Atherton, 1967).

55   Lewis's work is described in M. Lewis and L. Rosenblum (eds.), *The ori-
          gins of fear* (New York: Wiley, 1975).

55   On the emergence of symbolic competence, see H. Werner and B. Kaplan
          (eds.), *Symbol formation* (New York: Wiley, 1967); and D. Wolf (ed.),
          "Early symbolization," *New Directions for Child Development*, 1979, 3.

57   On early language production, see L. Bloom, *One word at a time: The use
          of single word utterances before syntax* (The Hague: Mouton, 1973).

61   On tadpole creatures, see R. Hofmann, "The bonhomme têtard: A develop-
          mental stage in human figure drawing" (paper presented at the Jean
          Piaget Society, Philadelphia, June 1976); and R. Arnheim, *Art and visual
          perception: The new version* (Berkeley: University of California Press,
          1974), chap. 4.

62   C. Golomb's findings appear in *Young children's sculpture and drawing: A
          study in representational development* (Cambridge, Mass.: Harvard Uni-
          versity Press, 1974).

62   Freeman reports his findings in "How young children try to plan draw-
          ings," in G. Butterworth (ed.) *The child's representation of the world* (New
          York: Plenum, 1977).

66   On children's tendencies to classify objects at a certain level of generality,
          see E. Rosch, C. B. Mervis, W. D. Gray, D. M. Johnson, and P. Boyes-Braem,
          "Basic objects in natural categories," *Cognitive Psychology*, 1976, 8, pp.
          382–439.

69   Clark's original study was reported in A. B. Clark, "The child's attitude
          toward perspective problems," *Studies in Education* (Stanford University,
          1896–97), pp. 283–94. Lewis's replication of 1971 is reported in B. Lark-
          Horovitz *et al.*, *Understanding children's art*, p. 104.

70   On the resemblance between children's solutions and those formed in pre-
          literate cultures, see L. Adam, *Primitive art* (Harmondsworth, England:
          Penguin, 1949); and F. Boas, *Primitive art* (New York: Free Press, 1965).

73   Two good sources of information about deviant drawings are J. Di Leo,
          Young children and their drawings (New York: Brunner/Mazel, 1970);
          and J. Di Leo, *Children's drawings as diagnostic aids* (New York: Brunner/
          Mazel, 1973).

91   Ed Emberley's work appears in *Make a world* (Boston: Little, Brown, 1972).

99   On childhood synesthesia, see H. Gardner, *The arts and human develop-
          ment* (New York: Wiley, 1973), chap. 4 and the references cited therein.

115   On young girls and horses, see S. Fein, *Heidi's horse* (Pleasant Hills, Calif.:
          Exelrod Press, 1976).

133   Nelson Goodman's criteria for the aesthetic are laid out in *Languages of
          art* (Indianapolis: Bobbs-Merrill, 1968).

133   Carothers's study is described in T. Carothers and H. Gardner, "When
          children's drawings become works of art," *Developmental Psychology*, 1979.

136–37   Diana Korzenik's work is chronicled in "Children's drawings: Changes in
          representation between the ages of five and seven" (unpublished doctoral
          dissertation, Harvard Graduate School of Education, 1972).

141   The quotation from Picasso appears in F. de Meredieu, *Le dessin d'enfant*
          (Paris: Editions universitaires Jean-Pierre de Large, 1974), p. 13. The Mal-
          raux quote comes from *The voices of silence* (Garden City: Doubleday,
          1953), p. 285.

148   On literalism and its dangers, see J. Silverman, E. Winner, and H. Gardner,
          "On going beyond the literal: The development of sensitivity to artistic
          symbols," *Semiotica*, 1976, 18, pp. 291–312; V. Lowenfeld and W. Brittain,
          Creative and mental growth (New York: Macmillan, 1970); and H. Read,
          Education through art (New York: Pantheon, n.d.).

148   On the opposite view of literalism, see H. Gardner, "Unfolding or training:
          On the optimal approach to art education," in E. Eisner (ed.), *The arts,
          human development, and education* (Berkeley, Calif.: McCutchan Publish-
          ing Co., 1976).

PAGE

149   On decline in flavor, see S. W. Ives, J. Silverman, H. Kelly, and H. Gardner, "Artistic development in the early school years: A cross-media study of storytelling, drawing, and clay modelling," *Harvard Project Zero Technical Report #8*, 1979.

149   On literalism in language, see H. Gardner, E. Winner, R. Bechhofer, and D. Wolf, "The development of figurative language," in K. Nelson (ed.), *Children's language* (New York: Gardner Press, 1978).

151   On mixed laterality and its concomitant learning problems, see S. Witelson, Neural and cognitive correlates of developmental dyslexia: Age and sex differences, in C. Shagass *et al* (eds.) *Psychopathology and brain dysfunction* (New York: Raven Press, 1977).

152   The quotation from R. Alschuler and L. Hattwick can be found in their *Painting and personality: A study of young children*, revised edition (Chicago: University of Chicago Press, 1969), p. 9.

155   On early writing, see E. Ferreiro, "Vers une théorie génétique de l'apprentissage de la lecture," *Schweizerische Zeitschrift für Psychologie und ihre Anwendungen*, 1977, 36, pp. 109–30.

155   The study of trains appears in G. Hildreth, *The child mind in evolution* (New York: Kings Crown Press, 1941).

157   On the learning of drawing conventions, see J. Goodnow, *Children drawing* (Cambridge, Mass.: Harvard University Press, 1977).

159   The information on cross-cultural drawing comes from a conversation with Professor Alexander Alland of Columbia University on 22 November 1978.

163   Leondar's remarks are in her article, "The arts in alternative schools," *Journal of Aesthetic Education*, 1971, 5, p. 80.

167   The quotation from Quentin Bell appears in B. Wilson and M. Wilson, "An iconoclastic view of the imagery sources in the drawings of young people," *Art Education*, 1977, 30, pp. 5–11.

169   V. Lowenfeld, *Creative and Mental Growth* (New York: Macmillan, 1947).

169   E. H. Gombrich's views can be gleaned from *Art and illusion* (New York: Pantheon, 1960).

169   The Wilsons' point of view appears in their article cited in note for page 167.

172   The Egyptian study is described in B. Wilson and M. Wilson, "Cognicomics, art learning, and art teaching," paper delivered at the National Art Education Association, Houston, Texas, March 1978.

172   The study done at Stirling University is reported in W. Phillips, S. B. Hobbs, and F. R. Pratt, "Intellectual realism in children's drawings of cubes," *Cognition*, 1978, 6, pp. 15–33.

175   The unusual patient forms the subject of a case report: W. Wapner, T. Judd, and H. Gardner, "Visual agnosia in an artist," *Cortex*, 1978, 14, pp. 343–64.

180   The quotation from Alexander Marshack appears in his pamphlet, *Ice age art* (New York: American Museum of Natural History, 1978). Further information on paleolithic art can be found in B. Rensberger, "The world's oldest works of art," *New York Times Magazine*, 21 May 1978, pp. 27–42; and A. Marshack, "The art and symbols of ice age man," *Human Nature*, September 1978, pp. 32–41.

180   An invaluable source book on infantile autism is Bernard Rimland's *Infantile autism* (New York: Appleton-Century, 1964).

181   Since the publication of *Nadia*, Clara Park has pointed out examples of other precocious autistic artists. See her review of *Nadia* in *Journal of Autism and Childhood Schizophrenia*, 1978, 8, pp. 457–72.

184   The quotation about Nadia comes from a discussion by E. Newson, in G. Butterworth (ed.), *The child's representation of the world* (New York: Plenum, 1977). Other information appears in L. Selfe, *Nadia: A case of extraordinary drawing ability in an autistic child* (New York: Academic Press, 1977).

190   William Hogarth's comments on the training of visual memory can be found in H. Read, *Education through art* (New York: Pantheon, n.d.), p. 42.

208   An excellent account of *The Last Supper* is given in Leo Steinberg, "Leonardo's Last Supper," *The Art Quarterly*, 1973, 36, pp. 297–410.

210   The quotations from Leonardo's notebooks are found in *The notebooks of Leonardo da Vinci*, ed. by Pamela Taylor (New York: Mentor, 1960), pp. 30–32, 28, 63, 53, 74, and 62.

215   I am indebted to Thomas Carothers for his trenchant account of the ex-

PAGE

hibit at the Israel National Museum in the winter of 1979, and to Ellen
Winner for her supplementary notes.

216   John Willats's research is reported in "How children learn to draw realistic pictures," *Quarterly Journal of Experimental Psychology*, 1977, 29, pp.
367–682; and "How children learn to represent three-dimensional space in
drawings," in G. Butterworth (ed.), *The child's representation of the world*
(New York: Plenum, 1977).

220   Rodolphe Töppfer's facial caricatures can be seen in his "Essai du physiognomie," discussed in E. H. Gombrich, *Art and illusion* (New York: Bol-
lingen Foundation, 1960), pp. 339–41.

221   The early works by Picasso have been reprinted in Juan-Eduardo Cirlot
(ed.), *Picasso: Birth of a genius* (New York: Praeger, 1972). Klee's early
works appear in J. Glaesemer (ed.), *Paul Klee: Handzeichnungen I. Kind-
heit* (Bern: Kunstmuseum, 1973).

231   The study by J. Getzels and M. Csikszentmihalyi comprises their book *The
creative vision* (New York: Wiley, 1976). The quotation is on p. 224.

233   Otto Rank's views are put forth in his *Art and artist* (New York: Knopf,
1932).

252   Suzi Gablik's views are presented in her *Progress in art* (New York: Riz-
zoli, 1976); the quotations are from pp. 154, 45, and 12.

254   Henry Schaefer-Simmern's magnum opus is *The unfolding of artistic activity* (Berkeley: University of California Press, 1948); his remarks are
found on p. 8.

257   See Karl Popper, *The open society and its enemies* (Princeton: Princeton
University Press, 1966), and *The poverty of historicism* (New York: Harper
& Row, 1977).

260   The quotation from Christopher Alexander comes from pp. 223 and 225 of
his paper, "The origin of creative power in children," *British Journal of
Aesthetics*, 1962, 2, pp. 207–26.

264   Picasso's remark is quoted in Rudolf Arnheim, *The genesis of a painting:
Picasso's Guernica* (Berkeley: University of California Press, 1962), p. 31;
the other quotations from Arnheim come from pp. 30, 80–81, 131–34.

266   Saul Steinberg's remark appeared in the *New York Times* of 16 April 1978,
p. 48.

269   On Otto Rank's views, see the note to chapter 8, p. 233.

AUTHOR/ARTIST INDEX

Page numbers in *Italics* indicate illustrations

SUBJECT INDEX

Page numbers in *Italics* indicate illustrations

277